THE BEDFORD SERIES IN HISTORY AND CULTURE

Victors and Vanquished
Spanish and Nahua Views of the Fall of the Mexica Empire

SECOND EDITION

Edited with an Introduction by

Stuart B. Schwartz

Yale University

Tatiana Seijas

Pennsylvania State University

bedford/st.martin's
Macmillan Learning
Boston | New York

For Bedford/St. Martin's
Vice President, Editorial, Macmillan Learning Humanities: Edwin Hill
Program Director for History: Michael Rosenberg
Senior Program Manager for History: William J. Lombardo
History Marketing Manager: Melissa Rodriguez
Director of Content Development: Jane Knetzger
Associate Editor: Mary Posman Starowicz
Content Project Manager: Lidia MacDonald-Carr
Senior Project Workflow Manager: Lisa McDowell
Production Supervisor: Robert Cherry
Media Project Manager: Michelle Camisa
Manager of Publishing Services: Andrea Cava
Project Management: Lumina Datamatics, Inc.
Composition: Lumina Datamatics, Inc.
Cartographer: Mapping Specialists, Ltd.
Text Permissions Researcher: Lenny Benhke, Lumina Datamatics, Inc.
Permissions Manager: Kalina Ingham
Senior Art Director: Anna Palchik
Cover Design: William Boardman
Cover Art: Image courtesy of The Latin American Library, Tulane University
Printing and Binding: LSC Communications

Manufactured in the United States of America.

2
f e

For information, write: Bedford/St. Martin's, 75 Arlington Street, Boston, MA 02116

ISBN 978-1-319-09485-0

Acknowledgments
Text acknowledgments and copyrights appear at the back of the book on page 251, which constitute an extension of the copyright page. Art acknowledgments and copyrights appear on the same page as the art selections they cover.

At the time of publication all Internet URLs published in this text were found to accurately link to their intended website. If you do find a broken link, please forward the information to history@macmillan.com so that it can be corrected for the next printing.

For our students

Foreword

The Bedford Series in History and Culture is designed so that readers can study the past as historians do.

The historian's first task is finding the evidence. Documents, letters, memoirs, interviews, pictures, movies, novels, or poems can provide facts and clues. Then the historian questions and compares the sources. There is more to do than in a courtroom, for hearsay evidence is welcome, and the historian is usually looking for answers beyond act and motive. Different views of an event may be as important as a single verdict. How a story is told may yield as much information as what it says.

Along the way the historian seeks help from other historians and perhaps from specialists in other disciplines. Finally, it is time to write, to decide on an interpretation and how to arrange the evidence for readers.

Each book in this series contains an important historical document or group of documents, each document a witness from the past and open to interpretation in different ways. The documents are combined with some element of historical narrative—an introduction or a biographical essay, for example—that provides students with an analysis of the primary source material and important background information about the world in which it was produced.

Each book in the series focuses on a specific topic within a specific historical period. Each provides a basis for lively thought and discussion about several aspects of the topic and the historian's role. Each is short enough (and inexpensive enough) to be a reasonable one-week assignment in a college course. Whether as classroom or personal reading, each book in the series provides firsthand experience of the challenge—and fun—of discovering, recreating, and interpreting the past.

Lynn Hunt
David W. Blight
Bonnie G. Smith

Preface

The history of the fall of the "Aztec" Empire has captured the imagination of readers since the sixteenth century. Contemporary Spanish chroniclers were enthralled by the tale of a great civilization conquered and destroyed by a determined and ruthless band of conquistadors led by Hernando (Hernán) Cortés, which was equally fascinating to nineteenth-century historians like the American William Prescott. This conflict continues to demand the attention of present-day scholars, who now speak of Spanish and allied Indigenous soldiers jointly defeating the Mexica Empire (Triple Alliance). The relevance of this story of epic proportions has not diminished with time and generates strong emotions even today.

While the outlines of the story are familiar, the interpretation of events, of rights and wrongs, and of the personalities of the major actors has changed radically over the years. This shift is related to changing attitudes toward European expansion, a richer reckoning of Indigenous societies, and more critical attitudes about the so-called conquest of the Americas. It is also the result of increased accessibility to new sources, mainly produced by Indigenous peoples of Mexico. Together these changes have produced a New Conquest History, largely based on a new philology that employs texts written in Indigenous languages during the subsequent century.

In this second edition we have sought to integrate some of these recent advances in the field of Mesoamerican ethnohistory, to update the bibliography, and to enrich the narrative by incorporating new evidence and interpretations. Readers will find an updated introduction, extensively revised headnotes, and ten new sources—both text and visual—that help to reframe this conflict from an enthohistorical perspective.

The primary objective of this volume is to introduce students to this history by a reading of excerpts from two main sources: from the Spanish side, *The True History of the Conquest of New Spain* by conquistador Bernal Díaz del Castillo; and from the "Aztec" side, the

Florentine Codex, which represents the testimony of survivors. Additional texts—including numerous new visuals—paint a broader, richer canvas, fleshing out the complicated struggle and conveying to the reader a sense that there was not simply a "Spanish" or an "Indian" view. Rather, the sources reveal a variety of visions and opinions, influenced and mediated by personal interests, ethnic biases, political considerations, and other factors. Indigenous accounts were no less influenced by such considerations than were European ones.

The war also raises the question of how to judge who were the winners and losers. We have chosen the title "Victors and Vanquished: Spanish and Nahua Views of the Fall of the Mexica Empire" for this revision, because in military terms the Spaniards and their Indigenous allies won and the Mexica lost. This new subtitle better captures the nuance of the fact that thousands of Indigenous soldiers were militarily on the winning side, even though subsequently they too fell into a dependent status within the colonial state. In the war's aftermath, the Indigenous peoples of central Mexico demonstrated considerable ability to accommodate, adapt, and resist the challenges that a new political system imposed. Historians of Mexico are continually faced with the dilemma of what to emphasize: the resilience of Indigenous cultures, or the disruption and exploitation that Spanish colonization represented. The title is as much a question, as it is a description of a permanent condition.

The book begins with an introduction to the societies of central Mexico and Iberia prior to contact. It also discusses the major sources from which the selections have been chosen. The book then presents these documents divided into eight chapters, proceeding chronologically. Beginning with accounts of omens that preceded the encounter, the following chapters cover early Spanish contacts with Yucatan, the first encounter of Spaniards and Mexicas, the march to the Mexica capital, the flight of Spaniards from Tenochtitlan, and the bitter last struggles. While the book is about the fall of the Mexica Empire, rather than the "conquest" of the rest of Mexico and subsequent history, a final chapter discusses the later attempts to impose a colonial regime, and the creative resistance of Indigenous peoples to those efforts.

A short introduction precedes each chapter, setting the historical context of the selections and discussing their relevance to the overall story. Each chapter includes both Indigenous and Spanish sources, although it is sometimes difficult to separate materials by such labels since crosscultural influences were already at work shortly after the war. Each selection has an accompanying headnote. Notes have been kept to a minimum and are intended to serve as an introductory guide to sources, primarily those in English. A chronology of events, updated study questions for students, a listing of the principal individuals mentioned in the texts, a glossary of Indigenous language terms, and a bibliography as a guide to further research are also included.

NOTE ON SOURCES AND CONVENTIONS USED

Historians continually confront the question of sources. Nahuas and Spaniards differed in what they chose to record and remember about these events, as well as in the ways they recorded them. We address this matter of representation by including a number of Indigenous sources of a pictorial nature so that readers can begin to understand the Nahua perception and interpretation of events and some of the conventions used to record them. The fall of the Mexica Empire presents an opportunity to consider heroism, greed, and despair, but it also challenges us to think about problems that confront all historians: Can we understand and interpret other cultures? How can we evaluate conflicting sources? How can we read and understand such differing styles of representation?

A few words are in order about some of the conventions used. First, scholars today infrequently use the term "Aztec," because members of this society did not employ it for themselves. The Spaniards first heard of these people as Culhua or Mexica, but that too was somewhat inaccurate. Most of the peoples of the great imperial state of central Mexico were speakers of Nahuatl, and culturally it is accurate to refer to them as Nahua peoples. They were also, however, divided into a number of separate political units and different ethnicities. Thus, while both the people of Tenochtitlan and Tlaxcala spoke Nahuatl and shared many cultural attributes, they were bitter enemies. The occupants of the great capital city of Tenochtitlan and the neighboring island community of Tlatelolco were the core of the empire. Both referred to themselves not as "Aztecs" but as "Mexica," and scholars now use "Mexica" to designate this society, recognizing that they had strong local identities as Tenochca and Tlatelolca and that there were many ethnic groups, as well as peoples of other cities, associated with them. We use the term "Mexica" to refer specifically to the residents of the island capital and try where possible to use the ethnic designation of other groups when they are mentioned. We also use "Indigenous" (more so than "native" or

Indian) as a broad adjective for the peoples of Mesoamerica, similar to the word "European," which references geography and certain cultural distinctions.

There is considerable variation in the texts as to the spelling and pronunciation of names and terms. Spaniards wrote what they heard or thought they heard. Sometimes Spanish could not reproduce Nahuatl sounds, and so variations abound in the sources. Take for example the various forms used for the name of the Mexica ruler—Motecuhzoma (closest to Nahuatl), Moctezuma, Montezuma, and so forth, or for his successor Cuauhtémoc (Quauhtemoctzin, Guatemoc, etc.). We chose to standardize the forms used in the introductions but to leave the original selections alone to retain their flavor. To clarify matters, we have indicated in parentheses the standardized form after the first appearance of a variation. Sixteenth-century Spanish usage presents its own set of difficulties. Accents were often left "in the inkwell" and orthography was not standardized. Bernal Díaz referred to Diego Belazquez, yet the modern spelling of his name would be Velázquez. Hernando Cortés is often referred to as Hernán in popular history, especially in English, and some contemporaries called him Fernando, but we use his given name of Hernando. In obvious cases, we have not altered the selections and only where necessary have we tried to standardize according to modern usage. We note the sources of all translations, which remain as they were originally published. All other translations are by T. Seijas. Finally, footnotes that appeared in the original publications are asterisked.

ACKNOWLEDGMENTS

We are grateful for the suggestions of Bradley Benton, Amber E. Brian, William F. Connell, Byron E. Hamann, Mary Miller, Matthew Restall, Jennifer Saracino, John F. Schwaller, Amara Solari, and Peter Villela for the new edition. Thank you as well to Christopher M. Valesey.

We would also like to thank the team at Bedford/St. Martin's for their work, particularly Program Director Michael Rosenberg, Senior Program Manager Laura Arcari, Senior Program Manager William Lombardo, History Marketing Manager Melissa Rodriquez, Associate Editor Mary Posman Starowicz, Content Project Manager Lidia MacDonald-Carr, and Cover Designer William Boardman.

This volume is born out of our experiences as students of the Early Modern World, of cultural encounters, and as teachers of Latin

American history. Our classroom experience has taught us that there are few stories as fascinating or as troubling as the fall of the Mexica Empire. It is a history that raises significant methodological and episte-mological questions that are important to all of us fascinated by the past and hopeful of understanding cultures different from our own.

Stuart B. Schwartz

Tatiana Seijas

Contents

APPENDIXES

Maps and Illustrations

PART ONE

Introduction: States in Conflict

Early modern history includes few stories of drama and tragedy equal to the fall of the Mexica Empire.[1] A small contingent of Spanish adventurers arrived on the Mexican coast in 1519. Two years later, alongside thousands of Indigenous soldiers and joined by hundreds of additional Spaniards, Hernando Cortés led an overthrow of a great imperial state that had dominated the land and held sway over millions of people for close to a century. The loss of population from warfare, famine, and disease was incalculable. Subsequently, Indigenous societies struggled to survive and adapt to Spanish governance and to Catholicism as the new state religion. These events represented both the death of a political state, or more exactly states, and the birth of a new colonial regime in its place.

A LONG TRADITION: THE INDIGENOUS PEOPLES OF MESOAMERICA

The Mexica were not the only people who occupied the lands of central Mexico, but they were the most powerful at the time of European contact. Their story has come to symbolize what happened to all the peoples of Mesoamerica (the cultural region that extended from the modern U.S. Southwest to Nicaragua). One of the reasons for their representative role has been the survival of a Mexica version of these events that parallels, confirms, and contradicts the Spanish accounts. The Mexica and other peoples of Mexico had their own systems of recording and remembering events through a combination of pictographic representation and oral history, and they adopted the Roman alphabet to write both in their own languages, including Nahuatl, and in Spanish. So there exists, possibly more so than for any other Indigenous society of the time in the Americas, a written record of Nahua perceptions of European contact.

The Mexica who ruled central Mexico from their island capital Tenochtitlan were the heirs of ancient cultural traditions. Agrarian societies based on the cultivation of maize and other crops developed in Mesoamerica from about 2000 BCE, such as the Olmecs. Centuries later, Maya peoples created a number of flourishing city-states in southern Mexico and Central America between 600 and 900 CE, with high levels of social stratification and cultural attainments. Archaeologists categorize these centuries as Mesoamerica's Classic Period. Ongoing research reveals that Mayas made great achievements in architecture, sculpture, mathematics, astronomy, and other disciplines at places like Tikal (Guatemala), Copán (Honduras), and Palenque (Mexico). At roughly the same time, the great city-state of Teotihuacán, near Mexico City, developed its own distinctive culture that spread through conquest, trade, and missionary activity to other regional centers in Mesoamerica. For reasons still not fully understood, Teotihuacán first fell into decline and then to invaders around 750 CE, and the Classic Maya cities were abandoned circa 900 CE. By about 1000 CE, the Classic Period had ended and a period of instability followed (see Map 1).

Although the reasons for the end of the Classic Period are much debated, pressure from outside forces was an important factor, especially in central Mexico. Migratory peoples from the north constantly exerted pressure on Teotihuacán's stable agricultural areas in order to secure more resources. After Teotihuacán's decline, the Toltecs developed as the next great power in the region, establishing their capital at Tula (Tollan) in the modern state of Hidalgo. Urban life, as such, continued to flourish in what archaeologists call the Post-Classic Period. By military means and through trade, the Toltecs established control over much of central Mexico and their influence eventually reached as far as the Maya cities of Yucatan. Yet, by 1175 the Toltecs also succumbed, apparently once again to new waves of peoples from the north.

During these cycles of imperial formation and dissolution, the Toltecs were especially important for the way later peoples in the region viewed

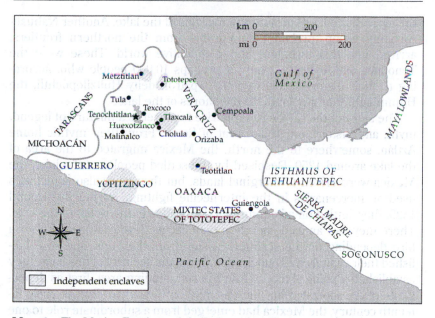

Map 1. *The Mexica Empire and the Independent Enclaves, c. 1519.*
Adapted from Figure 11 in *Religion and Empire: The Dynamics of Aztec and Inca Expansion* by Geoffrey W. Conrad and Arthur A. Demarest (Cambridge: Cambridge University Press, 1984, 1995), 45. Reprinted with permission.

their history. For the Mexica and other city-states who came afterward, Tula exemplified all the positives of urban life: monumental buildings, institutions for the arts and sciences, markets with varied trade goods, and so forth. Claiming descent from the Toltecs, as the families in some of the later city-states did, gave their descendants legitimacy, authority, and political advantage.

After the fall of Tula, central Mexico was without a central authority. Many peoples lived there, speaking a variety of languages—Otomí, Purépecha, Totonaco, and especially Nahuatl. Nahuas shared many cultural elements, but they were divided politically into a number of separate city-states (*altepetl*), only a few of which could claim descent from the Toltec nobility. By the twelfth century, the population had concentrated around Lake Texcoco, a series of brackish and freshwater lakes in Mexico's Central Valley. Larger cities like Azcapotzalco and Texcoco clashed and struggled for regional dominance and control of the agricultural lands around the margins of the lake. Another Nahuatl-speaking group, probably immigrants from the northern frontiers, arrived into this turbulent and competitive world. These were the Tenochca or Mexica, a group of perhaps 10,000 people who, according to their histories, followed their patron deity Huitzilopochtli, the Hummingbird of the South, to the shores of the lake.[2]

The story of the Mexicas' rapid rise to power is a mixture of legend, myth, and history, much like that of Rome. From their mythic home Aztlán, somewhere to the north, the Mexica migrated to the area of the lake around 1250. Despised by the settled peoples of the lake, the Mexica were driven to marginal lands, but they were also sometimes used as mercenaries in the internecine fighting. Eventually, around 1325, they settled on adjoining marshy islands in the midst of the lake. There they saw an eagle perched on a cactus devouring a snake (or a bird depending on the account), a sign from the gods, and so established their capital city Tenochtitlan. From the security of this base, they established a political foothold in the surrounding area, first as dependents of Azcapotzalco but increasingly on their own. By the early fifteenth century, the Mexica had emerged from a subordinate role to one of increasing influence. Under their ruler or *tlahtoani* (orator) Itzcoatl (1426–1440) and later under Moctezuma I (1440–1468), the Mexica came to control much of central Mexico and neighboring peoples like the Totonacs on the Gulf coast and the Mixtecs to the south in Oaxaca.[3] By 1470 the Mexica had become the dominant power of central Mexico, extracting tribute from peoples who lived hundreds of miles away.

Increasing centralization and other changes within Mexica society accompanied the process of Mexica imperial expansion. Perhaps under the influence of Tlacaeleltzin, who served as a sort of prime minister under a number of rulers over a sixty-year period, Mexica society became more militarized. The imperial cult of warfare celebrated victories with great pomp and display, which included the state-sanctioned killing of war captives. The traditional clan or *calpulli* system survived, but the division between the Mexica nobility (*pipiltin*) and the commoners (*macehualtin*) grew ever wider. Tenochtitlan conquered and then politically integrated the neighboring island city of Tlatelolco in the early 1470s, but its people continued to maintain a separate local identity as Tlatelolcans. Tenochtitlan then created an alliance with the lakeside cities of Texcoco and Tlacopan. Despite the alliance, Tenochtitlan always remained the predominant power. Some neighboring peoples remained politically independent and hostile to the Mexica. The Purépecha

(Tarascans) in Michoacán to the north were never conquered, and other Nahuas to the east in city-states such as Tlaxcala, Huejotzingo, and Metztitlán remained bitter enemies.[4]

The Mexica Empire reached its greatest extent in the first decades of the sixteenth century, but its power, while real, was also fragile. Subject peoples were restive and occasionally rebelled; traditional enemies continued to pose a formidable threat to their rule. The stability of the ruling alliance itself was also precarious, as court factions and ruling families jockeyed for advantage in each of the cities where Tenochtitlan's partners looked on its power with envy and fear.

TENOCHTITLAN: THE FOUNDATION OF HEAVEN

Tenochtitlan, a backdrop to much of the story narrated in the following texts, was a world-class metropolis. To the Mexica, it was "the foundation of heaven"—the political, symbolic, and ritual center of their universe. From humble beginnings as the small settlement of a marginal people, Tenochtitlan became a mighty capital covering approximately five square miles with a population estimated to be as high as 300,000 people. Its core was a central complex of palaces and temples surrounded by an enclosing wall. This central temple precinct (*plaza mayor*) was dominated by a sixty-meter-high great pyramid with twin temples: one to Tlaloc, the Mesoamerican deity of water and rain; and one to Huitzilopochtli, a war deity and patron of the Mexica. Some eighty other palaces and temples stood around the temple precinct, including the ruler's residence and the seminary and military academy. Beyond the enclosing wall were other palaces, temples, markets, and residential buildings, some of them two stories high with gardens on their roofs. The architecture and craftsmanship, especially of the public buildings, was remarkable. "It could not be bettered anywhere," noted one Spanish eyewitness. Tlatelolco, at first a separate city on an adjacent island, was eventually incorporated as part of greater Tenochtitlan. It too had palaces and temples but was most famous for its great marketplace.

Because of its location in the midst of the water and its maze of canals, a number of the first Spanish visitors to Tenochtitlan compared the city to Venice. The island location gave the city its peculiar character with the constant traffic of canoes carrying goods to and from the city.[5] Fresh water was supplied by aqueducts, and away from the city center many families farmed "floating gardens" (*chinampas*), rectangular plots of silt on which multiple harvests could be made in a single year in a

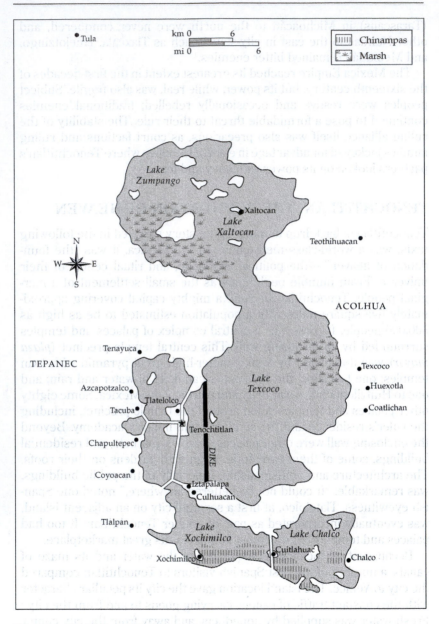

Map 2. *The Valley of Mexico.*
Adapted from Figure 12 in *Religion and Empire: The Dynamics of Aztec and Inca Expansion* by Geoffrey W. Conrad and Arthur A. Demarest (Cambridge: Cambridge University Press, 1984, 1995), 12. Reprinted with permission.

kind of hydroponic agriculture.[6] A dike held out the brackish waters of the eastern side of the lake and protected crops near the city. Four great causeways extended from the lakeshore to connect the city to the other cities and towns that surrounded the lake. Bernal Díaz, the young soldier who saw the city in 1519, gave voice to the awe that many of his companions felt:

> Gazing on such wonderful sights, we did not know what to say, or whether what appeared before us was real, for on one side, on the land there were great cities, and in the lake ever so many more, and the lake was crowded with canoes, and in the causeway were many bridges at intervals, and in front of us stood the great city of Mexico.

Tenochtitlan was much more than Bernal Díaz perceived. In many ways it was also a plan of the Mexica social and religious universe—a city built of "mortar and metaphor," in the words of art historian Barbara Mundy. Its causeways represented the four cardinal directions. Neighborhoods were organized in pairs of twenty communal corporate groups (*calpulli*) and in temple-maintenance groups, each with its own temple and school to look after. Thus, the cosmology and calendar were physically represented by the city's organization and by the arrangement of different sectors of the population.

The Tenochtitlan of 1519, in the autumn of Mexica greatness, was a great urban center rivaling Venice, London, or Paris in complexity and size. The city seemed to be an impregnable fortress and a symbol of the very favor of the gods. Little did the Mexica suspect that in three short years much of it would be rubble, with temple stones turned into masonry for Spanish churches.

MEXICA SOCIETY

As in most belief systems, Mexica religion was a powerful and uniting force that penetrated most aspects of life. Basic issues of human existence were of primary concern: What is life? What constitutes moral behavior? Is there life after death? What is the proper relationship between human beings and the gods? Religious thinkers and philosophers wondered if the pleasures of this life were transient, or if life was simply a "veil of tears." As part of the great Mesoamerican tradition, Mexica religion had a complex cosmology and theology that sought to explain the existence of the universe and the relationships within it.

Although there was recognition of a unifying life-giving force, Mexica religion had a vast pantheon of deities. Often the same basic force could manifest itself in male and female forms. Xochipilli, a solar fertility god, for example, was the counterpart to Xochiquetzal, the goddess of flowers and sexual love. The Mexica honored this extensive pantheon through the yearly religious calendar by complex ritual and ceremonial activities of feasting, fasting, dancing, penance, and sacrifice. Mexica deities can be grouped into three major categories. The first consisted of the creator deities who brought the universe into being and whose actions formed the core of Mexica cosmology. Tonatiuh, the sun god and turquoise prince, and Tezcatlipoca, god of the night sky, were especially important. A second category included deities associated with settled agriculture, like Tlaloc and his sister Chicomecoatl, the goddess of maize. Finally, there were the deities who formed part of the imperial cult of war. Chief among them was the Mexica's main patron, the Hummingbird of the South, Huitzilopochtli.

The ancient Mesoamerican deity Quetzalcoatl, the Feathered Serpent, was also prominent, as he had been among the Toltecs. The Mexica wished to claim legitimacy on their military prowess but also as cultural descendants of the Toltecs. To that end, Moctezuma Xocoyotzin (Moctezuma II) built a great temple to Quetzalcoatl in Tenochtitlan. Notably, a number of postcontact accounts connected Cortés to legends about the Toltec king Topiltzin, who had taken Quetzalcoatl's name before he was forced to leave the Toltec capital Tula. Topiltzin-Quetzalcoatl had migrated with his followers down to the coast and departed on a raft made of snakes for "the Red Land," or Yucatan. Linking legend and fact, archaeologists have found evidence of a Toltec presence and the cult of the Feathered Serpent in Yucatan after 990. It was said that Topiltzin-Quetzalcoatl would someday return to reclaim his position and lands.

Perhaps to appease Spanish missionaries, some Nahua informants and later historians claimed that the Quetzalcoatl of the myths was a bearded white man who opposed human sacrifice and the cult of war. Topiltzin-Quetzalcoatl had been born in the year one-reed (*ce-acatl*) and had supposedly left Tula in the year one-reed as well, exactly fifty-two years later, or one cycle of the Mexica calendar. Curiously, the year of Cortés's arrival, 1519, also corresponded to the year one-reed in the Mexica calendar. Seeking to explain Moctezuma's vacillation in the face of the Spanish challenge, some Nahua historians claimed that the emperor truly believed Cortés to be the returning god-ruler that the prophecies foretold. Cortés's letters contain no mention of this theme, but later Nahua accounts and those of Spanish chroniclers like Bernal Díaz usually mention it. Cortés's arrival in the year one-reed is either the fulfillment of prophecy, extraordinary coincidence, the later Nahua construction of a tale to fit the circumstances, or the intentional use of the Mesoamerican calendar and legends to bolster Spanish claims.[7]

A powerful political and military force sustained Mexica society. The Mexica mobilized large armies or legions and sent them long distances to expand their economic reach and political sovereignty. Mexica armies usually campaigned in the dry season from December to April when farmers, who comprised the bulk of the troops, were free from labor in the fields and when transport was easier. This was also the time when food was available to support the army along its march. Veteran soldiers, whose accomplishments were recognized by specific uniforms, decorative clothing, hairstyles, and other symbols, led the armies. These men belonged to distinguished military organizations, such as the league of the Eagle, which were similar to the medieval European orders of knighthood. Although sometimes a simple threat of force was enough to gain submission, faced with resistance, the Mexica were an implacable foe. From the comments of their hostile neighbors and from Spanish observations, it is clear that the Mexica were a commanding and dreaded military threat.

Mexica military might depended on complex organization and training.[8] Boys were prepared from birth for a soldier's life and death and inculcated with military virtues. Military accomplishment was the measure of manhood and a means of social mobility. Campaigns had a strong individual component. While the Nahua peoples had projectile weapons like spear throwers (*atlatl*) and bows and arrows, their preferred weapons were those designed for close combat, where individual skill and bravery could best be demonstrated. In this way, battle was a scene for personal demonstrations of bravery, where the individual taking of a captive was the greatest achievement. Their primary weapon was a sword set with razor-sharp obsidian blades designed for slashing and incapacitating rather than killing an enemy. These were lethal weapons; Spanish accounts tell of a horse's head lopped off by a blow from a single thrust.

Warfare for the Mexica served as an economic and political tool, but it was also a way of life with deep religious meaning, much like it was for Spaniards. The Mexica believed that the gods, especially Huitzilopochtli, required "precious water," or human blood, to nourish them. The best and most noble sacrifice as a messenger to the gods was that of a military opponent. Thus the presentation of captives for sacrifice was a main goal of battle and an occasion of great religious significance surrounded by ritual obligations and responsibilities. These state-sanctioned deaths were usually accompanied by a strict set of observances including forms of ritual cannibalism. As the Mexica and their allies controlled more and more of the country and subjected additional neighbors to their control, it became difficult to find suitable opponents. Migratory peoples, derisively called *Chichimecas* ("barbarians"), who lived in the frontiers of the Mexica Empire were held in low esteem and seen as unworthy opponents or sacrifices. War with other Nahua peoples who were political opponents, but who shared the same culture as the Mexica, was considered best. Sometimes they fought in arranged battles or *xochiyaoyotl* ("flower wars") designed for each side to demonstrate its valor and to have the opportunity to take appropriate captives. The cities of Tlaxcala, Huejotzingo, and Cholula, all of which joined Cortés as allies, were traditional opponents in these flower wars.

Despite the Mexicas' experience in warfare, their political objectives put them at a disadvantage in the face of Spanish aims and, more importantly, of the resentment of Nahua soldiers from subjugated city-states, who rallied to overthrow Moctezuma. Spanish weapons like the unwieldy harquebus were a surprise factor in the earliest battles, but Mexica warriors were quick to adjust their practices, seizing Spanish weaponry and turning their firearms against them. By the end, much of the fighting on the ground took place between Indigenous soldiers, and the Mexica were simply outnumbered.

The military alliance between Cortés's men and Indigenous elites from city-states like Tlaxcala and Texcoco brought about the fall of the Mexica Empire. This fact, ignored by Spanish aggrandizers, was not lost to contemporaries or even to historians in the following centuries. In 1794, a Portuguese commentator made it quite clear: "Cortés would not be so celebrated in history . . . if he did not have on his side the valiant Tlaxcalteca Indians, the sworn enemies of the Mexicas."[9]

RENAISSANCE CONQUISTADORS

Early sixteenth-century Spain was a society in transition and only recently a unified monarchy. The marriage of Ferdinand, prince of Aragon, to Isabella, princess of Castile, in 1469 created the political basis of modern Spain. For some seven centuries, the Iberian peninsula had been a multicultural region where Muslims, Christians, and Jews lived in close and continuous if often hostile contact and proximity. The Catholic kings moved to end that coexistence and free themselves of internal religious challenges. To that end, they established the Holy Office of the Inquisition in 1479, a court charged with enforcing religious orthodoxy and social control, especially among people who had recently converted from Judaism and Islam. Then, in 1492, Granada, the last Muslim kingdom, fell to Catholic arms. A few months later the Catholic kings forced the Jews either to convert or to leave the country. Political and religious unification worked in tandem to elevate the monarchy.

The last two decades of the fifteenth century were a time of consolidation and war. The Iberian Peninsula had been part of the Roman Empire, and that experience was reflected in its language, laws, and military orientation, as were the Germanic traditions brought by later invaders. Campaigns had mobilized thousands of young men and convinced them to make their fortune through military prowess, courage, and skill. Throughout Europe the use of arms and horses was a privilege of the nobility, but in Spain many young men of common birth knew these skills and used them to their advantage. By the early sixteenth century, through Aragon's interests in Italy, Spain also became involved in conflicts further afield, and these wars provided additional military experience.

The voyages of Christopher Columbus beginning in 1492 opened up a new outlet for Spanish military and political activity. The colonization and exploitation of the Caribbean was fully under way by 1500. Spaniards established control of the major islands along with a few places on the mainland. The native populations suffered rapid decline as a result of war, enslavement and forced labor, and the impact of Old World diseases. Ongoing explorations and raids raised individual Spaniards' hopes of fame and fortune, and all were justified as colonial expeditions that extended the sovereignty of the Spanish crown and the truth of the Roman Catholic faith. With each new territory brought under Spanish control, a few reaped the rewards, usually the leaders and their close associates, but many others were left unsatisfied. There never seemed to be enough treasure. The crown always received its 20 percent of the booty, and the "Indians" assigned to labor for Spanish colonizers actively resisted imposed control or disappeared in the face of mistreatment and social disruption.

Cortés's expedition to the mainland of Mexico was in no way unusual. It followed two earlier ones that had gone westward from Cuba to nearby Yucatan, about 120 miles away, in search of new islands and new kingdoms to colonize. The difference was not in the expedition's leadership, composition, or goals, but in the nature of the Indigenous societies they encountered. In Yucatan and central Mexico, Spaniards encountered for the first time states organized in large kingdoms and with the military capacity to oppose them. The Spaniards and the Mexica were well-suited opponents. Both were the heirs of a long process of social development and fusion, both had a warrior ethos, both held fervently to a religious faith, and both justified their imperial expansion in terms of theological ideals.

Great controversy exists over the size of the Mesoamerican population when the Europeans arrived. Most estimates place the population of Tenochtitlan at some 250,000 inhabitants in the early 1500s (similar to Paris). Historical demographers Woodrow Borah and S. F. Cook estimated that central Mexico alone had a population of about twenty-five million people in 1519. Not all scholars agree, and some have placed the estimate at half that figure or less, but all concede that central Mexico was the most densely populated region of the Americas at the moment of contact. By 1580, only about one million Indigenous people remained. The process of colonization constituted a horrifying demographic disaster.[10]

The size of the invading force of Spaniards is easier to calculate. Various participants spoke of the numbers involved. Bernal Díaz noted that Cortés's original expedition had 550 men. With the addition of other Spaniards, including a few women, after 1520, Cortés's forces swelled to perhaps over 1,500, but many were lost in subsequent fighting. Before the final siege of Tenochtitlan on April 28, 1521, Cortés reviewed his troops and counted 86 horsemen, 118 musketeers and crossbowmen, and 700 foot soldiers, as well as perhaps another 400 men who manned the ships he ordered built to sail on the lake.

Chroniclers have pointed to these numbers to glorify Spanish conquistadors, but their victory is much less impressive if we consider the number of Indigenous allies who fought with the Spaniards. In the first entry into Tenochtitlan, Cortés's forces included perhaps 2,000 Tlaxcalan allies. In the final siege of the city, not only Tlaxcalans but also troops from Huejotzingo, Texcoco, Cholula, and many other towns and cities fought with the Spaniards in the last battles. Cortés himself noted 50,000 Tlaxcalans alone at the final siege, and over 75,000 native allies fighting alongside Spanish units. Bernal Díaz mentioned 100,000 allies in the engagements, and later Indigenous chroniclers speak of even higher numbers. Such figures emphasize the fact that in many ways the fall of Tenochtitlan and the conquest of the Mexica Empire was as much a struggle among Indigenous peoples as it was a clash of the Old and New Worlds. In terms of scale, the long battle for Tenochtitlan was a major military effort, equal to the great contemporaneous wars in Europe and elsewhere.

THE SPANISH SOURCES

We know a great deal about the fall of the Mexica Empire because participants and observers on both sides recorded their impressions, opinions, and stories, including Spaniards who participated directly in the fighting. These accounts reflect the personal, political, economic, and social interests of their authors. Hernando Cortés, the leader of the Spanish expedition, wrote a number of reports or letters that were sent back to the Spanish king. These were quickly published and became the basis of the "official" story of the conquest. Cortés's observations were realistic and direct, lacking the fantasy found in other, earlier European observations of the New World. Naturally, Cortés's reports tended to justify his decisions and actions and placed him always in a positive light.[11] Later, Francisco López de Gómara, a distinguished author, met Cortés, who hired him to write a history of the conquest. Using Cortés's letters, notes, and personal papers, López de Gómara produced in 1553 a laudatory biography, very favorable to his patron.[12] Luckily, these official versions were not the only accounts from the Spanish side.

Bernal Díaz del Castillo wrote the great chronicle of the war against the Mexica. Like many of the conquistadors he was not a military man by profession, but he knew the use of arms and served as a foot soldier.[13] The events of his youth marked him deeply, and Díaz had a remarkable memory and eye for detail, which he used effectively in his narrative. By the time he began to write down his version of the events, Diaz was an old soldier, veteran of the great campaigns of the conquest, and frustrated by the hopes of his youth. He wished to set the record straight about the efforts of the common men like himself, who had delivered a mighty empire to their king. Here is how Díaz introduced himself and his book:

> I, Bernal Díaz del Castillo, citizen and *regidor* (alderman) of the most loyal city of Santiago de Guatemala, one of the first discoverers and conquerors of New Spain and its provinces . . . a native of the very noble and distinguished town of Medina del Campo . . . speak about that which concerns myself and all the true conquistadors my companions who served His Majesty by discovering, conquering, pacifying, and settling most of the provinces of New Spain, and that it is one of the best countries yet discovered in the New World, we found this out by our own efforts without His Majesty knowing anything about it.

Here in this introductory paragraph we see some of the motives that drove Díaz and his companions: localism, pride in their origins, a great sense of self-worth and accomplishment, a hope for recognition (and reward), and a desire to set down a "true" story of their deeds and triumphs.

We know relatively little about Díaz's early life. Born around 1496, of honorable but not titled family, he received some education. As a teenager he left home and made his way to Seville, and in 1514, at the age of nineteen, he joined a great expedition under Pedrarias Dávila that sailed for Castilla del Oro, modern-day Panama. The expedition was something of a disaster. Disgruntled and disappointed, many men, Bernal Díaz among them, abandoned the region. From Panama he made his way to the island of Cuba, where he settled for a few years. Then in 1517, he signed on to a new expedition under Francisco Hernández de Córdoba that explored the coast of Yucatan, and, after some stiff fighting, Díaz returned to Cuba with reports of a densely populated land where people wore fine cotton garments, lived in stone dwellings, cultivated fields of maize, and possessed gold. The Spaniards had encountered the Maya kingdoms of Yucatan. The governor of Cuba, Diego Velázquez, impressed by these reports, immediately organized another expedition under a nephew named Juan de Grijalva, and Bernal Díaz signed on yet again. The result was more trading, exploring, and fighting up the coast, as far north as modern-day Veracruz. During this time, Spaniards, through trade and plunder, accumulated more gold and, through their native translators, they learned of the existence of a great empire that lay in the interior of the country. Grijalva returned to Cuba, where the gold and the reports moved the governor to immediately start plans for yet another, larger expedition to the west. By 1519, when this third expedition set sail under Hernando Cortés, Bernal Díaz was a young man of twenty-three with military experience in three expeditions, and, as he liked to point out, he had been to Mexico twice before Cortés.

The events of the conquest of Tenochtitlan are the core of Bernal Díaz's account. Subsequently, frustrated in his hopes for wealth in Mexico, he participated in the colonization of Guatemala, and there he remained with a grant of Indigenous laborers (*encomienda*) to support him as a member of the local elite, a town councilman, and a man of some stature, respected but not very wealthy.

Garrulous and with a prodigious memory, Díaz must have been asked on numerous occasions to retell the stories of the conquest, of the glories of the Mexica capital, the hardships of marches and battles, the appearance of Moctezuma, and the exploits of Cortés and his men.

When he began to write them down is unclear, but by the mid-1550s he had composed a number of chapters. Perhaps there was a political motive behind the origins of the work. The struggle for control of Indigenous laborers between the colonists and the crown during the 1540s may have motivated Díaz to set the record straight by pointing out what the conquerors had in fact accomplished. We know he had taken an active role in defending the colonists' behavior against the criticism of reformist clerics like Bartolomé de Las Casas who wished to eradicate slavery and forced labor.

Whatever the origins of the project, Bernal Díaz was shocked to learn that others had published first. The work of Francisco López de Gómara fell into his hands, as did some of the other chronicles of the conquest. Although López de Gómara and the others wrote with an elegance that the old soldier could not hope to match, and Díaz was tempted to give up the endeavor altogether, these were books by scholars who had not been eyewitnesses like him, and they contained many factual errors. Above all, the work of López de Gómara, like Cortés's own letters, celebrated the captain's role and gave little credit to the common soldiers, men like Díaz who felt they had been overlooked. Díaz called his book *The True History of the Conquest of New Spain* because it was written against the "false" histories of López de Gómara and others. The old battler wished to set the record straight and, in doing so, bring his own accomplishments and those of his companions to the forefront so those in authority might reward them.

Much of the book was written in the 1560s when Bernal Díaz was in his seventies. Friends who read the manuscript were impressed that he could remember so many details about the campaigns and his companions. Perhaps they doubted his accuracy. Here was his response:

> I replied it was not so remarkable, because there were only 550 of us and we were always together conversing before and after campaigns and following a battle it soon became known who were killed or who were sacrificed; when we came from a bloody and doubtful battle, we always counted our dead—I retained in my memories all the details about them and if I could paint or sculpt, I would fashion them as they were, their figures, their faces, and their manners—I would like to paint all of them, according to life, with the full expression of courage which was on their faces when they entered battle.

Díaz's "true history" was completed about 1567 and sent to Spain in 1575. There it remained unnoticed in the papers of the Council of the

Indies until other historians began to make use of it at the beginning of the seventeenth century. It was not published until 1632, long after Bernal Díaz, the last of the Spanish conquerors of Tenochtitlan, had passed away.

Years after the conquest in the following generation, a number of authors like the Dominican friar Diego Durán or the judge Alonso de Zorita wrote about Nahua society. These works often incorporated evidence from eyewitness accounts and sometimes provided new information, but they also reflected the interests of their times and their authors. They have been used sparingly in this collection.

INDIGENOUS HISTORICAL TRADITIONS

There are different ways of thinking about, narrating, and recording the past. For the peoples of central Mexico, there was a profound belief in a cycle of time in which events repeated themselves, making prediction possible. History was the foundation of society, and recounting the past served both political and religious ends. In 1427, the Mexica ruler Itzcoatl ordered that all historical accounts and manuscripts be destroyed so that only the "official" record would survive to guide the memory of the Mexica rise to power as Huitzilopochtli's chosen people. In this effort, the Mexica rulers, like the ancient Egyptian pharaohs, displayed a practical concern for how the past could be used to legitimize power and to influence the future.

History was also a sacred trust, and remembrance of the past was essential for the continuation of Mexica identity. The historian Tezozómoc in his *Crónica Mexicayotl* captured the Nahua importance of history in this verse:

> Thus they have come to tell it,
> thus they have come to record it in their narration
> and for us they have painted it in their codices,
> the ancient men, the ancient women.
> They were our grandfathers, our grandmothers . . .
> Their account was repeated,
> they left it to us;
> they bequeathed it forever
> to us who live now,
> to us who come down from them.
> Never will it be lost, never will it be forgotten,
> that which they came to do,

that which they record in their paintings:
their renown, their history, their memory.
Thus in the future
never will it perish, never will it be forgotten
always will we treasure it,
we their children, their grandchildren . . .
we who carry their blood and their color,
we will tell it, we will pass it on
to those who do not yet live, who are to be born,
the children of the Mexicans, the children of the Tenochcans.[14]

The cadence or rhythm of such texts suggests that they were recited out loud. The drawings and symbols used to record legends and the events of history served as a basis for an accompanying oral tradition, in which commentaries and analyses of the written or pictorial record created a composite kind of history that made up the Nahua form of presentation. The artist-scribe (*tlahcuiloh*), "the master of the black ink and the red ink," as the Nahua poetically referred to him, was a respected and essential figure in the preservation of history and culture. We should note, however, that this skill and knowledge was socially limited. Only a few people, almost always boys, were trained to be a *tlahcuiloh,* and the books or codices they produced became the exclusive possessions of the priesthood, rulers, and nobility.[15]

Prior to the arrival of the Spaniards, the peoples of central Mexico used a system of images that were ordered in patterns based on a number of criteria to record and transmit knowledge. Unlike the European tradition where writing and painting were discrete activities, for the Nahuas, Mixtecs, and others, the two activities were fused and often accompanied by oral explanation as well. Rather than employing alphabetic script, peoples in central Mexico used patterned images accompanied by symbols or glyphs that readers could readily identify. These were usually painted into books on deerskin or a paper made from the maguey plant and then folded into panels like an accordion. It is not known exactly how a text was read, but the scale of objects, their position on the page, and their relationship to each other determined how they were interpreted.

There were a number of genres or types of texts. Precontact books recorded annals or the chronology of important events, prophecies, calendric information, rituals, lists of merchant goods, boundaries, and tribute or tax records. Because the Spaniards later came to believe that these texts preserved the ancient religion of the conquered peoples, they destroyed many of them, so that few precontact texts survive to this day. About five hundred Mexican codices are known to have survived, but less than twenty of these predate the fall of Tenochtitlan. The vast majority of surviving codices were created afterwards and reflect some European influences.

Several authors have argued that the use of symbols and images was a communicational disadvantage for Indigenous peoples, but this position rests on a highly questionable distinction between European alphabetic writing and native pictorial forms.[16] Ethnohistorians have rightly criticized this contention for privileging alphabetic writing and disregarding the effectiveness of the composite nature of Mesoamerican texts. Contemporary European observers recognized the value of native documentation. For Fray Diego Durán, for example, the Mesoamerican recording system was highly effective. He stated:

> They have written and painted it all in books and large sheets (*papeles*), with the count of the years, the months, and days in which things happened. They have written in these paintings their legends and laws, their customs, etc. all with great order and care. From this they have most excellent historians that, with these paintings, compose the fullest history of their forbearers.[17]

In the years immediately following the conquest, a double-headed process took place that altered native ways of perceiving and recording. The tradition of the *tlahcuiloh* who had been specially trained in seminaries and academies underwent modification through their contact with Europeans. Nahua artists and scholars continued to use the old forms of symbolic representation and glyphs, but they were also influenced by images and techniques introduced from European art and writing. Perspective, shading, and other techniques were now used alongside traditional methods of composition and presentation. Indigenous peoples also adopted alphabetic writing. Through missionary instruction and schools, a generation of native youth learned Spanish and Latin and also began to write their Indigenous languages, including Nahuatl, Mixtec, Mayan, Purépecha, and others, in the Roman alphabet. The two traditions were sometimes combined, as in the case of the *Florentine Codex* or the *Codex Mendoza,* to produce a new "colonial" kind of writing. The mixture of the two traditions created a new kind of text altogether. A large number of these postcontact texts exist, reflecting various degrees of Indigenous and European elements and presenting a variety of viewpoints.

Among the various postcontact native texts are a number that record aspects of the fall of the Mexica Empire. The peoples of Mexico did not form a single political entity, and these political and ethnic divisions contributed to the fall of Tenochtitlan. Those subject to the Mexica used the arrival of the Spaniards to break free from imperial control. Traditional enemies of Tenochtitlan like Tlaxcala, after initial opposition, allied with the Spaniards, and even some former partners of Tenochtitlan like Texcoco abandoned the alliance during the war. The later accounts of the conquest reflected these political and ethnic differences. Narratives produced by Nahua intellectuals from Tlaxcala, Texcoco, Chalco, and other city-states told the story from their perspective and usually in a way favorable to their historical role and the glory of their city-state. We note specifically the works of Fernando de Alva Ixtlilxochitl of Texcoco and of Chalco historian Domingo Francisco de San Anton Muñón Chimalpahin Quauhtlehuanitzin.[18] This volume includes excerpts from both and from several other non-Mexica postcontact native sources.[19] Readers should be aware that these sources do not form an "Indigenous" vision of events that can be placed in opposition to a "European" view. The native sources are often at odds with each other over details and interpretations of events, and just like the Spanish sources, they reflect their authors' social, political, geographic, and other interests.

Of all the Nahua accounts, one group or collection stands out above all the others. It was a collaborative effort, compiled by a Spanish friar who employed native research assistants. As early as 1533, some missionaries advocated recording and collecting information on the culture of the Indigenous peoples of Mexico as a way of facilitating their conversion. Of these projects, by far the most ambitious and complete was that of Fray Bernardino de Sahagún. Around 1547 Sahagún began to interview Nahua informants who had lived before and during the conquest. The work was done with the help of young Nahua scholars who had been trained in the elite Mexica academy (*calmecac*) for religious and military leaders and had been subsequently instructed by missionaries. They collected information on the calendar, rituals, social organization, and philosophy of the Nahuas.

This research was done in three different locales: Tepepulco, Tlatelolco, and Tenochtitlan. The information was crosschecked in a method akin to what a modern anthropologist might do. Informants sometimes drew pictures illustrating their responses and then added commentary, which was then translated by Sahagún's assistants.

The text that resulted was organized in parallel columns of Nahuatl and Spanish translation and commentary, with accompanying illustrations that represent the Nahua tradition of painting historical narratives. This tripartite organization invited readers to study the narrative in both languages and to interpret the images alongside the words in order to capture the full meaning. The text, which Sahagún titled "General History of the Things of New Spain," went through a number of manuscript versions, but the most famous today is called the *Florentine Codex* because it is housed in the Laurenziana Library in Florence, Italy. Scholars rightly identify the Codex as one of the greatest ethnographic works ever done; it is a remarkable encyclopedia of Nahua society that is simultaneously a dictionary and a grammar as well.[20]

The sixteenth-century missionary project aimed at the Indigenous peoples of New Spain (Mexico) provides a context for Sahagún's work. First-generation missionaries (Franciscans, Dominicans, Augustinians, and Jesuits after 1574) were often men of considerable ability and fervent beliefs, but there were profound differences among the orders on how best to convert the native peoples. Some missionaries were more willing to look for parallels in native religions, arguing it would lead people to convert more easily. The first Franciscans, including Sahagún, emphasized the learning of native languages and an understanding of local custom and behavior as a way to bring converts to Christianity. As he put it, "These people are our brothers, descendants from the trunk of Adam like ourselves, they are our fellowmen whom we are obliged to love as ourselves."[21] Despite his repulsion at their "pagan" worship, Sahagún came to appreciate and even celebrate much of Nahua culture. Others did not share his enthusiasm. The rival Dominican Order, which was much less sympathetic to the integration of some Indigenous beliefs into Catholic practice, opposed Sahagún's methods, as did more conservative elements within the Franciscan Order itself. The primary fear was that Sahagún's approach preserved too much of the ancient beliefs (which were deemed to be the work of the devil). At one point the manuscripts were taken from him, presumably because some missionaries and civil authorities wanted to eliminate the old ways completely. Although Sahagún regained his manuscripts in 1575, the project later encountered political difficulties in Spain. Sahagún's great opus remained in manuscript form until it was finally published in 1829.

Book Twelve of the *Florentine Codex*, titled "How the War Was Fought Here in Mexico," is essentially a Mexica account of the events, filtered through Sahagún and his informants. In terms of content and length, this book is the most important Nahua version of the fall of the Mexica empire, but it does have its biases and problems. First, many of the informants were from Tlatelolco, the junior member of the Triple Alliance. Thus, the accounts tend to be highly critical of Tenochtitlan and especially of its leader Moctezuma, laying the blame for defeat on his indecision and weakness, and viewing any successes as due to the bravery of the Tlatelolcans. Second, the accounts were written down some thirty years after the events described, and it is difficult to know to what extent the passage of time clouded memories and provided time for reflection on events. Also unknown is the extent to which the subsequent conversion of the informants to Catholicism may have colored their view of their historical past. Scattered throughout the texts are postcontact elements. The ancient deities are called "devils," and metaphors such as "lusting after gold like pigs" are used even though there were no domestic swine in Mexico before the Spanish brought them. It is difficult to tell how much the young Nahua translators, already tied to Spanish culture, shaded meanings, molded their informants' accounts, or even misunderstood what the elders told them. Nevertheless, these accounts provide the basis of our knowledge of Nahua views of the conquest and its aftermath. They are surely native texts, but they are postcontact and they reflect the subject position and colonial situation of the Nahua peoples at the time they were recorded.

The Nahua accounts have been translated into English a number of times, but the truest and the one represented in this volume is that of James Lockhart. He was for many years a professor of Latin American history at the University of California in Los Angeles, where he worked on postcontact Nahuatl texts and trained a generation of graduate students in the philological and historical skills needed to use and analyze these documents. His translations of Book Twelve directly from the Nahuatl are particularly important because they are sensitive to the literal meaning of the Nahuatl and also to its common usage and the problems of converting it into idiomatic English. Lockhart pointed out that Sahagún's original translation into Spanish was often a paraphrase in which the friar inserted commentary and other observations. To what extent Book Twelve of the *Florentine Codex* is Sahagún's interpretation, or to what extent it is really a Nahua account, is open to much debate, but Lockhart was convinced that these texts reflect Indigenous "ideas, frameworks, and imperatives." In terms of language, narrative technique, and structure, Book Twelve presents an Indigenous view of the war, albeit a partial one biased by the passage of time, localism, and the peculiar circumstance of its composition. The translated Nahuatl text is included here alongside illustrations from the original because readers were meant to analyze the words and images together.

Another important Nahua account is the *Lienzo de Tlaxcala*, which was created circa 1552 as a series of paintings on a cotton canvas. The source depicts the political structure of Tlaxcala and celebrates the alliance between Tlaxcalans and Spaniards.[22] The Lienzo was originally commissioned by members of the town council of Tlaxcala to be taken to Spain on a diplomatic delegation. The original Lienzo, now lost, has primarily come down to us through a 1773 copy housed at the National Museum of Anthropology in Mexico City, and a lithograph facsimile copy (of the sixteenth-century original) printed in the late nineteenth century. The Lienzo underlines the importance of visual images to the Indigenous peoples of central Mexico as a way of recording the past.[23] European art and writing also influenced the Tlaxcalan artists, which can be seen in the left-to-right reading order and the manner of drawing the figures. Traditional iconographic conventions such as burning temples signifying defeat or the stylized presentation of soldiers point to a continuing Nahua artistic and representational tradition.

The Nahua and Spanish accounts differ in their form, structure, and content. Both Bernal Díaz and Cortés, whatever their differences, sought to tell a connected story, linking events in chronological order, mixing discussions of personality with analyses of motives and actions. The Nahua accounts are more episodic, a series of vignettes in which feats of individual bravery and the designs of uniforms receive as much attention as the decisions of leaders. This construction is typical of Indigenous historical traditions, where visual images were often used alongside oral accounts. The fact that those pictures that accompanied Sahagún's manuscript lack the detail of the written texts seems to confirm their use as markers or aides and the composite nature of Nahua texts. Traditional Nahua ways of remembering depended on song, dance, and formal oratory as well as on images. It is difficult to know how the Nahua understood the symbols they saw, when metaphor replaced literal understandings, or when irony was used. With the adaptation of the Roman alphabet to write Nahuatl, a whole new range of possibilities and cultural fusions opened up in terms of writing history. The Nahua texts and paintings of the conquest provide a rich and complex vision of history but one that is opaque and complicated as well.

We must also recognize the "silences" in the documents. Certain groups or sectors of society are not represented in the surviving sources. The voices of the majority of people went unrecorded due to class and gender biases. Literacy was limited among both Europeans and Nahua to certain groups in society. Although Bernal Díaz is seen as a representative of the common man, he was not from the lowest rungs of society but rather from the provincial middle class and, unlike many of his companions, he was educated. The Nahua accounts were written often by or for the nobility. How Mexica commoners (*macehualtin*) saw these events remains open to question. Furthermore, women obviously experienced the violence of war, but no sources on the events of the conquest written by women have survived, although we know that Maria Bártola, a sister of Cuitlahuac, the emperor who succeeded Moctezuma, wrote histories in both Spanish and Nahuatl. Much more is known about the perspective of women in the postcontact period.[24]

CONCLUSION

The outline of the fall of Tenochtitlan and the end of the Mexica Empire has been known for a long time, but in the past three decades newly uncovered sources, especially those written in Indigenous languages after the conquest, and new interpretative strategies have led to a far more nuanced understanding of these events. This New Conquest History no longer presents the simple triumphant narrative of Spanish courage and technology that became popular in the nineteenth century. This new history, instead, incorporates the activities and strategies of Indigenous peoples who allied with the Spanish or who joined the Tenochca in their defense, with considerable regional and ethnic variations. There is also a new emphasis on common people rather than on the exploits of a few military men. The story of the fall of the Mexica Empire challenges us to think about the problems that confront all historians. How can we understand and interpret other cultures? How can we evaluate conflicting sources? How can we read and understand such divergent styles of representation? And, how can we try to recapture the presence of those whose voices have been lost? The sources in the following chapters invite readers to answer these questions and also to imagine the experiences of those men and women who were caught up in this epic encounter.

NOTES

[1]For a thoughtful analysis of the mythologies that sustain popular narratives about Spaniards "conquering" the Americas, see Matthew Restall, *Seven Myths of the Spanish Conquest* (New York: Oxford University Press, 2003).

[2]Some good introductions to Mexica history can be found in Davíd Carrasco, *The Aztecs: A Very Short Introduction* (Oxford: Oxford University Press, 2012); Deborah L. Nichols and Enrique Rodríguez-Alegría, eds., *The Oxford Handbook of the Aztecs* (New York: Oxford University Press, 2016).

[3]An excellent history is Kevin Terraciano, *The Mixtecs of Colonial Oaxaca: Ñudzahui History, Sixteenth through Eighteenth Centuries* (Stanford: Stanford University Press, 2001).

[4]On the Purépecha state, see Helen Perlstein Pollard, *Taríacuri's Legacy: The Prehispanic Tarascan State* (Norman: University of Oklahoma Press, 1993); James Krippner-Martínez, *Rereading the Conquest: Power, Politics, and the History of Early Colonial Michoacán, Mexico, 1521–1565* (University Park: Pennsylvania State University Press, 2001); Rodrigo Martínez Baracs, *Convivencia y utopía: El gobierno indio y español de la "ciudad Mechuacan," 1521–1580* (México: INAH, 2005).

[5]Richard Conway, "Lakes, Canoes, and the Aquatic Communities of Xochimilco and Chalco, New Spain," *Ethnohistory* 59, no. 3 (2012).

[6]For this unique ecology, see Teresa Rojas Rabiela, *La agricultura chinampera: compilación histórica*, 2 ed. (Chapingo: Universidad Autónoma de Chapingo, 1993).

[7]For a discussion of the origins of the omens, see Camilla Townsend, "Burying the White Gods: New Perspectives on the Conquest of Mexico," *American Historical Review* 108, no. 3 (2003).

[8]For the military capabilities of both Nahuas and Spaniards, see Ross Hassig, *Aztec Warfare: Imperial Expansion and Political Control* (Norman: University of Oklahoma Press, 1988).

[9]José Joaquim da Cunha de Azeredo Coutinho, *Ensaio económico sobre o comércio de Portugal e suas colónias* (Lisboa: Banco de Portugal, 1992. 1794), 50.

[10]Sherburne F. Cook and Woodrow W. Borah, *Essays in Population History: Mexico and the Caribbean*, 3 vols. (Berkeley: University of California Press, 1971); David P. Henige, *Numbers from Nowhere: The American Indian Contact Population Debate* (Norman: University of Oklahoma Press, 1998). For a broader perspective, see Suzanne Austin Alchon, *A Pest in the Land: New World Epidemics in a Global Perspective* (Albuquerque: University of New Mexico Press, 2003).

[11]Anthony Pagden, ed., *Hernán Cortés: Letters from Mexico* (New Haven: Yale University Press, 1986); Hernán Cortés, *Cartas y documentos* (México: Editorial Porrúa, 1963). Cortés's letters have been subjected to analysis since they were first published. See, for example, Beatriz Pastor Bodmer, *The Armature of Conquest: Spanish Accounts of the Discovery of America, 1492–1589* (Stanford: Stanford University Press, 1992); Rolena Adorno, *The Polemics of Possession in Spanish American Narrative* (New Haven: Yale University Press, 2007).

[12]Francisco López de Gómara, *Cortés: The Life of the Conqueror*, trans. Lesley B. Simpson (Berkeley: University of California Press, 1966); *La conquista de México* (Madrid: Historia 16, 1987).

[13]There are a number of studies of Díaz and his book. See, for example, Carmelo Sáenz de Santa María, *Historia de una historia: La crónica de Bernal Díaz del Castillo* (Madrid: CSIC, 1984). For a biography in English, see Herbert Cerwin, *Bernal Díaz: Historian of the Conquest* (Norman: University of Oklahoma Press, 1963). We find unconvincing the doubts raised about Díaz's authorship by Christian Duverger, *Crónica*

de la eternidad: ¿Quién escribió la Historia verdadera de la conquista de la nueva España? (México: Taurus, 2013).

[14]Miguel León Portilla, *Pre-Columbian Literatures of Mexico*, trans. Grace Lobanov (Norman: University of Oklahoma Press, 1986), 117.

[15]On writing traditions, see Joyce Marcus, *Mesoamerican Writing Systems: Propaganda, Myth, and History in Four Ancient Civilizations* (Princeton: Princeton University Press, 1992); Donald Robertson, *Mexican Manuscript Painting of the Early Colonial Period: The Metropolitan Schools*, 2 ed. (Norman: University of Oklahoma Press, 1994); and Elizabeth H. Boone, *Stories in Red and Black: Pictorial Histories of the Aztecs and Mixtecs* (Austin: University of Texas Press, 2000).

[16]The ways in which alphabetic languages were linked to power in the conquest of America have been emphasized by Walter Mignolo, *The Darker Side of the Renaissance: Literacy, Territoriality, and Colonization* (Ann Arbor: University of Michigan Press, 1995); Tzvetan Todorov, *The Conquest of America: The Question of the Other*, 2 ed. (Norman: University of Oklahoma Press, 1999). Lockhart, by contrast, emphasized the adaptability of Nahuatl and thus implicitly contested the idea of Indigenous linguistic limitations: James Lockhart, *The Nahuas after the Conquest: A Social and Cultural History of the Indians of Central Mexico, Sixteenth through Eighteenth Centuries* (Stanford: Stanford University Press, 1992). See also Miguel León-Portilla, "El binomio oralidad y códices en Mesoamerica," *Estudios de Cultura Nahuatl* 27 (1997).

[17]Diego Durán, *Historia de las Indias de Nueva España e islas de Tierra Firme*, 2 vols., vol. 2 (México: Imprenta de Ignacio Escalante, 1880), 257.

[18]On Chimalpahin, see Susan Schroeder, *Chimalpahin and the Kingdoms of Chalco* (Tucson: University of Arizona Press, 1991). On Alva Ixtlilxochitl, see Amber Brian, *Alva Ixtlilxochitl's Native Archive and the Circulation of Knowledge in Colonial Mexico* (Nashville: Vanderbilt University Press, 2016).

[19]For a brief annotated listing of Indigenous codices relate to the conquest, see Hugh Thomas, *Conquest: Montezuma, Cortés, and the Fall of Old Mexico* (New York: Simon & Schuster, 1993), 774–84. The Latin American Originals series out of The Pennsylvania State University Press has published a number of translations of primary sources originally written in Indigenous languages about the conquest period.

[20]Fray Bernardino de Sahagún, *The Florentine Codex: Historia general de las cosas de Nueva España* (1577), https://www.wdl.org/en/item/10096/. For the English translation, see Arthur J. O. Anderson and Charles E. Dibble, eds., *Florentine Codex: General History of the Things of New Spain*, 12 vols. (Salt Lake City: University of Utah Press, 1982). For its construction, see Diana Magaloni Kerpel and Cuauhtémoc Medina, *The Colors of the New World: Artists, Materials, and the Creation of the Florentine Codex* (Los Angeles: Getty Publications, 2014).

[21]Angel María Garibay K., ed. *Historia general de las cosas de Nueva España*, 4 vols., vol. 1 (México: Porrúa, 1956), 31.

[22]For an insightful analysis of the Lienzo's original composition and its reconstruction, see Byron E. Hamann, "Object, Image, Cleverness: The Lienzo de Tlaxcala," *Art History* 36, no. 3 (2013). The reconstructed piece is online at http://www.mesolore.org/viewer/view/2/The-Lienzo-de-Tlaxcala.

[23]For the writing of history in Tlaxcala, see Travis Barton Kranz, "Visual Persuasion: Sixteenth-Century Tlaxcalan Pictorials in Response to the Conquest of Mexico," in *The Conquest All Over Again: Nahuas and Zapotecs Thinking, Writing, and Painting Spanish Colonialism*, ed. Susan Schroeder (Eastbourne, UK: Sussex Academic Press, 2010).

[24]Susan Schroeder, Stephanie G. Wood, et al., *Indian Women of Early Mexico* (Norman: University of Oklahoma Press, 1997). Lisa Sousa, *The Woman Who Turned Into a Jaguar, and Other Narratives of Native Women in Archives of Colonial Mexico* (Stanford: Stanford University Press, 2017).

PART TWO

Omens

The Documents

1

Omens

Omens and signs were an important aspect of Nahuatl history, employed to explain events and to foretell the future. The first source in this section, from the *Tovar Codex*, illustrates this cultural inclination. It represents the legendary founding of the Mexica capital at the place where their ancestors first saw an eagle perched on a cactus and recognized it as a sign for them to settle in Tenochtitlan. Nahua accounts of the fall of the Mexica Empire also emphasized signs and omens that preceded the Spaniards' arrival as a way of deciphering the unfolding events.

Although the omens described in the following selections appear to predate Spanish contact and to be native in origin, a closer look raises serious questions. There is much evidence suggesting that the Nahua peoples were not alarmed by the arrival of the Spaniards, and rather saw them as simply another group of dangerous outsiders who needed to be controlled or accommodated. After the conquest, on the other hand, some people from Tenochtitlan-Tlatelolco, where the impact of the war was most profound, considered otherworldly explanations. Nahua emphasis on eight miraculous omens—the usual number when the Nahua considered sets of anything—was probably a postcontact interpretation. Informants may have wished to placate the Spaniards who wrote down these accounts, and they may also have resented Moctezuma's failure to provide leadership. In the accounts of the omens, the story of the return of Quetzalcoatl begins to play a role in explaining Moctezuma's behavior from the outset of events, but that too was a subsequent gloss.

Omens announcing a cataclysmic change were not limited to the Nahua version of events, as we see from the third selection, drawn from the *Chronicles of Michoacán*, a text based on information gathered from Purépecha peoples, traditional enemies of the Mexica. They too discussed with Spanish friars that miraculous events had preceded the fall

28

of the Mexica Empire. Finally, Spanish accounts, like the fourth selection, also tended to incorporate a version of the omens, perhaps as a way of justifying colonialism by underlining the preordained nature of the conquest from a Christian perspective.

1

JUAN DE TOVAR

Mexican Eagle and Cactus

From *History of the Arrival of Indians to Populate Mexico*

This selection from a manuscript by Juan de Tovar illustrates the use of symbolism in Mexica history. Tovar was a Jesuit, son of a conquistador, who traveled widely in central Mexico to record its history. Fluent in Nahuatl and Otomí, Tovar sought to preserve Indigenous traditions in his principal work, Historia de la venida de los indios *(c.1580s), a copy of which is housed at the John Carter Brown Library. The manuscript, commonly called the* Tovar Codex, *employed drawings in the Mesoamerican tradition alongside Spanish commentary.*

This image depicts the legendary founding of Tenochtitlan, which occurred after migrants led by Tenoch (on right) witnessed an awaited sign: an eagle with a prey in its beak atop a flowering cactus located in the middle of a lake. In most depictions the eagle holds a snake instead of a bird. The historical importance of this omen is borne out in the modern-day flag of Mexico, which bears the eagle-on-a-cactus motif in memory of this event.

Juan de Tovar. "Historia de la benida de los yndios a poblar a Mexico . . ." (Mexico City, 1585), f.91v. Courtesy of the John Carter Brown Library at Brown University.

From the *Codex Tovar* (Mexico, c.1585). Courtesy of the John Carter Brown Library at Brown University.

2

FRAY BERNARDINO DE SAHAGÚN

From the *Florentine Codex*

The following selection from the Nahuatl text provided by Sahagún's research assistants reveals that some informants described wondrous signs at the inception of the story as indications of the events to come. Sahagún's assistants interviewed mainly people from Tlatelolco, but similar stories were also included in accounts that came from other Nahua communities. The illustration of the sixth omen should be read alongside the written description for a full rendering of the event.

Twelfth book, which speaks of how war was waged here in the altepetl of Mexico.

First chapter, where it is said that before the Spaniards came here to this land, and before the people who live here were known, there appeared and were seen signs and omens.

Ten years before the arrival of the Spaniards an omen first appeared in the sky, like a flame or tongue of fire, like the light of dawn. It appeared to be throwing off [sparks] and seemed to pierce the sky. It was wide at the bottom and narrow at the top. It looked as though it reached the very middle of the sky, its very heart and center. It showed itself off to the east. When it came out at midnight it appeared like the dawn. When dawn came, then the sun on coming out effaced it. For a full year it showed itself (it was in [the year] Twelve House that it began). And when it appeared there would be an outcry, and people would hit their hands against their mouths as they yelled. People were taken aback, they lamented.

The second omen that happened here in Mexico was that of its own accord the house of the devil Huitzilopochtli, what they call his mountain, named Tlacatecçan, burned and flared up; no one set fire to it, it just took fire itself. When the fire was seen, the wooden pillars were already burning. Tongues and tassels of flame were coming from inside; very quickly they consumed all the building's beams. Then there was an outcry. They

James Lockhart, ed., *We People Here: Nahuatl Accounts of the Conquest of Mexico* (Los Angeles: University of California Press, 1993), 50–56.

said, "O Mexica, let everyone come running, it must be put out, [bring] your water jars!" But when they threw water on it, trying to extinguish it, it blew up all the more. It could not be put out; it burned entirely.

The third omen was that a temple was struck by lightning, hit by a thunderbolt. It was just a building of straw at the temple complex of Xiuhteuctli, called Tzonmolco. The reason it was taken for an omen was that it was not raining hard, just drizzling. It was said that it was struck when the sun was shining, nor was thunder heard.

The fourth omen was that while the sun was still out a comet fell, in three parts. It began off to the west and headed in the direction of the east, looking as if it were sprinkling glowing coals. It had a long tail, which reached a great distance. When it was seen, there was a great outcry, like the sound of rattles.

The fifth omen was that the water [of the lake] boiled up; it was not the wind that caused it. It bubbled and made exploding sounds, rising high in the air. It reached the foundations of the houses; it flooded them, and they collapsed. This is the great lake that extends around us here in Mexico.

Figure 1. *"O my children, where am I to take you?"*
This section of the *Florentine Codex* shows the combined use of Spanish, Nahuatl, and pictorial renderings that makes this work truly unique.
Fray Bernardino de Sahagún, *The Florentine Codex: Historia general de las cosas de Nueva España,* Libro 12, f.2v, 1577.

The sixth omen was that many times a woman would be heard going along weeping and shouting. She cried out loudly at night, saying, "O my children, we are about to go forever." Sometimes she said, "O my children, where am I to take you?"

The seventh omen was that once the water folk were hunting or snaring and caught an ash-colored bird, like a crane. Then they went to the Tlillan calmecac to show it to Moteucçoma; the sun was inclining, it was still full day. On top of its head was something like a mirror, round, circular, seeming to be perforated, where the sky, the stars, and the Fire Drill [constellation] could be seen. And Moteucçoma took it for a very bad omen when he saw the stars and the Fire Drill. The second time he looked at the bird's head he saw something like a multitude of people coming along, coming bunched, outfitted for war, carried on the backs of deer. Then he called the soothsayers, the sages, and said to them, "Do you not know what I've seen, something like a multitude of people coming along?" But when they were going to answer him, what they saw disappeared, and they said nothing more.

The eighth omen was that many times people appeared, thistlepeople with two heads but one body; they took them to the Tlillan calmecac and showed them to Moteucçoma. When he had seen them, they disappeared.

3

FRAY MARTÍN DE JESÚS DE LA CORUÑA

From the *Chronicles of Michoacán*

The Purépecha peoples who dwelled to the northwest of Tenochtitlan lived in a relationship of respectful hostility with the Mexica. They too spoke about strange events previewing the arrival of the Spaniards. Their leaders (called cazonci*) had successfully resisted Mexica expansion into their area, the present-day Mexican state of Michoacán. Franciscan*

Chronicles of Michoacán, trans. and ed. Eugene R. Craine and Reginald C. Reindorp (Norman: University of Oklahoma Press, 1970), 53–54.

missionaries and Spanish soldiers made incursions starting in the 1520s, and by 1541, Fray Martín de Jesús de la Coruña had written a description of the province. Like Sahagún's work it was based on interviews with Purépecha informants, although the author's own biases and commentaries appear throughout the text.

These people say that during the four years before the Spaniards came to the land, their temples were burned from top to bottom, that they closed them and they would be burned again, and that the rock walls fell as their temples were made of flagstones. They did not know the cause of this except that they held it to be an augury. Likewise, they saw two large comets in the sky and thought that their gods were to conquer or destroy a village and that they were to do it for them. These people imitate parts of their dreams and do as much of what they dreamed as they can. They report their dreams to the chief priest who in turn conveys the information to the Cazonci. They say that the poor who bring in wood and sacrifice their ears dream about their gods who are reported as having told them that they would be given food and that they should marry such and such Christian girls. If this were a kind of omen they dared not tell it to the Cazonci. A priest related that, before the Spaniards came, he had dreamed that people would come bringing strange animals which turned out to be the horses which he had not known. In this dream these people entered the houses of the chief priests and slept there with their horses. They also brought many chickens that soiled the temples. He said he dreamed this two or three times in considerable fear for he did not know what it was until the Spaniards came to this province. When the Spaniards reached the city, they lodged in the houses of the chief priests with their horses where they held their prayer and kept their vigil. Before the Spaniards arrived they all had smallpox and measles, from which large numbers of people died, along with many lords and high families. All the Spaniards of the time are unanimous in that this disease was general throughout New Spain, for which reason it is to be given credence. The people are in accord in that measles and smallpox were unknown until the Spaniards brought them to the land.

4

DIEGO DURÁN

From *The History of the Indies of New Spain*

European authors who began to write about the peoples of Mesoamerica tended to incorporate some aspects of Indigenous history. Spanish writers like Diego Durán (1537–1587) sought to give their works a feeling of authenticity by including Nahua accounts of omens while also self-righteously suggesting the possible divine hand of God in the events of the conquest. Born in Seville, Durán came to Mexico as a child and learned to speak Nahuatl fluently; he resided in Texcoco, a center of indigenous culture. Durán became a member of the Dominican Order and eventually produced learned books on Nahua religion and history. His works were not published in his lifetime, but they circulated widely in manuscript form, and many other contemporary authors used them as a primary source. Included here is an example of the appropriation of omens into a Spanish explanation of Nahua actions, which also touches on the importance of pictographic representation as a historical method.

Montezuma remained concerned after hearing from Tlillancalqui [about the Spaniards] . . . and desired to know more about those who had happened upon his land, and where they had come from, and whose sons they were . . . and if they were to return. And with this preoccupation, he called on Tlillancalqui, and behind closed doors told him that he wished to see the manners of those men Tlillancalqui had seen. Montezuma asked him to have them [Spaniards] painted [*pintados*] in his presence, so that no one would know. Tlillancalqui said he would be pleased to have them painted, and thus called on the best painter in Mexico, who was an elderly man.

Secretly, Montezuma warned the painter that if anyone discovered what he was about to do, his lineage would disappear . . . The painter, fearful, replied that who was he to reveal the secret of such a powerful lord. Afterwards, all manner of colorful paints [*colores*] were brought [for the painter]. Tlillancalqui described to the painter what he had to portray, and the painter painted the ship Tlillancalqui had seen, and also the Spaniards with their long beards and white faces, and wearing clothes of different colors, and with hats on their heads and caps, and

Translation by T. Seijas. Durán, Diego. *Historia de las Indias de Nueva España y islas de Tierra Firme*. México: J.M. Andrade y F. Escalante, 1880.

carrying swords. Montezuma was amazed when he saw the Spaniards and looked at them for a long while, considering their appearance with great attention. Then he asked Tlillancalqui, "Did the paintings bear their likeness?" And he replied, "Yes my lord, without a lie or addition."

Montezuma ordered that the painter be paid for his work, and he said: "Brother, I beg you to tell me the truth; by chance do you know anything about what you have just painted? Did your ancestors leave you a painting or relation about these men arriving in my land? The painter responded: "Powerful Lord, I should not lie to you . . . it is well known that neither I, nor my ancestors ever had another discipline than to paint, and they did not leave accounts of what they painted for previous kings, so I do not know about anything about what you ask." . . . Montezuma ordered the painter to make inquiries with all the masters of his craft, and ask if they had a painting or relation from their own ancestors about the identity of the men who had come upon the land. The painter said he would do so and spent days making inquiries, but unable to learn anything, he told Montezuma that there was nothing to be found on the matter.

Seeking a different angle, Montezuma called on all the elderly painters of Malinalco . . . and Chalco and begged them to tell him if they knew anything about the people who were to return to his land, and if their ancestors had left them an account, or paintings, or effigies about them. [The painters showed Montezuma various paintings of fantastical beings, but he remained unsatisfied . . .]

Montezuma then called for the painters of Cuitlavac [Cuitláhuac] and those of Mizquic [Mixquic], saying that they were the wise heirs of the ancient Toltecs, and that they would surely know something. These painters went to Montezuma and brought their ancient paintings, and they told him that their ancestors had said that the children of Quetzalcoatl would return, and that they would possess the land that was once their dominion . . . But upon showing him the likeness of these men, Montezuma was not satisfied, as they did not conform to what had been painted for him previously.

Montezuma then called on the painters from Xochimilco, but Tlillancalqui who was present said: "Powerful Lord, you will tire and become uneasy from making inquiries from so many people, but there is one elderly man from Xochimilco whose name is Quilastli, very learned about antiquities, and if you would like, I will bring him before you and tell him about what you desire to know, and also ask him to bring his old paintings. Montezuma thanked him . . . The next day Tlillancalqui returned with the elderly painter who brought with him all the paintings about this business. The said painter was well received, for he was a venerable figure with a strong presence, and Montezuma begged him to declare what he knew about the men who were to come to this land. Quilastli responded: "Powerful Lord, I come before you willingly, even if must die for telling you the truth." And before showing Montezuma the papers, Quilastli told him the news, that the men who were to come to this land would arrive atop a large wooden mound with room for many men, which would serve as their house, where they would eat and sleep . . . and that these men would be bearded and white, dressed in different colors . . . and that some men would be riding beasts like deer and others would come flying like the wind upon eagles. And that these men would possess the land and populate all the towns, and that they would multiply, and would need to possess gold and silver and precious stones. [The painter said:] "In order for you to believe what I say is truth, examine what is painted here, my ancestors left me this painting." And taking out a very old painting, Quilastli showed Montezuma the ship . . . and the men on horseback, dressed in different colors and carrying swords.

Montezuma, seeing that these men conformed to what he had seen painted previously, was beside himself, and he began to cry in anguish. And revealing his heart to the old man, he said, "My brother, you should know that your ancestors were truly wise and knowledgeable, because those men you show in the painting arrived in this land only a few days ago, from where the sun rises, and they came in a wooden house . . . and dressed in the same way . . . Look at them painted here. But one thing consoles me, that I sent them a gift and asked them to leave in goodwill, and they obeyed me and left, and I do not know if they will return."

Quilastli responded, "It is possible, my powerful Lord, that they came and that they have left, but listen, and if what I say is false you may kill my family . . . Before two or three years pass, they will return to this land, because they visited merely to become acquainted with the route, in order to come back; and even though they said they were returning to their homeland, do not believe them; for they will come back once they are half way there."

Montezuma, acknowledging what the old man had said, and not pleased, said he did not want a wise man like himself to leave, but instead for him to be by his side. So Montezuma ordered that houses and land be given to Quilastli for his use and that of his children and family in Mexico City. And from then on Montezuma always had Quilastli by his side, doing nothing without his counsel. Then he sent a message to all the ports on the coast, where the sun raises, that everyone keep a careful lookout for anything coming from the sea, and that he be notified immediately. Since then, spies in watchtowers and citadels watched the sea. A year passed and then another and they [Spaniards] did not return, so Montezuma [turned his mind elsewhere] . . . People say that during the third year, when Montezuma had already forgotten, news came to him that a mound was at sea, and then two and three, going along the sea . . . And Montezuma, astonished, became distressed about what was about to happen . . .

2

Preparations

The sources included in this section narrate how Spaniards organized expeditions to the mainland of Mesoamerica from outposts in the Caribbean. The selection from Bernal Díaz begins after Grijalva's return to Cuba and then moves chronologically through the organizing of a new expedition under Hernando Cortés ("the General"), the return to Yucatan, and then the progress of the expedition up the Gulf coast of Mexico. The selection from Cortés's first letter to Charles V, king of Spain and Holy Roman Emperor, gives his (favorable and self-serving) interpretation of these events as well as explication for the founding of the town of Vera Cruz. Finally, the chapter includes a petition to the king by the town's newly organized municipal council to underline how Cortés and his followers employed legal constructs to defend their actions.

The selection from Díaz has three main themes. First is the importance of translators and of language itself in the process of encounter and conquest. The Spaniards understood this strategy from the outset, but they also had incredible luck. A Taino woman from Jamaica, who had been a castaway on the Yucatan coast and thus spoke Mayan, facilitated their first contacts with Maya peoples (Díaz and other Spaniards who had lived in the Caribbean understood and spoke Arawakan languages to varying degrees). Later, Cortés's expedition brought along as translators two Maya youths whom the Spaniards had previously captured. The Spaniards' major stroke of luck was discovering that two Spanish shipwreck survivors were living in Maya communities. Díaz recounts the story of the two: Jerónimo de Aguilar, who returned to become Cortés's Mayan translator; and Gonzalo Guerrero, who refused to return and instead remained with his wife, children, and adopted community. He later died leading Maya resistance against the Spaniards. Finally, Díaz tells in detail of the young Nahua noblewoman, an enslaved captive among the

Maya, who became Cortés's main translator, advisor, and confidante. Doña Marina or Malintzin is always treated with great respect in Díaz's account. The importance of language as a tool of conquest was never lost on Díaz.

A second theme is the military aspects of contact: weapons, equipment, logistics, and tactics. Díaz went beyond others in noting how Cortés often used demonstrations of European weaponry and horses for their psychological impact. At the same time, Díaz was also an astute observer of Indian weaponry and their military strategies. From his perspective, these were battles between worthy opponents in the tradition of European warfare.

The third theme is demonstrated by Díaz's awareness of the complexity of Indigenous states. He remarks on their system of writing or painting and communication, on their political system, and, negatively, on their religious practices. His descriptions of the first interviews with Moctezuma's ambassadors bear direct comparison with the Nahua accounts that appear in Chapter 3. At this time, the expedition also began to hear about "Culua" (Nahuatl language) and "Mexico." These were the first references to the Mexica Empire. While Díaz and his companions often misunderstood what they observed, they did differentiate among the various ethnicities and political loyalties of Indigenous peoples. This interaction was ethnography in the service of conquest.

The selections from Cortés and the petition expose the rivalry and political struggle represented by the enmity between Cortés and Diego Velázquez, the governor of Cuba. Cortés, having learned that there was a rich empire to conquer, broke away from the authority of Velázquez (just as Velázquez had earlier broken from the authority of the governor of Hispaniola). This political maneuvering was a relatively common pattern among the conquistadors. Typical of such struggles was an attempt to establish a new basis of authority (the foundation of the municipality of Vera Cruz) and the sending of a representative directly to Spain for royal approval, which Cortés certainly did. The conflict between the Cortés and Velázquez factions reemerges again and again in the story.

The excerpts from Cortés's first and second letters to Charles V explain the events that led to the foundation of Vera Cruz. It was a tricky business. Cortés had created a new municipality (staffed with his loyal followers) that abrogated his authority as granted by the governor of Cuba but established him as its representative. It was a legal sleight of hand. Cortés knew that this maneuver would be opposed by Governor Velázquez and by his supporters back in Spain, particularly Bishop Juan Rodríguez de Fonseca, head of the Council of the Indies. For this reason, Cortés gathered all the treasure acquired up to that point and dispatched

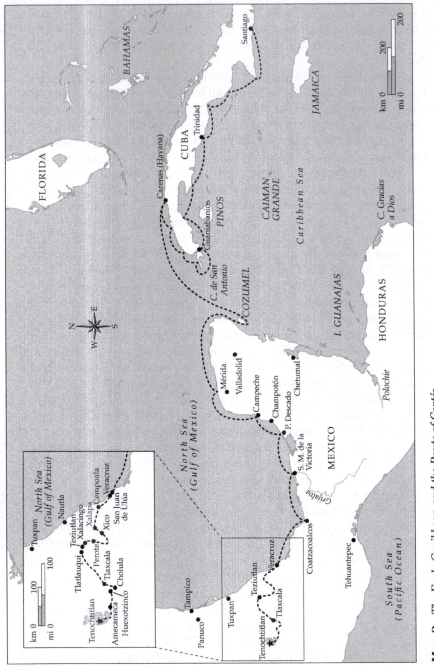

Map 3. *The Early Caribbean and the Route of Cortés.*
Adapted from *Itinerario de Hernán Cortés* from inside cover of *Hernán Cortés: Letters from Mexico* by Anthony Pagden. Copyright © 1986, 1992 by Yale University Press. Reprinted with permission.

it to the king along with his letter and two trusted representatives to plead his case. The decision to ground (not burn) the remaining ships was both to make use of the sailors as troops and to prevent dissidents of the Velázquez faction from reaching Cuba. Notice that Cortés's first letter is written in the third person in order to present a sense of objectivity despite the fact that his reports were, in fact, personal justifications. The extract from a petition made by the town council of Vera Cruz to Charles V offers a different rendering of the events leading to the town's foundation; it is included here for comparison and to illustrate Spaniards' emphasis on establishing the legal grounds for military conquest.

5

BERNAL DÍAZ

From *The True History of the Conquest of New Spain*

Díaz's account provides an outline of events but also considerable detail about his companions and the political and personal factions among them. The descriptions of the battles with Maya kingdoms, the story of the Spanish castaways, and that of Doña Marina (Malintzin) are highlights of the narrative.

After the return of the Captain Juan de Grijalva to Cuba, when the Governor Diego Velázquez understood how rich were these newly discovered lands, he ordered another fleet, much larger than the former one to be sent off . . . [Several] disputes arose over the choice of a captain for the expedition . . . Most of us soldiers who were there said that we should prefer to go again under Juan de Grijalva, for he was a good captain, and there was no fault to be found either with his person or his capacity for command. . . .

Bernal Díaz del Castillo, *The True History of the Conquest of New Spain,* trans. Alfred P. Maudslay, 2d series (London: Printed for the Hakluyt Society, 1908), 69–77, 90–103, 107–13, 118–35, 154–60.

Two great favorites of Diego . . . secretly formed a partnership with a gentleman named Hernando Cortés, a native of Medellin [Spain], who held a grant of Indians in the Island. . . . [They agreed to] divide between the three of them, the spoil of gold, silver and jewels which might fall to Cortés' share. For secretly Diego Velázquez was sending [the expedition] to trade and not to form a settlement, as was apparent afterwards from the instructions given about it, although it was announced and published that the expedition was for the purpose of founding a settlement.

When this arrangement had been made, Duero and the accountant went to work in such a way with Diego Velázquez, and addressed such honied words to him, praising Cortés highly, as the very man for the position of Captain, as in addition to being energetic he knew how to command and ensure respect, and as one who would be faithful in everything entrusted to him, both in regard to the fleet and in everything else . . . When the appointment was made public, some persons were pleased and others annoyed . . .

Before going any further I wish to say that the valiant and energetic Hernando Cortés was a gentleman by birth (*hijo-d'algo*) by four lines of descent. . . . Although he was such a valiant, energetic, and daring captain, I will not from now on, call him by any of these epithets of valiant, or energetic, nor will I speak of him as Marqués del Valle, but simply as Hernando Cortés. For the name Cortés alone was held in as high respect throughout the Indies as well as in Spain, as was the name of Alexander in Macedonia, and those of Julius Caesar and Pompey and Scipio among the Romans, and Hannibal among the Carthaginians . . . And the valiant Cortés himself was better pleased not to be called by lofty titles but simply by his name, and so I will call him for the future. . . .

As soon as Hernando Cortés had been appointed General . . . he began to search for all sorts of arms, guns, powder and crossbows and every kind of warlike stores which he could get together, and all sorts of articles to be used for barter, and other things necessary for the expedition. . . .

We assembled at Santiago de Cuba, whence we set out with the fleet more than three hundred and fifty soldiers in number. . . .

As soon as we arrived in port we went on shore with all the soldiers to the town of Cozumel, but we found no Indians there as they had all fled. So we were ordered to go on to another town about a league distant, and there also the natives had fled and taken to the bush, but they could not carry off their property and left behind their poultry and other things and Pedro de Alvarado ordered forty of the fowls to be taken.

In an Idol house there were some altar ornaments made of old cloths and some little chests containing diadems, Idols, beads and pendants of gold of poor quality, and here we captured two Indians and an Indian woman, and we returned to the town where we had disembarked.

While we were there Cortés arrived with all the fleet, and after taking up his lodging the first thing he did was to order the pilot Camacho to be put in irons for not having waited for him at sea as he had been ordered to do. When he saw the town without any people in it, and heard that Pedro de Alvarado had gone to the other town and had taken fowls and cloths and other things of small value from the Idols, and some gold which was half copper, he showed that he was very angry both at that and at the pilot not having waited for him, and he reprimanded Pedro de Alvarado severely, and told him that we should never pacify the country in that way by robbing the natives of their property, and he sent for the two Indians and the woman whom we had captured, and through Melchorejo . . . the man we had brought from Cape Catoche who understood the language well, he spoke to them telling them to go and summon the Caciques and Indians of their town, and he told them not to be afraid, and he ordered the gold and the cloths and all the rest to be given back to them, and for the fowls (which had already been eaten) he ordered them to be given beads and little bells, and in addition he gave to each Indian a Spanish shirt.

So they went off to summon the lord of the town, and the next day the Cacique and all his people arrived, women and children and all the inhabitants of the town, and they went about among us as though they had been used to us all their lives, and Cortés ordered us not to annoy them in any way. Here in this Island Cortés began to rule energetically, and Our Lord so favored him that whatever he put his hand to it turned out well for him, especially in pacifying the people and towns of these lands, as we shall see further on.

When we had been in Cozumel three days Cortés ordered a muster of his forces so as to see how many of us there were, and he found that we numbered five hundred and eight, not counting the shipmasters, pilots and sailors, who numbered about one hundred. There were sixteen horses and mares all fit to be used for sport or as chargers.

There were eleven ships both great and small, and one a sort of launch which a certain Gines Nortes brought laden with supplies.

There were thirty two crossbowmen and thirteen musketeers;— *escopeteros*, as they were then called and brass guns, and four falconets, and much powder and ball. . . .

As Cortés was most diligent in all matters, he sent for me and a Biscayan named Martin Ramos, and asked us what we thought about those words which the Indians of Campeche had used when we went there . . . when they cried out "Castilan, Castilan" . . . We again related to Cortés all that we had seen and heard about the matter, and he said that he also had often thought about it, and that perhaps there might be some Spaniards living in the country, and added "It seems to me that it would be well to ask these Caciques of Cozumel if they know anything about them." So through Melchorejo . . . [who] knew the language of Cozumel very well, all the chiefs were questioned, and every one of them said that they had known of certain Spaniards and gave descriptions of them, and said that some Caciques, who lived about two days' journey inland, kept them as slaves, and that here in Cozumel were some Indian traders who spoke to them only a few days ago.

We were all delighted at this news, and Cortés told the Caciques that they must go at once and summon the Spaniards, taking with them letters . . . and he he gave shirts to the Caciques and Indians who went with the letters and spoke reassuringly to them, and told them that when they returned he would give them some more beads. The Cacique advised Cortés to send a ransom to the owners who held these men as slaves, so that they should be allowed to come, and Cortés did so, and gave to the messengers all manner of beads. Then he ordered the two smallest vessels to be got ready (one of them was little larger than a launch [ship]) and twenty men with guns and crossbows, under the command of Diego de Ordás, and he sent them off to the coast near Cape Catoche where the larger vessel was to wait for eight days while the smaller vessel should go backwards and forwards and bring news of what was being done, for the land of Cape Catoche was only four leagues distant, and the one country could be seen from the other.

In the letter Cortés said:—"Gentlemen and brothers, here in Cozumel I have learnt that you are captives in the hands of a Cacique, and I pray you that you come here to Cozumel at once, and for this purpose I have sent a ship with soldiers, in case you have need of them, and a ransom to be paid to those Indians with whom you are living. The ship will wait eight days for you. Come in all haste, and you will be welcomed and protected. I am here at this Island with five hundred soldiers and eleven ships, in which I go on, please God, to a town called Tabasco or Potonchan."

The two vessels were soon dispatched with the two Indian traders from Cozumel who carried the letters, and they crossed the strait in three hours and the messengers with the letters and ransom were landed. In two days the letters were delivered to a Spaniard named Jerónimo de Aguilar, for that we found to be his name, and so I shall call him in future. When he had read the letter and received the ransom of beads which we had sent to him he was delighted, and carried the ransom to the Cacique his master, and begged leave to depart, and the Cacique at once gave him leave to go wherever he pleased.

Aguilar set out for the place, five leagues distant, where his companion Gonzalo Guerrero was living, but when he read the letter to him he answered, "Brother Aguilar, I am married and have three children and the Indians look on me as a Cacique and captain in wartime,—You go and God be with you, but I have my face tattooed and my ears pierced, what would the Spaniards say should they see me in this guise? And look how handsome these boys of mine are, for God's sake give me those green beads you have brought and I will give the beads to them and say that my brothers have sent them from my own country." And the Indian wife of Gonzalo spoke to Aguilar in her own tongue very angrily and said to him, "What is this slave coming here for talking to my husband,—go off with you, and don't trouble us with any more words."

Then Aguilar reminded Gonzalo that he was a Christian and said that he should not imperil his soul for the sake of an Indian woman, and as for his wife and children he could take them with him if he did not wish to desert them. But by no words or admonishments could he be persuaded to come. . . .

When Jerónimo de Aguilar saw that Gonzalo would not accompany him he went at once, with the two Indian messengers, to the place where the ship had been awaiting his coming, but when he arrived he saw no ship for she had already departed. The eight days during which Ordás had been ordered to await and one day more had already expired, and seeing that Aguilar had not arrived Ordás returned to Cozumel without bringing any news about that for which he had come.

When Aguilar saw that there was no ship there he became very sad, and returned to his master and to the town where he usually lived.

Now I will leave this and say that when Cortés saw Ordás return without success or any news of the Spaniards or Indian messengers he was very angry, and said haughtily to Ordás that he thought that he would have done better than to return without the Spaniards or any news of them, for it was quite clear that they were prisoners in that country. . . .

[M]any Indians both the natives of the towns near Cape Catoche and those from other parts of Yucatan came on pilgrimages to the Island of Cozumel, for it appeared that there were some very hideous idols kept in a certain oratory on Cozumel to which it was the custom of the people of the land to offer sacrifices at that season. One morning the courtyard of the oratory where the Idols were kept was crowded with Indians, and many of them both men and women were burning a resin like our incense. As this was a new sight to us we stood round watching it with attention, and presently an old Indian with a long cloak, who was the priest of the Idols (and I have already said that the priests in New Spain are called Papás [fathers]) went up on the top of the oratory and began to preach to the people. Cortés and all of us were wondering what would be the result of that black sermon. Cortés asked Melchorejo, who understood the language well, what the old Indian was saying, for he was informed that he was preaching evil things, and he sent for the Cacique and all the principal chiefs and the priest himself, and, as well as he could through the aid of our interpreter, he told them that if we were to be brothers they must cast those most evil Idols out of their temple, for they were not gods at all but very evil things which led them astray and could lead their souls to hell. Then he spoke to them about good and holy things, and told them to set up in the place of their Idols an image of Our Lady which he gave them, and a cross, which would always aid them and bring good harvests and would save their souls, and he told them in a very excellent way other things about our holy faith.

The Priest and the Caciques answered that their forefathers had worshipped those Idols because they were good, and that they did not dare to do otherwise, and that if we cast out their Idols we would see how much harm it would do us, for we should be lost at sea. Then Cortés ordered us to break the Idols to pieces and roll them down the steps, and this we did; then he ordered lime to be brought, of which there was a good store in the town, and Indian masons, and he set up a very fair altar on which we placed the figure of Our Lady; and he ordered two of our party . . . . who were carpenters and joiners to make a cross of some rough timber which was there, and it was placed in a small chapel near the altar and the priest named Juan Díaz said mass there, and the Cacique and the heathen priest and all the Indians stood watching us with attention. . . .

When the Spaniard who was a prisoner among the Indians, knew for certain that we had returned to Cozumel with the ships, he was very joyful and gave thanks to God, and he came in all haste with the two Indians who had carried the letters and ransom, and embarked in a canoe, and as he was able to pay well with the green beads we had sent him, he soon hired a canoe and six Indian rowers, and they rowed so fast that, meeting no head wind, in a very short time they crossed the strait between the two shores, which is a distance of about four leagues.

When they arrived on the coast of Cozumel and were disembarking, some soldiers who had gone out hunting (for there were wild pigs on the island) told Cortés that a large canoe, which had come from the direction of Cape Catoche, had arrived near the town. Cortés sent Andrés de Tápia and two other soldiers to go and see, for it was a new thing for Indians to come fearlessly in large canoes into our neighborhood.

So they set out, and as soon as the Indians who came in the canoe which Aguilar had hired caught sight of the Spaniards, they were frightened and wished to get back into the canoe and flee away. Aguilar told them in their own language not to be afraid, that these men were his brothers. When Andrés de Tápia saw that they were only Indians (for Aguilar looked neither more nor less than an Indian), he at once sent word to Cortés by a Spaniard that they were Cozumel Indians who had come in the canoe. As soon as the men had landed, the Spaniard in words badly articulated and worse pronounced, cried *Dios y Santa Maria de Sevilla*, and Tápia went at once to embrace him. The other soldier who had accompanied Tápia when he saw what had happened, promptly ran to Cortés to beg a reward for the good news, for it was a Spaniard who had come in the canoe, and we were all delighted when we heard it.

Tápia soon brought the Spaniard to Cortés, but before he arrived where Cortés was standing, several Spaniards asked Tápia where the Spaniard was? although he was walking by his side, for they could not distinguish him from an Indian as he was naturally brown and he had his hair shorn like an Indian slave, and carried a paddle on his shoulder, he was shod with one old sandal and the other was tied to his belt, he had on a ragged old cloak, and a worse loin cloth with which he covered his nakedness, and he had tied up, in a bundle in his cloak, a Book of Hours, old and worn.

When Cortés saw him in this state, he too was deceived like the other soldiers, and asked Tápia "Where is the Spaniard?" On hearing this, the Spaniard squatted down on his haunches as the Indians do and said "I am he." Cortés at once ordered him to be given a shirt and doublet and drawers and a cape and sandals, for he had no other clothes, and asked him about himself and what his name was and when he came to this country. The man replied, pronouncing with difficulty, that he was called Jerónimo de Aguilar, a native of Ecija, and that he had taken holy orders, that eight years had passed since he and fifteen other men and two women left Darien [Panama] for the Island of Santo Domingo, where he had some disputes and a law-suit . . . and he said that they were carrying ten thousand gold dollars and the legal documents of the case, and that the ship in which they sailed, struck on the Alacranes [Scorpion Reef] so that she could not be floated, and that he and his companions and the two women got into the ship's boat, thinking to reach the Island of Cuba or Jamaica, but that the currents were very strong and carried them to this land, and that the Calachiones of that district had divided them among themselves, and that many of his companions had been sacrificed to the Idols, and that others had died of disease, and the women had died of overwork only a short time before, for they had been made to grind corn; that the Indians had intended him for a sacrifice, but that one night he escaped and fled to the Cacique with whom since then he had been living (I don't remember the name that he gave) and that none were left of all his party except himself and a certain Gonzalo Guerrero, whom he had gone to summon, but he would not come.

When Cortés heard all this, he gave thanks to God, and said that he would have him well looked after and rewarded. He questioned Aguilar about the country and the towns, but Aguilar replied that having been a slave, he knew only about hewing wood and drawing water and digging in the fields, that he had only once travelled as far as four leagues from home when he was sent with a load, but, as it was heavier than he could carry, he fell ill, but that he understood that there were very many towns.

When questioned about Gonzalo Guerrero, he said that he was married and had three sons, and that his face was tattooed and his ears and lower lip were pierced, that he was a seaman and a native of Palos, and that the Indians considered him to be very valiant; that when a little more than a year ago a captain and three vessels arrived at Cape Catoche, (it seems probable that this was when we came with Francisco Hernández de Córdova) it was at the suggestion of Guerrero that the Indians attacked them, and that he was there himself in the company of the Cacique of the large town . . . . When Cortés heard this he exclaimed "I wish I had him in my hands for it will never do to leave him here."

When the Caciques of Cozumel found out that Aguilar could speak their language, they gave him to eat of their best, and Aguilar advised them always to respect and revere the holy image of Our Lady and the Cross, for they would find that it would benefit them greatly.

On the advice of Aguilar the Caciques asked Cortés to give them a letter of recommendation, so that if any other Spaniards came to that port they would treat the Indians well and do them no harm, and this letter was given to them. After bidding the people good-bye with many caresses and promises we set sail for the Rio de Grijalva.

[There follows a description of armed conflict with Maya soldiers in Tabasco . . .]

[W]e were marching along when we met all the forces of the enemy which were moving in search of us, and all the men wore great feather crests and they carried drums and trumpets, and their faces were colored black and white, and they were armed with large bows and arrows, lances and shields and swords shaped like our two-handed swords, and many slings and stones and fire-hardened javelins, and all wore quilted cotton armor. As they approached us their squadrons were so numerous that they covered the whole plain, and they rushed on us like mad dogs completely surrounding us, and they let fly such a cloud of arrows, javelins and stones that on the first assault they wounded over seventy of us, and fighting hand to hand they did us great damage with their lances, and one soldier fell dead at once from an arrow wound in the ear, and they kept on shooting and wounding us. With our muskets and crossbows and with good sword play we did not fail as stout fighters, and when they came to feel the edge of our swords little by little they fell back, but it was only so as to shoot at us in greater safety. Mesa, our artilleryman, killed many of them with his cannon, for they were formed in great squadrons and they did not open out so that he could fire at them as he pleased, but with all the hurts and wounds which we gave them, we could not drive them off. I said to Diego de Ordás "it seems to me that we ought to close up and charge them," for in truth they suffered greatly from the strokes and thrusts of our swords, and that was why they fell away from us, both from fear of these swords, and the better to shoot their arrows and hurl their javelins and the hail of stones. Ordás replied that it was not good advice, for there were three hundred Indians to every one of us, and that we could not hold out against such a multitude,—so there we stood enduring their attack. However, we did agree to get as near as we could to them, as I had advised Ordás, so as to give them a bad time with our swordsmanship, and they suffered so much from it that they retreated towards a swamp. . . .

I remember that when we fired shots the Indians gave great shouts and whistles and threw dust and rubbish into the air so that we should not see the damage done to them, and they sounded their trumpets and drums and shouted and whistled and cried "Alala! alala!"

Just at this time we caught sight of our horsemen, and as the great Indian host was crazed with its attack on us, it did not at once perceive them coming up behind their backs, and as the plain was level ground and the horsemen were good riders, and many of the horses were very handy and fine gallopers, they came quickly on the enemy and speared them as they chose. As soon as we saw the horsemen we fell on the Indians with such energy that with us attacking on one side and the horsemen on the other, they soon turned tail. The Indians thought that the horse and its rider was all one animal, for they had never seen horses up to this time.

The savannas and fields were crowded with Indians running to take refuge in the thick woods near by.

After we had defeated the enemy Cortés told us that he had not been able to come to us sooner as there was a swamp in the way, and he had to fight his way through another force of warriors before he could reach us, and three horsemen and five horses had been wounded.

As soon as the horsemen had dismounted under some trees and houses, we returned thanks to God for giving us so complete a victory.

. . . This was the first battle that we fought under Cortés in New Spain.

After this we bound up the hurts of the wounded with cloths, for we had nothing else, and we doctored the horses by searing their wounds with the fat from the body of a dead Indian which we cut up to get out the fat, and we went to look at the dead lying on the plain and there were more than eight hundred of them, the greater number killed by thrusts, the others by the cannon, muskets and crossbows, and many were stretched on the ground half dead. Where the horsemen had passed, numbers of them lay dead or groaning from their wounds. The battle lasted over an hour, and the Indians fought all the time like brave warriors, until the horsemen came up.

We took five prisoners, two of them Captains. As it was late and we had had enough of fighting, and we had not eaten anything, we returned to our camp. Then we buried the two soldiers who had been killed, one by a wound in the ear, and the other by a wound in the throat, and we seared the wounds of the others and of the horses with the fat of the Indian, and after posting sentinels and guards, we had supper and rested. . . .

I have already said that we captured five Indians during the battle of whom two were captains. When Aguilar spoke to these men he found out from what they said that they were fit persons to be sent as messengers, and he advised Cortés to free them, so that they might go and talk to the Caciques of the town and any others they might see. These two messengers were given green and blue beads, and Aguilar spoke many pleasant and flattering words to them, telling them that they had nothing to fear as we wished to treat them like brothers, that it was their own fault that they had made war on us, and that now they had better collect together all the Caciques of the different towns as we wished to talk to them, and he gave them much other advice in a gentle way so as to gain their good will. The messengers went off willingly and spoke to the Caciques and chief men, and told them all we wished them to know about our desire for peace.

When our envoys had been listened to, it was settled among them that fifteen Indian slaves, all with stained faces and ragged cloaks and loin cloths, should at once be sent to us with fowls and baked fish and maize cakes. When these men came before Cortés he received them graciously, but Aguilar the interpreter asked them rather angrily why they had come with their faces in that state, that it looked more as though they came to fight than to treat for peace; and he told them to go back to the Caciques and inform them, that if they wished for peace in the way we offered it, chieftains should come and treat for it, as was always the custom, and that they should not send slaves. But even these painted faced slaves were treated with consideration by us and blue beads were sent by them in sign of peace, and to soothe their feelings.

The next day thirty Indian Chieftains, clad in good cloaks, came to visit us and brought fowls, fish, fruit and maize cakes, and asked leave from Cortés to burn and bury the bodies of the dead who had fallen in the recent battles, so that they should not smell badly or be eaten by lions and tigers. Permission was at once given them and they hastened to bring many people to bury and burn the bodies according to their customs.

Cortés learnt from the Caciques that over eight hundred men were missing, not counting those who had been carried off wounded.

They said that they could not tarry with us either to discuss the matter or make peace, for on the morrow the chieftains and leaders of all the towns would have assembled, and that then they would agree about a peace.

As Cortés was very sagacious about everything, he said, laughing, to us soldiers who happened to be in his company, "Do you know, gentlemen, that it seems to me that the Indians are terrified at the horses and may think that they and the cannon alone make war on them.

I have thought of something which will confirm this belief, and that is to bring the mare belonging to Juan Sedeño, which foaled the other day on board ship, and tie her up where I am now standing and also to bring the stallion of Ortiz the musician, which is very excitable, near enough to scent the mare, and when he has scented her to lead each of them off separately so that the Caciques who are coming shall not hear the horse neighing as they approach, not until they are standing before me and are talking to me." We did just as Cortés ordered and brought the horse and mare, and the horse soon detected the scent of her in Cortés's quarters. In addition to this Cortés ordered the largest cannon that we possessed to be loaded with a large ball and a good charge of powder.

About mid-day forty Indians arrived, all of them Caciques of good bearing, wearing rich mantles such as are used by them. They saluted Cortés and all of us, and brought incense and fumigated all of us who were present, and they asked pardon for their past behavior, and said that henceforth they would be friendly.

Cortés, through Aguilar the Interpreter, answered them in a rather grave manner, as though he were angry, that they well knew how many times he had asked them to maintain peace, that the fault was theirs, and that now they deserved to be put to death, they and all the people of their towns, but that as we were the vassals of a great King and Lord named the Emperor Don Carlos, who had sent us to these countries, and ordered us to help and favor those who would enter his royal service, that if they were now as well disposed as they said they were, that we would take this course, but that if they were not, some of those Tepustles would jump out and kill them (they call iron Tepustle [*tepoztli*] in their language) for some of the Tepustles were still angry because they had made war on us. At this moment the order was secretly given to put a match to the cannon which had been loaded, and it went off with such a thunderclap as was wanted, and the ball went buzzing over the hills, and as it was midday and very still it made a great noise, and the Caciques were terrified on hearing it. As they had never seen anything like it they believed what Cortés had told them was true. Then Cortés told them, through Aguilar, not to be afraid for he had given orders that no harm should be done to them.

Just then the horse that had scented the mare was brought and tied up not far distant from where Cortés was talking to the Caciques, and, as the mare had been tied up at the place where Cortés and the Indians were talking, the horse began to paw the ground and neigh and become wild with excitement, looking all the time towards the Indians and the place whence the scent of the mare had reached him, and the Caciques thought that he was roaring at them and they were terrified. When Cortés observed their state of mind, he rose from his seat and went to the horse and told two orderlies to lead it far away, and said to the Indians that he had told the horse not to be angry as they were friendly and wished to make peace.

While this was going on there arrived more than thirty Indian carriers, whom the natives call Tamenes [*tlamemeh*], who brought a meal of fowls and fish and fruits and other food, and it appears that they had lagged behind and could not reach us at the same time as the Caciques.

Cortés had a long conversation with these chieftains and Caciques and they told him that they would all come on the next day and would bring a present and would discuss other matters, and then they went away quite contented. . . .

Early the next morning, the 15th March, 1519, many Caciques and chiefs of Tabasco and the neighboring towns arrived and paid great respect to us all, and they brought a present of gold, consisting of four diadems and some gold lizards, and two [ornaments] like little dogs, and earrings, and five ducks, and two masks with Indian faces, and two gold soles for sandals, and some other things of little value. I do not remember how much the things were worth; and they brought cloth, such as they make and wear, which was quilted stuff. My readers will have heard from those who know that province that there is nothing of much value in it.

This present, however, was worth nothing in comparison with the twenty women that were given us, among them one very excellent woman called Doña Marina, for so she was named when she became a Christian. I will leave off talking about her and the other women who were brought to us, and will tell how Cortés received this present with pleasure and went aside with all the Caciques, and with Aguilar, the interpreter, to hold converse, and he told them that he gave them thanks for what they had brought with them, but there was one thing that he must ask of them, namely, that they should re-occupy the town with all their people, women and children, and he wished to see it repeopled within two days, for he would recognize that as a sign of true peace. The Caciques sent at once to summon all the inhabitants with their women and children and within two days they were again settled in the town.

One other thing Cortés asked of the chiefs and that was to give up their idols and sacrifices, and this they said they would do, and, through

Aguilar, Cortés told them as well as he was able about matters concerning our holy faith, how we were Christians and worshipped one true and only God, and he showed them an image of Our Lady with her precious Son in her arms and explained to them that we paid the greatest reverence to it as it was the image of the Mother of our Lord God who was in heaven. The Caciques replied that they liked the look of the great Teleciguata (for in their language great ladies are called Teleciguatas) and [begged] that she might be given them to keep in their town, and Cortés said that the image should be given to them and ordered them to make a well-constructed altar, and this they did at once. . . .

When all this had been settled Cortés asked the Caciques what was their reason for attacking us three times when we had asked them to keep the peace; the chief replied that he had already asked pardon for their acts and had been forgiven, that the Cacique of Chanpoton, his brother, had advised it, and that he feared to be accused of cowardice, for he had already been reproached and dishonored for not having attacked the other captain who had come with four ships, (he must have meant Juan de Grijalva) and he also said that the Indian whom we had brought as an Interpreter, who escaped in the night, had advised them to attack us both by day and night.

Cortés then ordered this man to be brought before him without fail, but they replied that when he saw that the battle was going against them, he had taken to flight, and they knew not where he was although search had been made for him; but we came to know that they had offered him as a sacrifice because his counsel had cost them so dear.

Cortés also asked them where they procured their gold and jewels, and they replied, from the direction of the setting sun, and said "Culua" and "Mexica," and as we did not know what Mexica and Culua meant we paid little attention to it.

Then we brought another interpreter named Francisco, whom we had captured during Grijalva's expedition, who has already been mentioned by me, but he understood nothing of the Tabasco language only that of Culua which is the Mexican tongue. By means of signs he told Cortés that Culua was far ahead, and he repeated "Mexico" which we did not understand.

So the talk ceased until the next day when the sacred image of Our Lady and the Cross were set up on the altar and we all paid reverence to them, and Padre Fray Bartolomé de Olmedo said mass and all the Caciques and chiefs were present and we gave the name of Santa María de la Victoria to the town, and by this name the town of Tabasco is now called. The same friar, with Aguilar as interpreter, preached many good things about our holy faith to the twenty Indian women who had been given us, telling them not to believe in the Idols which they had been wont to trust in, for they were evil things and not gods, and that they should offer no more sacrifices to them for they would lead them astray, but that they should worship our Lord Jesus Christ, and immediately afterwards they were baptized. One Indian lady who was given to us here was christened Doña Marina, and she was truly a great chieftainess and the daughter of great Caciques and the mistress of vassals, and this her appearance clearly showed. Later on I will relate why it was and in what manner she was brought here. I do not clearly remember the names of all the other women, and it is not worth while to name any of them; however, they were the first women to become Christians in New Spain.

Cortés allotted one of them to each of his captains and Doña Marina, as she was good looking and intelligent and without embarrassment [*entremetida*], he gave to Alonso Hernández Puertocarrero, who I have already said was a distinguished gentleman, and cousin of the Count of Medellin. When Puertocarrero went to Spain, Doña Marina lived with Cortés, and bore him a son named Don Martin Cortés. . . .

Before telling about the great Montezuma and his famous City of Mexico and the Mexicans, I wish to give some account of Doña Marina, who from her childhood had been the mistress and Cacica* of towns and vassals. It happened in this way:

Her father and mother were chiefs and Caciques of a town called Paynala, which had other towns subject to it, and stood about eight leagues from the town of Coatzacoalcos. Her father died while she was still a little child, and her mother married another Cacique, a young man, and bore him a son. It seems that the father and mother had a great affection for this son and it was agreed between them that he should succeed to their honours when their days were done. So that there should be no impediment to this, they gave the little girl, Doña Marina, to some Indians from Xicalango* and this they did by night so as to escape observation, and they then spread the report that she had

---

*Feminine form of *cacique*.

*Xicalango, on the southern side of the Laguna de Términos [in present-day Campeche], was an outlying stronghold of the Mexica Empire.

died, and as it happened at this time that a child of one of their Indian slaves died they gave out that it was their daughter and the heiress who was dead.

The Indians of Xicalango gave the child to the people of Tabasco, and the Tabasco people gave her to Cortés. I myself knew her mother, and the old woman's son and her half-brother, when he was already grown up and ruled the town jointly with his mother, for the second husband of the old lady was dead. When they became Christians, the old lady was called Marta and the son Lázaro. I knew all this very well because in the year 1523 after the conquest of Mexico and the other provinces, when Cristóbal de Olid revolted in Honduras, and Cortés was on his way there, he passed through Coatzacoalcos and I and the greater number of the settlers of that town accompanied him on that expedition as I shall relate in the proper time and place. As Doña Marina proved herself such an excellent woman and good interpreter throughout the wars in New Spain, Tlaxcala and Mexico (as I shall show later on) Cortés always took her with him, and during that expedition she was married to a gentleman named Juan Jaramillo at the town of Orizaba, before certain witnesses, one of whom was named Aranda, a settler in Tabasco and this man told [me] about the marriage.

Doña Marina was a person of the greatest importance and was obeyed without question by the Indians throughout New Spain.

When Cortés was in the town of Coatzacoalcos he sent to summon to his presence all the Caciques of that province in order to make them a speech about our holy religion, and about their good treatment, and among the Caciques who assembled was the mother of Doña Marina and her half-brother, Lázaro.

Some time before this Doña Marina had told me that she belonged to that province and that she was the mistress of vassals, and Cortés also knew it well, as did Aguilar, the interpreter. In such a manner it was that mother, daughter and son came together, and it was easy enough to see that she was the daughter from the strong likeness she bore to her mother.

These relations were in great fear of Doña Marina, for they thought that she had sent for them to put them to death, and they were weeping.

When Doña Marina saw them in tears, she consoled them and told them to have no fear, that when they had given her over to the men from Xicalango, they knew not what they were doing, and she forgave them for doing it, and she gave them many jewels of gold, and raiment, and told them to return to their town, and said that God had been very gracious to her in freeing her from the worship of idols and making her a Christian, and letting her bear a son to her lord and master Cortés and in marrying her to such a gentleman as Juan Jaramillo, who was now her husband. That she would rather serve her husband and Cortés than anything else in the world, and would not exchange her place to be Cacica of all the provinces in New Spain. . . .

To go back to my subject: Doña Marina knew the language of Coatzacoalcos, which is that common to Mexico [Nahuatl], and she knew the language of Tabasco, as did also Jerónimo de Aguilar, who spoke the language of Yucatan and Tabasco, which is one and the same. So that these two could understand one another clearly, and Aguilar translated into Castilian for Cortés.

This was the great beginning of our conquests and thus, thanks be to God, things prospered with us. I have made a point of explaining this matter, because without the help of Doña Marina we could not have understood the language of New Spain and Mexico.

Here I will leave off, and go on later to tell how we disembarked in the Port of San Juan de Ulúa. . . .

6

HERNANDO CORTÉS

Letters to Charles V

After disregarding Governor Velázquez's instructions and feeling threatened by those still faithful to him, Cortés needed to justify his actions. Cortés's first report to the king, written while still in Yucatan, has never been found. In this short extract from his first surviving missive, the Letter from Vera Cruz, Cortés provides an account in which, for the greater service of God and the king, the men prevail on Cortés to take the actions he did. Written in the third person as though by a disinterested observer, the letter also reports the sending of treasure to the king, certainly done in hopes of gaining royal support for Cortés's actions. Those hopes also seem to lie behind his enthusiastic reports of the land and the promise of further riches. The tension between Cortés's supporters and the followers of Velázquez did not abate, and the final excerpt from Cortés's second letter explains the reason for his grounding of the ships.

Translated by T. Seijas. Fernando Cortés, "Cartas de Relación," in *Historiadores primitivos de Indias*, edited by Enrique de Vedia (Madrid: Impr. de M. Rivadeneyra, 1852), 8–9, 13.

Letter I

[July 10, 1519]

Many of us in the fleet are noblemen, knights and gentlemen, steadfast in our service to our Lord and your Majesties, and desirous of elevating the monarchy and expanding your sovereignty and royal income. To this end, we gathered together to speak with captain Hernando Cortés. We told him that this land was bountiful and surely rich, given the gold pieces that the visiting cacique had brought along, which was also a sign of the Indians' goodwill. It appeared to us, we continued, that Diego Velázquez had ordered captain Cortés to trade for all the available gold and then return to Fernandina Island [Cuba] for the sole profit of the said governor and captain.

We proposed, instead, that a town be founded and settled in your Majesties' name in order to guarantee just government as in your other kingdoms. Having Spaniards populate this land would increase your Majesties' sovereignty and revenue. . . . All in agreement, we jointly petitioned the captain to desist from trading, because to do so would only drain the land and also be a disservice to your majesties. . . . At the same time, we entreated with Cortés to designate a town for us to found, and also its governors and judges, in the name of your Majesties, adding our protests if he were not to do so. . . .

Seeing the convenience of our proposal, the captain responded on the following day that he was devoted to your majesties' service, and that irrespective of the profit that he would otherwise have made from trading, or of the capital he had invested in the fleet . . . that it nonetheless pleased him to do as we had asked. . . . So Cortés diligently set upon populating and founding . . . the rich town of the True Cross *[rica villa de la Vera Cruz]* . . .

The following day we came together as a municipal council and town hall, calling on Cortés, on behalf of your majesties, to show us the powers and instructions that Diego Velázques had given him to come to this place, which he promptly did. And having seen and read these . . . we understood that Cortés no longer held any power. . . . [His charge] had expired, so Cortés could no longer act as judge or captain. . . .

It seemed to us, our dearest Princes, that to maintain peace and unity among us, and to govern, we needed to place someone in your royal service, to act on your behalf in the said town as judge, captain, and head. . . . and seeing that no one else but Fernando Cortés could be given such a position. . . . given his great interest [*gran celo*] and desire to serve your Majesties, as well as his long experience in these parts and islands, about which he had always given good account, and having spent all that he owned to come here, as he did, we conferred on him, in the name of your Majesties, the charge of greater justice [*justicia mayor*] and of captain of your royal armed forces. . . . We received his pledge as required and welcomed him in our town hall and municipal council. . . .

After this, all of us together as a council agreed to write to your Majesties and to send you the gold and silver, and jewels that we have found in abundance in this land, in addition to the royal fifth that is your privilege, leaving nothing for ourselves, in order to demonstrate our goodwill. . . .

We elected as our representatives Alonso Fernandez Portocarrero and Francisco de Montejo, whom we dispatch to your majesties to kiss your royal hands and to supplicate for your favor on behalf of ourselves and of this town.

Letter II

[October 30, 1520]

As I mentioned in the first letter [*relación*] to your Majesty, a number of men in my company were servants and friends of Diego Velázquez. My actions in service of your Highness weighed on them, and some of them tried to rebel and leave me, especially four Spaniards . . . who, based on their unprovoked confession, had determined to seize a brigantine that was at port laden with bread and sausages, to kill the captain, and then to leave for Cuba to inform Diego Velázquez that I had set forth a sail ship to [inform] your Majesty [about Mexico]. . . . They had wanted his ship-guard to overtake the sail ship, which I subsequently learned he indeed attempted to do. . . . The four men confessed that others had the same intention of warning Velázquez. Based on these delinquents' confessions, I punished them accordingly, which seemed necessary at the time in the service of your Highness.

Apart from the servants and friends of Velázquez, a number of other men wanted to leave as well, seeing that the land was so great and with so many people, and that there were so few of us Spaniards. Given their intention, I considered that leaving the ships [as he marched inland] would only encourage them to rise against me, leaving me almost alone and hindering our service to God and your Highness.

So, under the pretense that the ships were un-navigable, I had them grounded on the coast, leaving these men without hope of departure. I thus secured my path, ensuring that I would have sufficient people to leave behind at the town [while he ventured towards the interior].

7

TOWN COUNCIL OF VERA CRUZ

Letter to Charles V

Both Bernal Díaz and Hernando Cortés emphasized the importance of the founding of the town of Vera Cruz (near present-day Veracruz). Cortés had sailed under the authority of Diego Velázquez, the governor of Cuba, with permission only to trade, so he needed a justification to strike out on his own. By founding a town and then electing mayors and a town council, which in turn recognized his military leadership, Cortés sought to create a legal basis for his subsequent actions. Knowing that Velázquez would try to stop him, that those among his company loyal to the governor would complain, and that the king might be displeased by this violation of the political hierarchy, Cortés did not include the pro-Velázquez men in the act of the city's foundation.

The selection included here is in the voice of Francisco Álvares Chico, speaking on behalf of the Spaniards who were not part of the municipal council. It is an acknowledgment that the council had decided to send a report to the king about the town's foundation, and that they consented to this new government. The petition was signed by 309 members of the expedition and therefore provides a partial catalog of the original company of the conquistadors of Mexico. The excerpt is couched in the legalistic language of a petition, but its intention is clearly to deny any authority to the governor of Cuba and to have Cortés appointed as captain general of this new conquest.

Petition made by the citizens of this town

[. . .] Very Noble Lords, Francisco Álvares Chico, representative of the Noble Town of Vera Cruz, appears before Your Graces [council members] and says that, as you well know, while in your council

---

John F. Schwaller and Helen Nader, *The First Letter from New Spain: The Lost Petition of Cortés and His Company, June 20, 1519* (Austin: University of Texas Press, 2014), 102–103.

considering those things most suitable to the service of our lord God and their highnesses, you informed me as representative of this town that . . . you decided to send a report with the gentlemen [*señores*] Alonso Hernández Puertocarrero and Francisco de Montejo, whom you authorized to negotiate on your behalf, and because I am obligated to be informed of whatever is most suitable to serve their highnesses and the well-being of this town, I have agreed with your graces to inform the citizens of this town of the content of the report and so give them a share in the favors that you ask his majesty to give you and those things that would be most suitable to provide for his royal service. . . .

Especially I note that your graces already know that in the report are some sections in which you ask his majesty not to give Diego Velázquez any responsibility or profit at all from this region, nor to grant it to him, both because of the harm and prejudice that all of us here would receive, and because it is obvious that having ceased to trade and do what Diego Velázquez wanted, and having settled and chosen a judge in His Majesty's name, and offered this land to his royal crown—land where Diego Velázquez would try to damage in any way possible those people involved in it, and if he were to come to this region no one would escape being hurt and thrown out, being persons who did not want to do what he wanted, rather what which would be to the service of their highnesses, as their subjects should do, and in this it seems appropriate [*bien*], because some people who have demonstrably shown themselves to be friends of the said Diego Velázquez [who are] wishing to disturb that service which might be done as which for your highnesses has been done and interfere with your royal crown, are set to bring them to justice, and if the said Diego Velázquez were to come, not only would the above mentioned delinquents remain without punishment, but even the rest of us who are here would suffer much damage to our persons and estates. . . .

3

Encounters

The Spaniards and the Mexica tried to make sense of each other based on their unique historical and cultural contexts. The Mexica mainly regarded the Spaniards as strange but understandable, simply a new kind of foreigner who needed to be expelled from their empire. The Spaniards viewed the Mexica through the lens of earlier encounters with Indigenous peoples in the Caribbean, and also based on their own traditions of diplomacy and contact with non-Europeans in the Mediterranean world.

The first selection in this chapter is from Cortés's earliest surviving letter to Charles V, in which he described the land and peoples he encountered. In order to provide the king with a common reference, he compared native customs to Islamic ("Moorish" or *Moro*) traditions, and also drew on biblical references. He focused on the religious practice of human sacrifice as a singularly reprehensible custom that justified the need to spread Catholicism, and by extension, the king's control over this land. This union of observation with self-serving emphases was typical of many European descriptions of the peoples of the Americas.

The second selection from Bernal Díaz provides insight into the importance of exchanging gifts for both the Spaniards and Nahuas. His report is also sensitive to the value of information, elaborating on Cortés's strategies to learn about the politics and wealth of the region, as well as how Nahua leaders similarly collected intelligence about the newcomers. Especially notable are his remarks on the importance of pictographic representation for the Mexica, and how those images were used to communicate information.

The Nahua selection is from the accounts gathered by Fray Bernardino de Sahagún about thirty years after the conquest. While its attention to certain details — the style of the capes offered as gifts, the costumes of the gods — seems authentic, the emphasis on Moctezuma's weakness and on the possible supernatural qualities of the strangers indicates a "shading" of the account made by those interviewed in order to criticize the failed Mexica leadership and probably to gratify the Spanish authorities of the time. The tendency to identify the Spaniards with a returning deity come to reclaim his kingdom—in some accounts Quetzalcoatl, the ancient god of the Toltecs—became a standard aspect of postcontact Indigenous accounts, and later those by Spanish chroniclers and mestizo historians. As discussed in the introduction, certain aspects of the story made this identification plausible. In some sense, myth, history, and propaganda were not discrete categories for the Nahua, and none was more "true" than the others. Traditionally, for peoples of Mesoamerica, history's main function was not so much to describe events as they "really" happened but rather to fit them into specific visions of the past and the future. The degree to which this concept of history influenced Sahagún's informants is open to debate.

8

HERNANDO CORTÉS

Letters to Charles V

The letters of Cortés were reports that mixed self-explanations and justifications with more general information of the kind to interest a king. Religion, politics, and ethnography are combined here along with observation and assessment. Cortés's preconceptions and previous experiences surely shaped his observations, and he likely "invented" some facts to fit his purposes.

Letter I

[July 10, 1519]

We send your highnesses this account [*relación*] in order to inform your Majesties of all the things of this land, its customs and wealth, and of the peoples who possess it, and of its laws or sects, and their rites and ceremonies.

Translated by T. Seijas. Fernando Cortés, "Cartas de Relación," in *Historiadores primitivos de Indias*, edited by Enrique de Vedia (Madrid: Impr. de M. Rivadeneyra, 1852), 9–10.

This land, oh powerful rulers, where we presently find ourselves, on your behalf, has fifty leagues of coastline on both sides of this town [Vera Cruz]. The coast is flat, with sand dunes that extend several leagues. Beyond these are fertile lands and beautiful banks, equal to those in Spain. The land is as pretty to see, as it is fruitful, sown neatly with native crops, with terrain for easy transport and to pasture all manner of livestock.

The land has all kinds of game, animals and birds, the same as our own, like deer, both red-deer and fallow-deer, wolves, foxes, partridges, doves, turtle-doves, pheasants, and jackrabbits—all no different than in Spain. . . .

There is a great range with beautiful mountains, some quite high, with the ocean and all the land visible from the highest one, which is so tall that the top is barely visible on a cloudy day. . . . On a clear day the summit appears higher than the clouds. It is so white we judge it to be covered in snow, though we have yet to tackle the peak. The native people say it is snow, but this region is so warm that we cannot confirm it.

We will endeavor to find out and give you, our royal Highnesses, further news of these matters and also tell you about this land's wealth in gold, silver, and gemstones, which you will be able to judge from the samples we are sending along. We believe there is as much gold here than in Solomon's mine, but since so little time has passed since our arrival, we have only been able to reconnoiter territory lying within five leagues of the sea, and along ten or twelve leagues of coastline, but we have seen much more while navigating.

The people who inhabit this land, from the island of Cozumel and the tip of Yucatan to our current location, are of medium-stature, with well-proportioned bodies. The people of each province distinguish themselves by certain signs [gestos]: some have piercings, wearing large and ugly earrings; while others have earplugs down to their mouths made of stones that look like mirrors; while others have lower-lid plugs down to their teeth, great circles of stone or gold, that hang down and deform their features.

Their clothing is like gauze [almaizal], highly decorated. The men cover their private parts and wear gauze [shirts] on their bodies made of thin cloth and painted in the manner of Moorish robes. The common women wear richly-colored cotton blankets [mantas] wrapped around the waist to their feet, and another that covers their breasts . . . while the principal women go around wearing large squares of thin cotton, embroidered, and made in the manner of wide robes [roquetes].

Their main food is maize, and some hamsters [cuyes] like in the other islands, and yucca like in Cuba, which is grilled rather than made into bread. They have their fish and fowl, raising many chickens like in Tierra Firme that are as big as turkeys.

Some towns are large and orderly. Where available, the important houses are made of stone and mortar, with smaller and shorter dwellings like the Moors. In places without stone, houses are made of adobe, which they enter from above, with straw roofs.

The houses of some of the elites [*principales*] are large and airy, with more than five patios inside each one, and with well-arranged rooms . . . with wells and pools of water, and quarters for their many slaves and servants.

Each of these principales has a large patio at the entrance of their homes, outside . . . where they keep altars for their idols (those made of stone, clay, and sticks), whom they serve and pay homage to in numerous ceremonies. . . . These temples or mosques [*mezquitas*] where they keep their idols are the best built structures in each town. They are decorated with feathers and richly decorated textiles, with great propriety.

Everyday before work begins, they burn incense in these mosques. Sometimes they offer their own blood as sacrifice, piercing their tongues, and others their ears, and others slash their bodies with blades. All of the blood that runs from them is offered to the idols. The blood is strewn about the mosques, other times thrown upwards to the sky, and with it other ceremonies. Nothing can begin before a sacrifice is made.

They have another horrible and abominable custom, worthy of being punished, worse than anything seen elsewhere. When they want to ask for something from their idols, for greater efficacy and to ensure acceptance of their petition, they take many girls and boys, and also older men and women, and in the presence of their idols, they open their chests and take out their hearts and entrails, burning these [organs] and offering the smoke as a sacrifice. A few of us have seen this [ceremony] and say it is the most terrible and horrifying thing that can ever be witnessed.

The Indians carry this out [ceremony] so frequently, or so we are informed and have also partly seen, that there is never a year when they do not kill and sacrifice fifty souls in each mosque, and this is a custom from Cozumel to the land we populate today. Know your Majesties, that given the size of this land, and the number of mosques, we have surmised that no year passes without the killing and sacrifice of three or four thousand souls.

Understand your Majesties that in order to avoid this grave wrong and harm, and certainly God our Lord would be served, these people must be introduced to and taught about our very holy Catholic faith. Their devotion, faith, and hope in these idols must be commuted to the divine might of God. . . . Our Lord caused these lands to be discovered in the name of your Highnesses . . . and by your guiding hand, [our] Faith will be brought to these barbarous peoples. Based on what we have learned about them, we believe that translators will surely make them understand the truth of our Faith, and [accept] their own error. . . .

We perhaps err in telling your Majesty about all the particularities of this land and people, because much of it has yet to be seen, except through the descriptions provided by the natives. As such, we have only dared to relate to you what we truly know. Your Majesties, if so served, might want to give an account to our holy father [pope], in order to commence the diligent and orderly conversion of these people, as much goodness will come of it.

His saintliness [pope] may then permit that those who are bad or who rebel, be first admonished, and then be punished and castigated as enemies of our Holy Faith. Such punishment will provide an occasion to instill fear in those who would resist knowing the truth. And, it would prevent the great wrongs done on behalf of the devil, such as . . . the killing and sacrifice of children, men, and women. We have also known and been informed as true that all of them are sodomites and commit this abominable sin.

Overall, we beg your Majesties to order that we be provided [with honors and payment], as is most convenient to God and your royal Highnesses, so that those of us who are here in your service may be favored and benefit [from the endeavor].

9

BERNAL DÍAZ

From *The True History of the Conquest of New Spain*

Bernal Díaz provides a revealing view of the first encounter with the Mexica representatives of Moctezuma, who begin to appear in this account as individuals. Díaz's attention to details like the ambassadors' gestures and the gifts exchanged provides a sense of the Spaniards' reaction to the meeting and of their desire to push forward toward Moctezuma's capital.

On Holy Thursday, the anniversary of the Last Supper of Our Lord, in the year 1519, we arrived with all the fleet at the port of San Juan de Ulúa [Vera Cruz], and as the Pilot Alaminos knew the place well

Bernal Díaz del Castillo, *The True History of the Conquest of New Spain*, trans. *Alfred P. Maudslay*, 2d series (London: Printed for the Hakluyt Society, 1908), 136–44.

from having come there with Juan de Grijalva he at once ordered the vessels to drop anchor where they would be safe from the northerly gales. The flagship hoisted her royal standards and pennants, and within half an hour of anchoring, two large canoes . . . came out to us, full of Mexican Indians. Seeing the big ship with the standards flying they knew that it was there they must go to speak with the captain; so they went direct to the flagship and going on board asked who was the Tatuan [*tlahtoani*], which in their language means the chief. Doña Marina who understood the language well, pointed him out. Then the Indians paid many marks of respect to Cortés, according to their usage, and bade him welcome, and said that their lord, a servant of the great Montezuma, had sent them to ask what kind of men we were and of what we were in search, and added that if we were in need of anything for ourselves or the ships, that we should tell them and they would supply it. Our Cortés thanked them through the two interpreters, Aguilar and Doña Marina, and ordered food and wine to be given them and some blue beads, and after they had drunk he told them that we came to see them and to trade with them and that our arrival in their country should cause them no uneasiness but be looked on by them as fortunate. The messengers returned on shore well content, and the next day, which was Good Friday, we disembarked with the horses and guns, on some sand hills which rise to a considerable height, for there was no level land, nothing but sand dunes; and the artilleryman Mesa placed the guns in position to the best of his judgment. Then we set up an altar where mass was said and we made huts and shelters for Cortés and the captains, and three hundred of the soldiers brought wood and made huts for themselves and we placed the horses where they would be safe and in this way was Good Friday passed.

The next day, Saturday, Easter Eve, many Indians arrived sent by a chief who was a governor under Montezuma, named Pitalpitoque (whom we afterwards called Ovandillo), and they brought axes and dressed wood for the huts of the captain Cortés and the other ranchos near to it, and covered them with large cloths on account of the strength of the sun, for as it was in Lent the heat was very great—and they brought fowls and maize cakes and plums, which were then in season, and I think that they brought some gold jewels, and they presented all these things to Cortés; and said that the next day a governor would come and would bring more food. Cortés thanked them heartily and ordered them to be given certain articles in exchange with which they went away well content. The next day, Easter Sunday, the governor whom they spoke of arrived. His name was Tendile, a man of affairs, and he brought with him Pitalpitoque who was also a man of importance amongst the natives and there followed them many Indians with presents of fowls and vegetables. Tendile ordered these people to stand aside on a hillock and with much humility he made three obeisances to Cortés according to their custom, and then to all the soldiers who were standing around. Cortés bade them welcome through our interpreters and embraced them and asked them to wait, as he wished presently to speak to them. Meanwhile he ordered an altar to be made as well as it could be done in the time, and Fray Bartolomé de Olmedo, who was a fine singer, chanted Mass, and Padre Juan Diaz assisted, and the two governors and the other chiefs who were with them looked on.

When Mass was over, Cortés and some of our captains and the two Indian officers of the great Montezuma dined together. When the tables had been cleared away—Cortés went aside with the two Caciques and our two interpreters and explained to them that we were Christians and vassals of the greatest lord on earth, called the Emperor Don Carlos, who had many great princes as his vassals and servants, and that it was at his orders that we had come to this country, because for many years he had heard rumors about the country and the great prince who ruled it. That he wished to be friends with this prince and to tell him many things in the name of the Emperor which things, when he knew and understood them, would please him greatly. Moreover he wished to trade with their prince and his Indians in good friendship, and he wanted to know where this prince would wish that they should meet so that they might confer together. Tendile replied somewhat proudly, and said—"You have only just now arrived and you already ask to speak with our prince; accept now this present which we give you in his name, and afterwards you will tell me what you think fitting." With that he took out a petaca—which is a sort of chest, many articles of gold beautifully and richly worked and ordered ten loads of white cloth made of cotton and feathers to be brought, wonderful things to see, and there were other things which I do not remember, besides quantities of food consisting of fowls of the country, fruit and baked fish.

Cortés received it all with smiles in a gracious manner and gave in return, beads or twisted glass and other small beads from Spain, and he begged them to send to their towns to ask the people to come and trade with us as he had brought many beads to exchange for gold, and they replied that they would do as he asked. As we afterwards found out, these two men, Tendile and Pitalpitoque, were the governors of the provinces named Cotustan, Tustepeque,[1] Guazpaltepeque and Tatalteco, and of some other townships lately conquered. Cortés then ordered his servants to bring an arm-chair, richly carved and inlaid and some margaritas, stones with many [intricate] designs in them, and a string of twisted glass beads packed in cotton scented with musk and a crimson cap with a golden medal engraved with a figure of St. George on horseback, lance in hand, slaying the dragon, and he told Tendile that he should send the chair to his prince Montezuma (for we already knew that he was so called) so that he could be seated in it when he, Cortés, came to see and speak with him, and that he should place the cap on his head, and that the stones and all the other things were presents from our lord the King, as a sign of his friendship, for he was aware that Montezuma was a great prince, and Cortés asked that a day and a place might be named where he could go to see Montezuma. Tendile received the present and said that his lord Montezuma was such a great prince that it would please him to know our great King and that he would carry the present to him at once and bring back a reply.

It appears that Tendile brought with him some clever painters such as they had in Mexico and ordered them to make pictures true to nature of the face and body of Cortés and all his captains, and of the soldiers, ships, sails and horses, and of Doña Marina and Aguilar, even of the two greyhounds, and the cannon and cannon balls, and all of the army we had brought with us, and he carried the pictures to his master. Cortés ordered our gunners to load the lombards [canons] with a great charge of powder so that they should make a great noise when they were fired off, and he told Pedro de Alvarado that he and all the horsemen should get ready so that these servants of Montezuma might see them gallop and told them to attach little bells to the horses' breastplates. Cortés also mounted his horse and said — "It would be well if we could gallop on these sand dunes but they will observe that even when on foot we get stuck in the sand — let us go out to the beach when the tide is low and gallop two and two;" — and to Pedro de Alvarado whose sorrel colored mare was a great galloper, and very handy, he gave charge of all the horsemen.

All this was carried out in the presence of the two ambassadors, and so that they should see the cannon fired, Cortés made as though he wished again to speak to them and a number of other chieftains, and the lombards were fired off, and as it was quite still at that moment, the stones went flying through the forest resounding with a great din, and

---

[1]The provinces were Cotaxtla, Tuxtepec or Tochtepec, Quetzaltepec, and Tlatlactetelco.

the two governors and all the other Indians were frightened by things so new to them, and ordered the painters to record them so that Montezuma might see.

It happened that one of the soldiers had a helmet half gilt but somewhat rusty and this Tendile noticed, for he was the more forward of the two ambassadors, and said that he wished to see it as it was like one that they possessed which had been left to them by their ancestors of the race from which they had sprung, and that it had been placed on the head of their of their god Huichilobos [Huitzilopochtli], and that their prince Montezuma would like to see this helmet. So it was given to him, and Cortés said to them that as he wished to know whether the gold of this country was the same as that we find in our rivers, they could return the helmet filled with grains of gold so that he could send it to our great Emperor.

After this, Tendile bade farewell to Cortés and to all of us and after many expressions of regard from Cortés he took leave of him and said that he would return with a reply without delay. After Tendile had departed we found out that besides being an Indian employed in matters of great importance, Tendile was the most active of the servants whom his master, Montezuma, had in his employ, and he went with all haste and narrated everything to his prince, and showed him the pictures which had been painted and the present which Cortés had sent. When the great Montezuma gazed on it he was struck with admiration and received it on his part with satisfaction. When he examined the helmet and that which was on his Huichilobos, he felt convinced that we belonged to the race which, as his forefathers had foretold would come to rule over that land. . . .

When Tendile departed with the present which the Captain Cortés gave him for his prince Montezuma, the other governor, Pitalpitoque, stayed in our camp and occupied some huts a little distance from ours, and they brought Indian women there to make maize bread, and brought fowls and fruit and fish, and supplied Cortés and the captains who fed with him. As for us soldiers, if we did not hunt for shellfish on the beach, or go out fishing, we did not get anything.

About that time, many Indians came from the towns already mentioned by me over which these two servants of Montezuma were governors, and some of them brought gold and jewels of little value, and fowls to exchange with us for our goods, which consisted of green beads and clear glass beads and other articles, and with this we managed to supply ourselves with food. Almost all the soldiers had brought things for barter, as we learnt in Grijalva's time that it was a good thing to bring beads—and in this manner six or seven days passed by.

Then one morning, Tendile arrived with more than one hundred laden Indians, accompanied by a great Mexican Cacique, who in his face, features and appearance bore a strong likeness to our Captain Cortés and the great Montezuma had sent him purposely, for it is said that when Tendile brought the portrait of Cortés all the chiefs who were in Montezuma's company said that a great chief named Quintalbor looked exactly like Cortés and that was the name of the Cacique who now arrived with Tendile; and as he was so like Cortés we called them in camp "our Cortés" and "the other Cortés."

To go back to my story, when these people arrived and came before our Captain they first of all kissed the earth and then fumigated him and all the soldiers who were standing around him, with incense which they brought in braziers of pottery. Cortés received them affectionately and seated them near himself, and that chief who came with the present (who I have already said was named Quintalbor) had been appointed spokesman together with Tendile. After welcoming us to the country and after many courteous speeches had passed he ordered the presents which he had brought to be displayed, and they were placed on mats which they call petates over which were spread cotton cloths.

The first article presented was a wheel like a sun, as big as a cart-wheel, with many sorts of pictures on it, the whole of fine gold, and a wonderful thing to behold, which those who afterwards weighed it said was worth more than ten thousand dollars. Then another wheel was presented of greater size made of silver of great brilliancy in imitation of the moon with other figures shown on it, and this was of great value as it was very heavy—and the chief brought back the helmet full of fine grains of gold, just as they are got out of the mines, and this was worth three thousand dollars. This gold in the helmet was worth more to us than if it had contained 20,000 [coins], because it showed us that there were good mines there. Then were brought twenty golden ducks, beautifully worked and very natural looking, and some [ornaments] like dogs, of the kind they keep, and many articles of gold worked in the shape of tigers and lions and monkeys, and ten collars beautifully worked and other necklaces; and twelve arrows and a bow with its string, and two rods like staffs of justice, five palms long, all in beautiful hollow work of fine gold. Then there were presented crests of gold and plumes of rich green feathers, and others of silver, and fans of the same materials, and deer copied in hollow gold and many other things that I cannot remember for it all happened so many years ago. And then over thirty loads of beautiful cotton cloth were brought worked with many patterns and decorated with many colored feathers, and so many other things were there that it is useless my trying to describe them for I know not how to do it. When all these things had been presented, this great Cacique Quintalbor and Tendile asked Cortés to accept this present with the same willingness with which his prince had sent it, and divide it among the taides* [teteu] and men who accompanied him. Cortés received the present with delight and then the ambassadors told Cortés that they wished to repeat what their prince, Montezuma, had sent them to say. First of all they told him that he was pleased that such valiant men, as he had heard that we were, should come to his country, for he knew all about what we had done at Tabasco, and that he would much like to see our great emperor who was such a mighty prince and whose fame was spread over so many lands, and that he would send him a present of precious stones; and that meanwhile we should stay in that port; that if he could assist us in any way he would do so with the greatest pleasure; but as to the interview, they should not worry about it; that there was no need for it and they (the ambassadors) urged many objections.

Cortés kept a good countenance, and returned his thanks to them, and with many flattering expressions gave each of the ambassadors two holland [fine linen] shirts and some blue glass beads and other things, and begged them to go back as his ambassadors to Mexico and to tell their prince, the great Montezuma, that as we had come across so many seas, and had journeyed from such distant lands solely to see and speak with him in person, that if we should return thus, that our great king and lord would not receive us well, and that wherever their prince Montezuma might be we wished to go and see him and do what he might order us to do. The ambassadors replied that they would go back and give this message to their prince, but as to the question of the desired interview — they considered it superfluous.

By these ambassadors Cortés sent what our poverty could afford as a gift to Montezuma: a glass cup of Florentine ware, engraved with trees and hunting scenes and gilt, and three holland shirts and other things, and he charged the messengers to bring a reply. The two governors set out and Pitalpitoque remained in camp; for it seems that the other servants of Montezuma had given him orders to see that food was brought to us from the neighboring towns. Here I will leave off, and then go on to tell what happened in our camp.

*Teules, "for so they call the idols which they worship" [teteu = gods].

10

FRAY BERNARDINO DE SAHAGÚN

From the *Florentine Codex*

The Nahua account contained in the Florentine Codex *provides considerable detail of the same meeting described by Díaz: the nobles involved, the exchange of gifts, and the way in which the encounter was reported to Moctezuma. Here the attention to detail is comparable to Díaz's account, but the focus on hostile aspects of the encounter, such as the Spaniards having chained their visitors, offers insight into their diverging goals. The descriptions of the Spaniards, their weapons, and animals have a sense of immediacy, but the commentary that these first meetings filled Moctezuma and others with forebodings of catastrophe must be regarded with considerable skepticism, as these accounts were collected several decades after the events occurred.*

Second chapter, when it is said how the first boat that came arrived . . . When those who came to the seashore were seen, they were going along by boat. Then Pinotl of Cuetlaxtlan, a high steward, went in person, taking other stewards with him: [second], Yaotzin, the steward of Mictlanquauhtla; third, the steward of Teocinyocan, named Teocinyocatl; fourth, Cuitlalpitoc, who was only a dependent, a subordinate leader; and fifth, Tentlil, also a subordinate leader.

These were the only ones who first went to see [the Spaniards]. They went as if to sell them things, so that they could spy on them and contemplate them. They gave them precious cloaks, precious goods, the very cloaks pertaining to Moteucçoma which no one else could don, which were assigned to him alone.

It was by boat that they went to see them. As they were doing it, Pinotzin said, "Let us not lie to the lord Moteucçoma, for you would live no longer. Let's just go, lest we die, so that he can hear the real truth." (Moteucçoma was his personal name, and Tlacateucth was his title as ruler.)

Then they embarked, launched off, and went out on the water; the water folk paddled for them. When they approached the Spaniards, they

James Lockhart, *We People Here: Nahuatl Accounts of the Conquest of Mexico*, Repertorium Columbianum, UCLA Center for Medieval and Renaissance Studies (Los Angeles: University of California Press, 1993), 56–86.

made the earth-eating gesture at the prow of the boat(s). They thought that it was Quetzalcoatl Topiltzin who had arrived.

The Spaniards called to them, saying to them, "Who are you? Where have you come from? Where is your homeland?"

Immediately they said, "It is from Mexico that we have come."

They answered them back, "If you are really Mexica, what is the name of the ruler of Mexico?"

They told them, "O our lords, Moteucçoma is his name."

Then they gave them all the different kinds of precious cloaks they carried, to wit, like those mentioned here: the sun-covered style, the blue-knotted style, the style covered with jars, the one with painted eagles, the style with serpent faces, the style with wind jewels, the style with (turkey blood), or with whirlpools, the style with smoking mirrors.

For all these things that they gave them, [the Spaniards] gave them things in return; they gave them green and yellow strings of beads, which one might imagine to be amber. And when they had taken them and looked at them, greatly did they marvel.

And [the Spaniards] took leave of them, saying to them, "Go off, while we go to Spain; we will not be long in getting to Mexico."

Thereupon they went, and [the local people] also came away, coming back. And when they came out on dry land, they came straight to Mexico, moving along in this direction day and night to come inform Moteucçoma, to tell him and report to him the truth [...]. They took the goods they had received.

Then they spoke to him: "O our lord, o master, destroy us [if you will, but] here is what we have seen and done at the place where your subordinates stand guard for you beside the ocean. For we went to see our lords the gods out on the water; we gave them all your cloaks, and here are the fine things belonging to them that they gave us. They said, 'If you have really come from Mexico, here is what you are to give the ruler Moteucçoma, whereby he will recognize us.'" They told him everything [the Spaniards] had told them out on the water.

And Moteucçoma said to them, "You are doubly welcome; take your rest. What I have seen is a secret. No one is to say anything, to let it escape from his lips, to let a word slip out, to open his mouth, to mention it, but it is to stay inside you."

Third chapter, where it is said what Moteucçoma ordered when he heard the statement of those who saw the first boat that came.

Thereupon Moteucçoma gave instructions to the man from Cuetlax-tlan and the rest, telling them, "Give orders that watch be kept everywhere along the coast, at [the places] called Nauhtlan, Toztlan, and

Mictlanquauhtla, wherever they will come to land." Then the stewards left and gave orders for watch to be kept.

And Moteucçoma assembled his lords, the Cihuacoatl Tlilpotonqui, the Tlacochcalcatl Quappiaztzin, the Ticocyahuacatl Quetzalaztatzin, and the Huitznahuatlailotlac Ecatenpatiltzin. He reported the account to them, and showed them, put before them, the beads they had brought.

He said to them, "We have beheld the fine blue turquoise; it is to be guarded well, the custodians are to take good care of it; if they let one piece get away from them, [their] homes, children, and women with child will be ours."

Then the year changed to the one following, Thirteen Rabbit, and when it was nearly over, at the end of the year Thirteen Rabbit, [the Spaniards] made an appearance and were seen once again. Then the stewards quickly came to tell Moteucçoma.

When he heard it, he quickly sent out a party. He thought and believed that it was Topiltzin Quetzalcoatl who had landed. For they were of the opinion that he would return, that he would appear, that he would come back to his seat of authority, because he had gone in that direction [eastward] when he left. And [Moteucçoma] sent five [people] to go to meet him and give him things. The leader had the official title of Teohua [custodian of the god] and the personal name of Yohualli ichan. The second was Tepoztecatl, the third Tiçahua, the fourth Huehuete-catl, and the fifth Hueicamecatl eca.

Fourth chapter, where it is said what orders Moteucçoma gave when he found out that the Spaniards had returned. The second time they came it was [with] don Hernando Cortés.

He said to them, "Come, o men of unique valor, do come. It is said that our lord has appeared at last. Do go to meet him; listen well, make good use of your ears, bring back in your ears a good record of what he says. Here is what you will take to our lord."

[First] were the appurtenances of Quetzalcoatl: a serpent mask, made of turquoise; a quetzal-feather head fan; a plaited neckband of green-stone beads, with a golden disk in the middle of it; and a shield with gold [strips] crossing each other, or with gold and seashells cross-ing, with quetzal feathers spread about the edge and with a quetzal-feather banner; and a mirror with quetzal feathers to be tied on his back; and this mirror for the back seemed to have a turquoise shield, with turquoise glued on it, and there were green-stone neck bands with golden shells on them; then there was the turquoise spear thrower, entirely of turquoise, with a kind of serpent head; and there were obsid-ian sandals.

The second set of things they went to give him were the appurtenances of Tezcatlipoca: a feather headpiece, covered with golden stars,
and his golden bell earplugs; and a seashell necklace; the chest orna-
ment, decorated with many small seashells, with its fringe made of
them; and a sleeveless jacket, painted all over, with eyes on its border
and teased feathers at the fringe; and a cloak with blue-green knots,
called a *tzitzilli*, tied on the back by taking its corners, also with a mirror
for the back over it; and another item, golden bells tied to the calves
of the legs; and another item, white sandals. [A third and fourth god's
costume was also sent.] . . .

These then were the things, called gods' appurtenances, that the
messengers carried with them, and they took many other things by way
of greeting: a shell-shaped gold headpiece with yellow parrot feathers
hanging from it, a golden miter, etc.

Then baskets were filled and carrying frames were adjusted. And
then Moteucçoma gave orders to the aforementioned five [emissaries],
saying to them, "Now go, don't tarry anywhere, and address yourselves
to our lord the god. Tell him, 'Your agent Moteucçoma has sent us;
here is what he is giving you. You have arrived in Mexico, your home.'"

And when they reached the coast, they were taken across [a river or
inlet] by boat at Xicalanco. There again they left by boat, taken by the
water folk. Everything went into the boats; the goods were placed in
boats. And when the boats were full, they left. They cast off and reached
[the Spaniards'] boat[s], bringing their own boat close.

Then [the Spaniards] said to them, "Who are you? Where have you
come from?"

Then [the emissaries] answered them, "Why, we have come from
Mexico."

Again [the Spaniards] replied to them, "Perhaps not. Perhaps you are
just claiming to be from there, perhaps you are making it up, perhaps
you are deceiving us."

But when they were convinced and satisfied, they hooked the prow of
the boat with an iron staff and hauled them in; then they also put down
a ladder.

Fifth chapter, where it is said what happened when Moteucçoma's
messengers went into don Hernando Cortés's boat.

Then they climbed up, carrying in their arms the goods. When they
had gotten up into the boat, each of them made the earth-eating gesture
before the Captain. Then they addressed him, saying,

"May the god attend: his agent Moteucçoma who is in charge in
Mexico for him addresses him and says, 'The god is doubly welcome.'"

Then they dressed up the Captain. They put on him the turquoise serpent mask attached to the quetzal-feather head fan, to which were fixed, from which hung the green-stone serpent earplugs. And they put the sleeveless jacket on him, and around his neck they put the plaited green-stone neckband with the golden disk in the middle. On his lower back they tied the back mirror, and also they tied behind him the cloak called a *tzitzilli*. And on his legs they placed the green-stone bands with the golden bells. And they gave him, placing it on his arm, the shield with gold and shells crossing, on whose edge were spread quetzal feathers, with a quetzal banner. And they laid the obsidian sandals before him.

And the other three outfits, the gods' appurtenances, they only arranged in rows before him.

When this had been done, the Captain said to them, "Is this everything you have by way of greeting and rapprochement?"

They answered, "That is all with which we have come, o our lord."

Then the Captain ordered that they be tied up: they put irons on their feet and necks. When this had been done they shot off the cannon. And at this point the messengers truly fainted and swooned; one after another they swayed and fell, losing consciousness. And the Spaniards lifted them into a sitting position and gave them wine to drink. Then they gave them food, fed them, with which they regained strength and got their breath back.

When this had been done the Captain said to them, "Do listen, I have found out and heard that by what they say these Mexica are very strong, great warriors, able to throw others down. Where there is one of them he can chase, push aside, overcome, and turn back his enemies, even though there should be ten or twenty. Now I wish to be satisfied, I want to see you, I want to try out how strong and manly you are." Then he gave them leather shields, iron swords, and iron lances. [He said,]

"Well now, very early in the morning, as dawn is about to come, we will struggle against each other, we will challenge each other, we will find out by comparison who will fall down first."

They answered the Captain, saying, "May the lord pay heed, this is not at all what his agent Moteucçoma ordered us. All we came to do was to greet and salute you. We were not charged with what the lord wishes. If we should do that, won't Moteucçoma be very angry with us because of it, won't he destroy us for it?"

Then the Captain said, "No indeed; it is simply to be done. I want to see and behold it, for word has gone to Spain that you are very strong, great warriors. Eat while it is still before dawn, and I will eat then too. Outfit yourselves well."

Figure 2. *Moctezuma's Messengers Board Cortés's Boat.*
Fray Bernardino de Sahagún, *The Florentine Codex: Historia general de las cosas de Nueva España*, Libro 12, f.8v, 1577.

Sixth chapter, where it is said how Moteucçoma's messengers came back here to Mexico to tell Moteucçoma what they had seen.

Then [Cortés] let them go. [The Spaniards] lowered them into their boat, and when they had descended into the boat, they paddled hard; each one paddled as hard as he could, and some used their hands to paddle. They fled with all possible speed, saying to one another as they came, "O warriors, exert all your strength, paddle hard! Let's not do something [wrong] here, lest something happen to us!"

By water they quickly reached the place called Xicalanco, where they did nothing but catch their breath, then again came running along as fast as possible. Then they reached Tecpantlayacac, whereupon they again left and came fleeing. They quickly got to Cuetlaxtlan, where they caught their breath and also quickly came away.

And the (ruler or steward) of Cuetlaxtlan said to them, "First take your rest for a day or so, until you recover your strength."

But they said to him, "No, rather we are going hurrying to talk to the lord ruler Moteucçoma, to tell him what we saw, these very terrifying things the like of which have never been seen. Should you be the very first to hear them?"

Then they quickly got on their way and soon reached Mexico. It was night when they got there; they came in by night.

During this time Moteucçoma neither slept nor touched food. Whatever he did, he was abstracted; it seemed as though he was ill at ease, frequently sighing. He tired and felt weak. He no longer found anything tasteful, enjoyable, or amusing.

Therefore he said, "What is to come of us? Who in the world must endure it? Will it not be me [as ruler]? My heart is tormented, as though chile water were poured on it; it greatly burns and smarts. Where in the world [are we to turn], o our lord?"

Then [the messengers] notified those who guarded [Moteucçoma], who kept watch at the head of his bed, saying to them, "Even if he is asleep, tell him. 'Those whom you sent out on the sea have come back.'"

But when they went to tell him, he replied, "I will not hear it here. I will hear it at the Coacalco; let them go there." And he gave orders, saying, "Let some captives be covered with chalk [for sacrifice]."

Then the messengers went to the Coacalco, and so did Moteucçoma. Thereupon the captives died in their presence; they cut open their chests and sprinkled their blood on the messengers. (The reason they did it was that they had gone to very dangerous places and had seen, gazed on the countenances of, and spoken to the gods.)

Figure 3. *Death of Captives.*
Fray Bernardino de Sahagún, *The Florentine Codex: Historia general de las cosas de Nueva España*, Libro 12, f.10v, 1577.

Seventh chapter, where is told the account that the messengers who went to see the boat gave to Moteucçoma.

When this was done, they talked to Moteucçoma, telling him what they had beheld, and they showed him what [the Spaniards'] food was like.

And when he heard what the messengers reported, he was greatly afraid and taken aback, and he was amazed at their food. It especially made him faint when he heard how the guns went off at [the Spaniards'] command, sounding like thunder, causing people actually to swoon, blocking the ears. And when it went off, something like a ball came out from inside, and fire went showering and spitting out. And the smoke that came from it had a very foul stench, striking one in the face. And if they shot at a hill, it seemed to crumble and come apart. And it turned a tree to dust; it seemed to make it vanish, as though someone had conjured it away. Their war gear was all iron. They clothed their bodies in iron, they put iron on their heads, their swords were iron, their bows were iron, and their shields and lances were iron.

And their deer that carried them were as tall as the roof. And they wrapped their bodies all over; only their faces could be seen, very white. Their faces were the color of limestone and their hair yellow-reddish, though some had black hair. They had long beards, also yellow-reddish. [The hair of some] was tightly curled. And their food was like fasting food, very large, white, not heavy, like chaff, like dried maize stalks, as tasty as maize stalk flour, a bit sweet or honeyed, honeyed and sweet to eat.

And their dogs were huge creatures, with their ears folded over and their jowls dragging. They had burning eyes, eyes like coals, yellow and fiery. They had thin, gaunt flanks with the rib lines showing; they were very tall. They did not keep quiet, they went about panting, with their tongues hanging down. They had spots like a jaguar's, they were varicolored.

When Moteucçoma heard it, he was greatly afraid; he seemed to faint away, he grew concerned and disturbed.

Eighth chapter, where it is said how Moteucçoma sent witches, wizards, and sorcerers to do something to the Spaniards.

Then at that time Moteucçoma sent out emissaries. Those whom he sent were all bad people, soothsayers and witches. He also sent elders, strong warriors, to see to all [the Spaniards] needed as to food: turkey hens, eggs, white tortillas, and whatever they might request, and to look after them well so that they would be satisfied in every way. He sent captives in case [the Spaniards] should drink their blood. And the emissaries did as indicated.

But when [the Spaniards] saw it, they were made sick to their stomachs, spitting, rubbing their eyelids, blinking, shaking their heads. And [the emissaries] sprinkled blood in the food, they bloodied it, which made their stomachs turn and disgusted them, because of the great stench of the blood.

Moteucçoma did this because he took them for gods, considered them gods, worshiped them as gods. They were called and given the name of gods who have come from heaven, and the blacks were called soiled gods. . . .

They say that Moteucçoma sent the witches, the rainmakers, to see what [the Spaniards] were like and perhaps be able to enchant them, cast spells on them, to use conjury or the evil eye on them or hurl something else at them, perhaps addressing some words of wizardry to them so that they would take sick, die, or turn back. But when they performed the assignment they had been given concerning the Spaniards, they could do nothing; they had no power at all. Then they quickly returned to tell Moteucçoma what they were like, how strong they were, [saying,] "We are not their match; we are as nothing."

Then Moteucçoma gave strict orders; he scolded and charged the stewards and all the lords and elders, under pain of death, that they see to and take care of everything [the Spaniards] might need. And when [the Spaniards] came onto dry land and finally started moving in this direction and coming along the road toward here, they were well cared for and made much of. They were always in the hands of someone as they came progressing; they were very well attended to.

Ninth chapter, where it is said how Moteucçoma wept, and the Mexica wept, when they found out that the Spaniards were very strong.

And Moteucçoma lamented his troubles at length; he was afraid and shocked. He told the troubles of the altepetl. And everyone was very afraid. Fear reigned, and shock, laments, and expressions of distress. People talked, assembled, gathered, wept for themselves and for others. Heads hung, there were tearful greetings, words of encouragement, and stroking of hair. Little children's heads were stroked. Fathers would say, "Alas, my children, how is it with you, that what is about to happen has happened to you?" And mothers said, "O my children, how is it with you who are to behold what is about to happen to us?"

And it was told, presented, made known, announced, and reported to Moteucçoma, and brought to his attention that a woman, one of us people here, came accompanying them as interpreter. Her name was Marina and her homeland was Tepeticpac, on the coast, where they first took her. . . .

4

The March Inland: Tlaxcala and Cholula

After the founding of Vera Cruz, Hernando Cortés sought to build alliances with nearby city-states, especially with Cempoala. According to his report, the Cempoalans had only recently been brought under Mexica domination and were restive under their overlords, so Cortés hoped they would ally with the Spaniards against the Mexica. This strategy of garnering support from Indigenous elites served him well throughout the wars that followed. After learning more about the Mexica Empire, Cortés decided to strike inland, leaving a garrison of about 150 men in Vera Cruz. The expedition consisted of several hundred Spaniards, Cempoalan soldiers, and a large number of Indigenous bearers (*tlamemeh*) with supplies. They trekked westward, climbing through the mountains that lay just beyond the coast and passing through a number of towns.

At various points the company received ambassadors, forward observers sent from Tenochtitlan by Moctezuma to gather information about the strangers. Cortés used a combination of diplomacy, bravado, and guile to try to impress these representatives, as well as to obtain local support for the mission, which by this time aimed to reach the Mexica capital and possibly force a confrontation. Informed about regional politics, Cortés chose to lead his force through Tlaxcala, an *altepetl* whose people were linguistically and culturally akin to the Mexica, but who were also their traditional political enemies.

Despite Cortés's diplomatic efforts, the Tlaxcalans understandably received the expedition with suspicion and hostility. The Tlaxcalan state was composed of four major political divisions, and its leadership was not united on the course of action to take against the invaders. Under the leadership of a young captain, Xicotencatl the Younger, certain Tlaxcalans and their Otomí allies carried out a military offensive that led to a number of open battles, which Bernal Díaz recounts in detail.

Eventually, the factions in favor of an alliance with the Spaniards won out, and the strangers were welcomed into the city with the usual presentations of food, supplies, and captive women. Some Tlaxcalans leaders like Mase Escasi and Xicotencatl the Elder, father of the hostile captain, seized the opportunity to join forces against the Mexica. For the Spaniards, cementing this alliance gave them a firm logistical base for further operations.

Cortés's alliance with Tlaxcala impressed Moctezuma's representatives, who realized that the strangers had gained a valuable if, for the Mexica, dangerous partner. Cortés's decision to march from Tlaxcala to the nearby city and religious center of Cholula, their traditional enemy, was likely taken at the urgings of Tlaxcalan military advisors, who hoped to take advantage of the new alliance to gain the upper hand over their regional competitors. Although the Spaniards were welcomed at first, fighting erupted in Cholula and resulted in a bloody massacre of the inhabitants, which was perhaps intended to show the Mexica leadership what Tlaxcalans and Spaniards were capable of doing together.

The story of the alliance with Tlaxcala is central to the course of subsequent events. Without Tlaxcalan support, the trajectory of the conquest of Tenochtitlan would have been very different. After the wars, Tlaxcala became a privileged province under Spanish colonial government, with Tlaxcalans receiving honors, rewards, and exemptions as acknowledgement of their critical role in dismantling the Mexica Empire. Some twentieth-century Mexican nationalists described the Tlaxcalans as traitors to a "native" cause, but such labels make little sense in the context of the ethnic rivalries and the contemporary geopolitics of central Mexico.

The selections on the campaign against Tlaxcala included here are excerpts from Bernal Díaz's account of the events. Another conquistador, Andrés de Tapia, narrates the Tlaxcala–Spanish attack on Cholula in a forthright manner. The Nahua sources for this part of the story include the Mexica views collected by Sahagún, as well the *Lienzo de Tlaxcala*—a sixteenth-century Tlaxcalan pictorial account that celebrates the Spanish–Tlaxcalan alliance.

11

BERNAL DÍAZ

From *The True History of the Conquest of New Spain*

Bernal Díaz conveys the feel of battle and the ferocity of the initial combat against Tlaxcala. Beyond the military tactics of each side, the narrative reveals the political fractures among the Tlaxcalans. During the encounter, it became increasingly clear that many Tlaxcalan military leaders wanted to ally with Cortés, with the end goal of waging war along with the Spaniards against their regional enemies.

After commending ourselves to God, with a happy confidence we set out on the following day for Tlaxcala, and as we were marching along, we met our two messengers who had been taken prisoners. It seems that the Indians who guarded them [in Tlaxcala] were perplexed by the warlike preparations and had been careless of their charge, and in fact, had let them out of prison. They arrived in such a state of terror at what they had seen and heard that they could hardly succeed in expressing themselves.

According to their account, when they were prisoners the Tlaxcalans had threatened them, saying: "Now we are going to kill those whom you call Teules, and eat their flesh, and we will see whether they are as valiant as you announce; and we shall eat your flesh too, you who come here with treasons and lies from that traitor Montezuma!" and for all that the messengers could say, that we were against the Mexicans, and wished to be brothers to the Tlaxcalans, they could not persuade them of its truth.

When Cortés and all of us heard those haughty words, and learned how they were prepared for war, although it gave us matter for serious thought, we all cried—"If this is so, forward—and good luck to us!" We commended ourselves to God and marched on, the Alferez [ensign] . . . , unfurling our banner and carrying it before us, for the people of the little town where we had slept, as well as the Cempoalans assured us that the Tlaxcalans would come out to meet us and resist our entry into their country.

Bernal Díaz del Castillo, *The True History of the Conquest of New Spain,* trans. Alfred P. Maudslay, 2d series (London: Printed for the Hakluyt Society, 1908), 225–30, 237–40, 243–45, 264–70.

Marching along as I have described, we discussed how the horsemen—in parties of three so as to help one another—should charge and return at a hard gallop with their lances held rather short, and when they broke through the hostile ranks should hold their lances before their faces and not stop to give thrusts, so that the Indians should not be able to seize hold of their lances; and if by chance a lance were seized, the horseman should use all his strength and put spurs to his horse, so that helped by the leverage of the lance held beneath his arm, the furious rush of the horse might enable him to wrench it from the grasp of the Indian, or should drag him along with it. It will be said today—what was the use of all this preparation when there were no hostile warriors in sight to attack us? I answer this by repeating the words of Cortés:—"Gentlemen and comrades, seeing how few of us there are, it behooves us to be always as well prepared and as much on the alert as though we saw the enemy approaching to attack us, and not only saw them approaching, but we should behave as though we were already fighting. . . .

In this way we marched about two leagues, when we came upon a fortress strongly built of stone and lime and some other cement, so strong that with iron pickaxes it was difficult to demolish it and it was constructed in such a way both for offence and defense, that it would be very difficult to capture. We halted to examine it, and Cortés asked the Indians from Zocotlan for what purpose the fortress had been built in such a way. They replied that, as war was always going on between the people of Tlaxcala and their lord, Montezuma, the Tlaxcalans had built this fort so strong the better to defend their towns, for we were already in their territory. We rested awhile and this, our entry into the land of Tlaxcala and the fortress, gave us plenty to think about. Cortés said: "Sirs, let us follow our banner which bears the sign of the holy cross, and through it we shall conquer!" Then one and all we answered him: "May good fortune attend our advance, for in God lies the true strength." So we began our march again in the order I have already noted.

We had not gone far when our scouts observed about thirty Indians who were spying. These carried two-handed swords, shields, lances and plumes of feathers. The swords are made with stones which cut worse than knives, so cleverly arranged, that one can neither break nor pull out the blades; they are as long as broadswords; and as I have already said, these spies wore devices and feather headdresses, and when our scouts observed them they came back to give us notice. Cortés then ordered the same scouts to follow the spies, and to try and capture one of them without hurting them; and then he sent five more mounted men as a support, in case there should be an ambush. Then all our army hastened on in good order and with quickstep, for our Indian friends who were with us said that there was sure to be a large body of warriors waiting in ambush.

When the thirty Indian spies saw the horsemen coming toward them, and beckoning to them with their hands, they would not wait for them to come up and capture one of them; furthermore, they defended themselves so well, that with their swords and lances they wounded some of the horses.

When our men saw how fiercely the Indians fought and that their horses were wounded, they were obliged to kill five of the Indians. As soon as this happened, a squadron of Tlaxcalans,* more than three thousand strong, which was lying in ambush, fell on them all of a sudden, with great fury and began to shower arrows on our horsemen who were now all together; and they made a good fight with their arrows and firehardened darts, and did wonders with their two-handed swords. At this moment we came up with our artillery, muskets and crossbows, and little by little the Indians gave way, but they had kept their ranks and fought well for a considerable time.

In this encounter they wounded four of our men and I think that one of them died of his wounds a few days later.

As it was now late the Tlaxcalans beat a retreat and we did not pursue them; they left about seventeen dead on the field, not counting many wounded. Where these skirmishes took place the ground was level and there were many houses and plantations of maize and magueys, which is the plant from which they make their wine.

We slept near a stream, and with the grease from a fat Indian whom we had killed and cut open, we dressed our wounds, for we had no oil, and we supped very well on some dogs which the Indians breed [for food] for all the houses were abandoned and the provisions carried off, and they had even taken the dogs with them, but these came back to their homes in the night, and there we captured them, and they proved good enough food.

All night we were on the alert with watches and patrols and scouts, and the horses bitted and saddled, in fear lest the Indians would attack us. . . .

---

*Probably Otomís from the Otomí town of Tecoac. Cortés says the chiefs of Tlaxcala sent messengers to say that the attack was made by communities (of Otomís?) without their knowledge.

The next morning, the 5th of September, 1519, we mustered the horses. There was not one of the wounded men who did not come forward to join the ranks and give as much help as he could. The crossbowmen were warned to use the store of darts very cautiously, some of them loading while the others were shooting, and the musketeers were to act in the same way, and the men with sword and shield were instructed to aim their cuts and thrusts at the bowels [of their enemies] so that they would not dare to come as close to us as they did before. The artillery was all ready for action, and the horsemen had already been instructed to aid one another and to hold their lances short, and not to stop to spear anyone except in the face and eyes—charging and returning at a hard gallop and no soldier was on any account to break away from the ranks. With our banner unfurled, and four of our comrades guarding the standard-bearer, Corral, we set out from our camp. We had not marched half a quarter of a league before we began to see the fields crowded with warriors with great feather crests and distinguishing devices, and to hear the blare of horns and trumpets.

Here would be a great opportunity to write down in proper order what happened to us in this most perilous and doubtful battle, for so many warriors surrounded us on all sides that [the situation] might be compared to a great plain, two leagues long and about the same breadth, and in its midst, four hundred men. Thus all the plain was swarming with warriors and we stood four hundred men in number, and of those many sick and wounded. And we knew for certain that this time our foe came with the determination to leave none of us alive excepting those who would be sacrificed to their idols.

To go back to our battle: How they began to charge on us! What a hail of stones sped from their slings! As for their bowmen, the javelins lay like corn on the threshing floor; all of them barbed and fire-hardened, which would pierce any armor and would reach the vitals where there is no protection; the men with swords and shields and other arms larger than swords, such as broadswords, and lances, how they pressed on us and with what valor and what mighty shouts and yells they charged upon us! The steady bearing of our artillery, musketeers and crossbowmen, was indeed a help to us, and we did the enemy much damage, and those of them who came close to us with their swords and broadswords met with such sword play from us that they were forced back and they did not close in on us so often as in the last battle. The horsemen were so skillful and bore themselves so valiantly that, after God who protected us, they were our bulwark. However, I saw that our troops were in considerable confusion, so that neither the shouts of Cortés nor the other captains availed to make them close up their ranks, and so many Indians charged down on us that it was only by a miracle of sword play that we could make them give way so that our ranks could be reformed.

One thing only saved our lives, and that was that the enemy were so numerous and so crowded one on another that the shots wrought havoc among them, and in addition to this they were not well commanded, for all the captains with their forces could not come into action, and from what we knew, since the last battle had been fought, there had been disputes and quarrels between the Captain Xicotenga and another captain the son of Chichimecatecle, over what the one had said to the other, that he had not fought well in the previous battle; to this the son of Chichimecatecle replied that he had fought better than Xicotenga and was ready to prove it by personal combat. So in this battle Chichimecatecle and his men would not help Xicotenga, and we knew for a certainty that he had also called on the company of Huexotzinco to abstain from fighting. Besides this, ever since the last battle they were afraid of the horses and the musketry, and the swords and crossbows, and our hard fighting; above all was the mercy of God which gave us strength to endure. So Xicotenga was not obeyed by two of the commanders, and we were doing great damage to his men, for we were killing many of them, and this they tried to conceal; for as they were so numerous, whenever one of their men was wounded, they immediately bound him up and carried him off on their shoulders, so that in this battle, as in the last, we never saw a dead man.

The enemy were already losing heart, and knowing that the followers of the other two captains whom I have already named, would not come to their assistance, they began to give way. It seems that in that battle we had killed one very important captain, not to mention others, and the enemy began to retreat in good order, our horsemen following them at a hard gallop for a short distance, for they could not sit their horses for fatigue, and when we found ourselves free from that multitude of warriors, we gave thanks to God.

In this engagement, one soldier was killed, and sixty were wounded, and all the horses were wounded as well. They gave me two wounds, one in the head with a stone, and one in the thigh with an arrow; but this did not prevent me from fighting, and keeping watch, and helping our soldiers, and all the soldiers who were wounded did the same; for if the wounds were not very dangerous, we had to fight and keep guard, wounded as we were, for few of us remained unwounded.

Then we returned to our camp, well contented, and giving thanks to God. We buried the dead in one of those houses which the Indians had built underground, so that the enemy should not see that we were mortals, but should believe that, as they said, we were Teules. We threw much earth over the top of the house, so that they should not smell the bodies, then we doctored all the wounded with the fat of the Indian, as I have related before. It was cold comfort to be even without salt or oil with which to cure the wounded. There was another want from which we suffered, and it was a severe one—and that was clothes with which to cover ourselves, for such a cold wind came from the snow mountains, that it made us shiver, for our lances and muskets and crossbows made a poor covering. That night we slept with more tranquility than on the night before, when we had so much duty to do, with scouting, spies, watchmen and patrols.

I will leave off here and relate what we did on the next day. In this battle we captured three Indian chieftains.

When we awoke and saw how all of us were wounded, even with two or three wounds, and how weary we were and how others were sick and clothed in rags, and knew that Xicotenga was always after us, and already over forty-five of our soldiers had been killed in battle, or succumbed to disease and chills, and another dozen of them were ill, and our Captain Cortés himself was suffering from fever as well as the Padre de la Merced, and what with our labors and the weight of our arms which we always carried on our backs, and other hardships from chills and the want of salt, for we could never find any to eat, we began to wonder what would be the outcome of all this fighting, and what we should do and where we should go when it was finished. To march into Mexico we thought too arduous an undertaking because of its great armies, and we said to one another that if those Tlaxcalans, which our Cempoalan friends had led us to believe were peacefully disposed, could reduce us to these straits, what would happen when we found ourselves at war with the great forces of Montezuma? In addition to this we had heard nothing from the Spaniards whom we had left settled in Villa Rica [Vera Cruz], nor they of us. As there were among us very excellent gentlemen and soldiers, steady and valiant men of good counsel, Cortés never said or did anything [important] without first asking well considered advice, and acting in concert with us. . . .

Let us leave this and say how Doña Marina who, although a native woman, possessed such manly valor that, although she had heard every day how the Indians were going to kill us and eat our flesh with chili, and had seen us surrounded in the late battles, and knew that all of us were wounded and sick, yet never allowed us to see any sign of fear in her, only a courage passing that of woman. So Doña Marina and Jerónimo de Aguilar spoke to the messengers whom we were now sending and told them that they must come and make peace at once, and that if it was not concluded within two days we should go and kill them all and destroy their country and would come to seek them in their city, and with these brave words they were dispatched to the capital where Xicotenga the elder and Mase Escasi were [residing]. . . .

As our Lord God, through his great loving kindness, was pleased to give us victory in those battles in Tlaxcala, our fame spread throughout the surrounding country, and reached the ears of the great Montezuma in the great City of Mexico; and if hitherto they took us for Teules, which is the same as their idols, from now on they held us in even greater respect as valiant warriors, and terror fell on the whole country at learning how, being so few in number and the Tlaxcalans in such great force, we had conquered them and that they had sued us for peace. So that now Montezuma, the great Prince of Mexico, powerful as he was, was in fear of our going to his city, and sent five chieftains, men of much importance, to our camp at Tlaxcala to bid us welcome, and say that he was rejoiced at our great victory against so many squadrons of warriors, and he sent a present, a matter of a thousand [coins] worth of gold, in very rich jeweled ornaments, worked in various shapes, and twenty loads of fine cotton cloth, and he sent word that he wished to become the vassal of our great Emperor, and that he was pleased that we were already near his city, on account of the good will that he bore Cortés and all his brothers, the Teules, who were with him (for so they called us) and that he [Cortés] should decide how much tribute he wished for every year for our great Emperor, and that he [Montezuma] would give it in gold and silver, cloth and chalchihuites [green stones], provided we would not come to Mexico. This was not because he would not receive us with the greatest willingness, but because the land was rough and sterile, and he would regret to see us undergo such hardships which perchance he might not be able to alleviate as well as he could wish. Cortés answered by saying that he highly appreciated the good will shown us, and the present which had been sent, and the offer to pay tribute to his Majesty, and he begged the messengers not to depart until he went to the capital of Tlaxcala, as he would dispatch them from that place, for they could then see how that war ended. . . . Cortés was talking to the ambassadors of Montezuma, as I have already said, and wanted to take some rest, for he was ill with fever and had purged himself the day before, when they came to tell him that the Captain Xicotenga was arriving with many other Caciques and Captains, all clothed in white and red cloaks, half of the cloak was white and the other half red, for this was the device and livery of Xicotenga, [who was approaching] in a very peaceful manner, and was bringing with him in his company about fifty chieftains.

When Xicotenga reached Cortés's quarters he paid him the greatest respect by his obeisance, and ordered much copal to be burned. Cortés, with the greatest show of affection, seated him by his side and Xicotenga said that he came on behalf of his father and of Mase Escasi and all the Caciques, and Commonwealth of Tlaxcala to pray Cortés to admit them to our friendship, and that he came to render obedience to our King and Lord, and to ask pardon for having taken up arms and made war upon us. That this had been done because they did not know who we were, and they had taken it for certain that we had come on behalf of their enemy Montezuma, and as it frequently happened that craft and cunning was used to gain entrance to their country so as to rob and pillage it, they had believed that this was now the case, and for that reason had endeavored to defend themselves and their country, and were obliged to show fight.

He said that they were a very poor people who possessed neither gold, nor silver, nor precious stones, nor cotton cloth, nor even salt to eat, because Montezuma gave them no opportunity to go out and search for it, and that although their ancestors possessed some gold and precious stones, they had been given to Montezuma on former occasions when, to save themselves from destruction, they had made peace or a truce, and this had been in times long past; so that if they had nothing to give now, we must pardon them for it, for poverty and not the want of good will was the cause of it. He made many complaints of Montezuma and his allies who were all hostile to them and made war on them, but they had defended themselves very well. Now they had thought to do the same against us, but they could not do it although they had gathered against us three times with all their warriors, and we must be invincible, and when they found this out about our persons they wished to become friends with us and the vassals of the great prince the Emperor Don Carlos, for they felt sure that in our company they and their women and children would be guarded and protected, and would not live in dread of the Mexican traitors, and he said many other words placing themselves and their city at our disposal.

Xicotenga was tall, broad shouldered and well made; his face was long, pockmarked and coarse, he was about thirty-five years old and of a dignified deportment.

Cortés thanked him very courteously, in a most flattering manner, and said that he would accept them as vassals of our King and Lord, and as our own friends. Then Xicotenga begged us to come to his city, for all the Caciques, elders and priests were waiting to receive us with great rejoicing. Cortés replied that he would go there promptly, and would start at once, were it not for some negotiations which he was carrying on with the great Montezuma, and that he would come after he had dispatched the messengers. Then Cortés spoke somewhat more sharply and severely about the attacks they had made on us both by day and night, adding that as it could not now be mended he would pardon it. Let them see to it that the peace we now were granting them was an enduring one, without any change, for otherwise he would kill them and destroy their city and that he [Xicotenga] should not expect further talk about peace, but only of war.

When Xicotenga and all the chieftains who had come with him heard these words they answered one and all, that the peace would be firm and true, and that to prove it they would all remain with us as hostages.

There was further conversation between Cortés and Xicotenga and most of his chiefs, and they were given blue and green beads for Xicotenga's father, for himself, and for the other Caciques, and were told to report that Cortés would soon set out for their city.

The Mexican Ambassadors were present during all these discussions and heard all the promises that were made, and the conclusion of peace weighed on them heavily, for they fully understood that it boded them no good. And when Xicotenga had taken his leave these Ambassadors of Montezuma half laughingly asked Cortés whether he believed any of those promises which were made on behalf of all Tlaxcala, [alleging] that it was all a trick which deserved no credence, and the words were those of traitors and deceivers; that their object was to attack and kill us as soon they had us within their city in a place where they could do so in safety; that we should bear in mind how often they had put forth all their strength to destroy us and had failed to do so, and had lost many killed and wounded, and that now they offered a sham peace so as to avenge themselves. Cortés answered them, with a brave face, that their alleged belief that such was the case did not trouble him, for even if it were true he would be glad of it so as to punish them [the Tlaxcalans] by taking their lives, that it did not matter to him whether they attacked him by day or by night, in the city or in the open, he did not mind one way or the other, and it was for the purpose of seeing whether they were telling the truth that he was determined to go to their city.

The Ambassadors seeing that he had made up his mind begged him to wait six days in our camp as they wished to send two of their companions with a message to their Lord Montezuma, and said that they would return with a reply within six days. To this Cortés agreed, on the one hand because, as I have said he was suffering from fever, and on the other because, although when the Ambassadors had made these statements he had appeared to attach no importance to them, he thought that there was a chance of their being true, and that until there was greater certainty of peace, they were of a nature requiring much consideration.

As at the time that this peace was made the towns all along the road that we had traversed from Vera Cruz were allied to us and friendly, Cortés wrote to Juan de Escalante who, as I have said, remained in the town to finish building the fort, and had under his command the sixty old or sick soldiers who had been left behind. In these letters he told them of the great mercies which our Lord Jesus Christ had vouchsafed to us in the victories which we had gained in our battles and encounters since we had entered the province of Tlaxcala, which had now sued for peace with us, and asked that all of them would give thanks to God for it. He also told them to see to it that they always kept on good terms with our friends in the towns of the Totonacs, and he told him to send at once two jars of wine which had been left behind, buried in a certain marked place in his lodgings, and some sacred wafers for the Mass, which had been brought from the Island of Cuba, for those which we had brought on this expedition were already finished.

These letters were most welcome, and Escalante wrote in reply to say what had happened in the town, and all that was asked for arrived very quickly.

About this time we set up a tall and sumptuous cross in our camp, and Cortés ordered the Indians of Tzumpantzingo and those who dwelt in the houses near our camp to whitewash it, and it was beautifully finished.

I must cease writing about this and return to our new friends the Caciques of Tlaxcala, who when they saw that we did not go to their city, came themselves to our camp and brought poultry and tunas,* which were then in season, each one brought some of the food which he had in his house and gave it to us with the greatest good will without asking

---

*Tuna: The prickly pear, the fruit of the Nopal Cactus (*Opuntia*).

anything in return, and they always begged Cortés to come with them soon to their city.

As we had promised to wait six days for the return of the Mexicans, Cortés put off the Tlaxcalans with fair speeches. When the time expired, according to their word, six chieftains, men of great importance, arrived from Mexico, and brought a rich present from the great Montezuma consisting of valuable gold jewels wrought in various shapes worth three thousand pesos in gold, and two hundred pieces of cloth, richly worked with feathers and other patterns. When they offered this present the Chieftains said to Cortés that their Lord Montezuma was delighted to hear of our success, but that he prayed him most earnestly on no account to go with the people of Tlaxcala to their town, nor to place any confidence in them, that they wished to get him there to rob him of his gold and cloth, for they were very poor, and did not possess a decent cotton cloak among them, and that the knowledge that Montezuma looked on us as friends, and was sending us gold and jewels and cloth, would still more induce the Tlaxcalans to rob us.

Cortés received the present with delight, and said that he thanked them for it and would repay their Lord Montezuma with good works, and if he should perceive that the Tlaxcalans had that in mind against which Montezuma had sent them to warn him, they would pay for it by having all their lives taken, but he felt sure they would be guilty of no such villainy, and he still meant to go and see what they would do.

While this discussion was proceeding, many other messengers from Tlaxcala came to tell Cortés that all the old Caciques from the Capital and from the whole province had arrived at our ranchos and huts, in order to see Cortés and all of us, and to take us to their city. When Cortés heard this he begged the Mexican Ambassadors to wait for three days for the reply to their prince, as he had at present to deliberate and decide about the past hostilities and the peace which was now offered, and the Ambassadors said that they would wait. . . .

12

ANDRÉS DE TAPIA

A Spanish View of the Cholula Massacre

Cortés's own report of the events in Cholula gave little detail of his bloody actions, but another Spanish observer, captain Andrés de Tapia, wrote a succinct and frank record of the destruction of that city. Tapia was Cortés's steward during the march inland. The first section is an excerpt of a deposition given by Tapia in 1529 during an investigation of Cortés's actions. The second section, written some fifteen years later, is from Tapia's concise account of the conquest, titled Relation of some things that happened to the very Illustrious Don Hernando Cortés, Marqués del Valle. *The two accounts differ in significant ways, but both are brutally honest about the two days of slaughter wrought by the Spaniards and Tlaxcalans at Cholula.*

Response to Questions about Cortés's Actions during the Conquest

Don Fernando summoned all the noblemen of the city, saying he wanted to leave [Cholula] and needed to talk with them beforehand. He asked that they bring many people to carry the Spaniards' belongings, and so they did, coming with four to five thousand Indians. They were all taken to the patios and corrals of the major temple. Once inside, he [Cortés] ordered the Spaniards who were present to kill all of them, and so they killed them. Once they were dead, he [Cortés] went out into the city with his men, and they killed everyone they encountered. He [Cortés] also ordered them to enter into the noblemen's houses and kill those who had fled or were hiding, and they set all the temples on fire. To this day, this witness [Tapia] ignores the cause, for he was told that the Indians wanted to rise and kill the Spaniards, but he had witnessed how they had welcomed them and given them food. This witness believes that more than twenty thousand were among those killed or captured on that date.

Translations by T. Seijas. Jorge Gurría Lacroix, ed. *Relación de méritos y servicios del conquistador Bernardino Vázquez de Tapia...* (México: UNAM, 1972), 82–3; Joaquín García Icazbalceta, ed. "Relación de Andrés de Tapia." In *Colección de documentos para la historia de México* (México: J. M. Andrade, 1858), 573–7.

"Relation of some things that happened to the very Illustrious Don Hernando Cortés, Marqués del Valle"

The marqués departed [from Tlaxcala] after gathering as much information as possible regarding the territory ahead, and the Indians from that province said they would show him the way along the road as far as they knew it. They also said that about four leagues away there was a city called Chitrula [Cholula], its own state, who were their enemies and friends and allies of Muteczuma, and that it was on our way. And so an expedition of Spaniards and forty thousand [Tlaxcalan] men of war left this city, apart from us, because that was the way the marqués commanded.

Having arrived at this city of Chitrula, one morning ten or twelve thousand men in squadrons came out bringing maize bread and some turkeys. Each squadron approached the marqués to bid him welcome, and then they withdrew. They [Cholulans] entreated and begged at various instances that the marqués not consent to the Tlaxcalans entering their territory. So the marqués ordered them to go back, but they [Tlaxcalans] repeatedly said: "Look, the people of this city are merchants, and not men of war, and they are men who have one heart and show another, and they always do things through trickery and lies, so we do not want to leave you, because we pledged to you our friendship." Regardless, the marqués ordered that all their men were to go back, but that if some of the nobles wished to remain, they could be quartered outside the city with some men to serve them, and that was the way it was done.

As we entered the city, everyone who lived there came out, the men in their squadrons, to greet the Spaniards they encountered, as we filed in. After the squadrons the remaining people emerged, [including] the ministers who served the idols, who were dressed in sleeveless robes, some closed in front, with hoods, with heavy cotton fringe, and others dressed in various ways. Many of them were playing flutes and trumpets, and carrying certain idols, which were covered, and many incense burners. And in this way they approached the marqués and then the other men, perfuming them with a resin they burned in the censers.

This city's principal god had been a man in past times, and they called him Quezalquate [Quetzalcoatl]. It is said that he founded this city and ordered them not to kill men, but instead to build edifices to the creator of the sun and the heavens and there offer him quail and hunted animal.

They were not to wish harm, nor hurt one another. He [the god] had worn a white vesture like a monk's tunic, and over it a mantle covered with red crosses. Here they have certain green stones, one of them [shaped like] a monkey's head, and they said that these had belonged to this god-man so they kept them as relics.

The marqués and his men stayed in this town for several days. From here, he sent several volunteers to explore a volcano that appeared along a high mountain range some five leagues away, which gave out much smoke. They were to look out from there in all directions and bring back news regarding the disposition of the land.

Certain persons of rank came to this city as messengers of Muteczuma, who made speeches over and over again. Sometimes they asked why and where we were going, because they did not have provisions for us to eat. At other times they said that Muteczuma did not want to see them because he would die of fright. Others said there was no road to get there [Tenochtitlan]. Seeing that the marqués was satisfied by all this, they made the people of the city tell us that where Muteczuma lived there were great numbers of lions and tigers and other wild beasts, and that Muteczuma let them loose whenever he wanted to, and that they would eat us and tear our bodies apart.

When they realized that nothing would deter us from our path, Muteczuma's messengers plotted with the people of the city to kill us. The way they proposed to do it was to take us to the left of the road leading to Mexico, where there were dangerous crossings formed by the waters flowing from the volcano's ridge. The earth there is sandy and soft, so a small stream of water can make a great ravine, and some of them are more than a hundred *estados* [measurement] deep. These are so narrow that tall trees are enough to make bridges across the ravines, and these exist, because we later saw them.

As we were preparing to leave, an Indian woman of this city of Cholula, the wife of one of the noblemen, told the woman who was our interpreter [Malintzin] along with the Christian, that she would like her to stay there, because she was very fond of her and it would be grievous to see her killed. Then she told her what they were plotting, which is how the marqués learned about it and delayed his departure for two days. He told them [Cholulans] that it did not surprise nor anger him when men fought against him, but that being told lies did weigh on him, so he warned them not to lie in their dealings with him, nor to resort to treachery.

They assured him they were his friends and always would be, and that they never lied to him and never would. Then they asked him when he wished to leave, and he said that on the following day. They said they wanted to assemble many men to send with him, but the marqués said he only wanted some slaves to carry the Spaniards' baggage. They insisted on sending an escort, but the marqués refused, repeating that he only wanted enough men to carry the baggage.

Next day, without warning, a large number of soldiers arrived with their weapons, the most valiant among them, saying they were slaves and bearers. The marqués said he wished to take his leave of all the lords of the city, and asked that they be summoned. This city did not have one lord, all men were captains of the republic, that is how they governed themselves. Later all these principal men arrived, all nobles, some thirty of them. The marqués took them into a courtyard of the house where he was lodged, and he said to them: "I have only ever spoken the truth to you, and I have given orders to all the Christians in my company to do you no harm, and no harm has been done you. Yet with bad intentions you asked that the Tlaxcalans not enter your territory. And even though you have not given me enough to eat as you should, I have not allowed my companions to take so much as a fowl. Also I have asked you not to lie to me. In payment for these good deeds, you have conspired to kill me and my companions, and you have brought men to fight me as soon as we were to reach the bad terrain over which you planned to lead us. For the malice you had planned, you will all die, and as a sign that you are traitors, I will destroy your city so that no memory remains of it. It is impossible for you to deny this, for I know it as well as I am saying it to you."

They were astonished, and kept looking at one another. There were guards to keep them from escaping, and outside in the large courtyards of the idols there were also men guarding the people who were to carry our baggage. The marqués then said to these dignitaries: "I want you to tell me the truth, even though I already know it, so that these messengers and everyone else may hear it from your lips and it not be said that I fabricated it."

Five or six at a time were taken aside, and each one confessed separately, without torture of any kind, that what the marqués had said was the truth. When he saw that they were in agreement with one another, he had them all gathered together again, and they all confessed that it was so. They said among themselves: "He is like our gods, who know everything; there is no denying him."

Then, the marqués had Muteczuma's messengers brought in, and said to them: "These men wanted to kill me, and they say that Muteczuma was involved, but I do not believe it because I consider him to be a friend, and I know that he is a great lord, and a lord does not lie. I believe they [Cholulans] wanted to do me this treacherous injury because they are scoundrels and people who have no lord. so they shall die. But you have nothing to fear, for you are the messengers of a lord I regard as a friend, who I have reason to believe is very good, and I will not tolerate that anything be said to the contrary."

Then he ordered that most of the noblemen be killed, leaving a few of them in chains. He also ordered the Spaniards in the other patios to give a signal that everyone be killed, and so it was done. They defended themselves the best they could, and tried to take the offensive, but since they were walled inside the courtyards with the entrances guarded, the majority of them died.

This done, the Spaniards and Indians in our company went out in squadrons to different parts of the city, killing the men and burning the houses. Shortly after, a number of people from Tlaxcala arrived, and they looted the city, destroyed everything possible, making off with a great amount of plunder.

Certain priests of the devil climbed to the top of the tower of the principal idol and refused to give themselves up, but stayed there to be burned, lamenting and telling their idol that it was wrong of him to forsake them. So everything possible was done to destroy this city, but the marqués ordered us to refrain from killing women and children. The work of destroying the city took two days. Many [of the residents] hid in the hills and fields, and others took refuge in the land of their enemies.

At the end of two days the marqués ordered the destruction ceased, and so it stopped. Within another two or three days, it appeared that many of the natives of the city had gathered together, for they sent word to the marqués begging for pardon and for permission to reoccupy the city, offering to be a protectorate of Tlaxcala. The marqués pardoned them.

13

FRAY BERNARDINO DE SAHAGÚN

From the *Florentine Codex*

The Nahua accounts collected by Sahagún emphasize the Spanish–Tlaxcalan alliance, and the Cholula massacre is described as an unprovoked act of violence.

James Lockhart, *We People Here: Nahuatl Accounts of the Conquest of Mexico*, Repertorium Columbianum, UCLA Center for Medieval and Renaissance Studies (Los Angeles: University of California Press, 1993), 90–98, 104–106.

Tenth chapter, where it is said how the Spaniards landed uncontested and came on their way in this direction, and how Moteucçoma left the great palace and went to his personal home.

Then Moteucçoma abandoned his patrimonial home, the great palace, and came back to his personal home.

When at last [the Spaniards] came, when they were coming along and moving this way, a certain person from Cempoallan, whose name was Tlacochcalcatl, whom they had taken when they first came to see the land and the various altepetl, also came interpreting for them, planning their route, conducting them, showing them the way, leading and guiding them.

And when they reached Tecoac, which is in the land of the Tlaxcalans, where their Otomis lived, the Otomis met them with hostilities and war. But they annihilated the Otomis of Tecoac, who were destroyed completely. They lanced and stabbed them, they shot them with guns, iron bolts, crossbows. Not just a few but a huge number of them were destroyed.

After the great defeat at Tecoac, when the Tlaxcalans heard it and found out about it and it was reported to them, they became limp with fear, they were made faint; fear took hold of them. Then they assembled, and all of them, including the lords and rulers, took counsel among themselves, considering the reports.

They said, "How is it to be with us? Should we face them? For the Otomis are great and valiant warriors, yet they thought nothing of them, they regarded them as nothing; in a very short time, in the blink of an eyelid, they destroyed the people. Now let us just submit to them, let us make friends with them, let us be friends, for something must be done about the common people."

Thereupon the Tlaxcalan rulers went to meet them, taking along food: turkey hens, eggs, white tortillas, fine tortillas. They said to them, "Welcome, our lords."

[The Spaniards] answered them back, "Where is your homeland? Where have you come from?"

They said, "We are Tlaxcalans. Welcome, you have arrived, you have reached the land of Tlaxcala, which is your home."

(But in olden times it was called Texcallan and the people Texcalans.)

Eleventh chapter, where it is said how the Spaniards reached Tlaxcala, [also] called Texcallan.

[The Tlaxcalans] guided, accompanied, and led them until they brought them to their palace(s) and placed them there. They showed them great honors, they gave them what they needed and attended to them, and then they gave them their daughters.

Then [the Spaniards] asked them, "Where is Mexico? What kind of a place is it? Is it still far?"

They answered them, "It's not far now. Perhaps one can get there in three days. It is a very favored place, and [the Mexica] are very strong, great warriors, conquerors, who go about conquering everywhere."

Now before this there had been friction between the Tlaxcalans and the Cholulans. They viewed each other with anger, fury, hate, and disgust; they could come together on nothing. Because of this they put [the Spaniards] up to killing them treacherously.

They said to them, "The Cholulans are very evil; they are our enemies. They are as strong as the Mexica, and they are the Mexica's friends."

When the Spaniards heard this, they went to Cholula. The Tlaxcalans and Cempoalans went with them, outfitted for war. When they arrived, there was a general summons and cry that all the noblemen, rulers, subordinate leaders, warriors, and commoners should come, and everyone assembled in the temple courtyard. When they had all come together, [the Spaniards and their friends] blocked the entrances, all of the places where one entered. Thereupon people were stabbed, struck, and killed. No such thing was in the minds of the Cholulans; they did not meet the Spaniards with weapons of war. It just seemed that they were stealthily and treacherously killed, because the Tlaxcalans persuaded [the Spaniards] to do it.

And a report of everything that was happening was given and relayed to Moteucçoma. Some of the messengers would be arriving as others were leaving; they just turned around and ran back. There was no time when they weren't listening, when reports weren't being given. And all the common people went about in a state of excitement; there were frequent disturbances, as if the earth moved and (quaked), as if everything were spinning before one's eyes. People took fright.

And after the dying in Cholula, [the Spaniards] set off on their way to Mexico, coming gathered and bunched, raising dust. Their iron lances and halberds seemed to sparkle, and their iron swords were curved like a stream of water. Their cuirasses and iron helmets seemed to make a clattering sound. Some of them came wearing iron all over, turned into iron beings, gleaming, so that they aroused great fear and were generally seen with fear and dread. Their dogs came in front, coming ahead of them, keeping to the front, panting, with their spittle hanging down.

Twelfth chapter, where it is said how Moteucçoma sent a great nobleman along with many other noblemen to go to meet the Spaniards, and what their gifts of greeting were when they greeted the Captain between Iztactepetl and Popocatepetl.

Thereupon Moteucçoma named and sent the noblemen and a great many other agents of his, with Tzihuacpopocatzin as their leader, to go meet [Cortés] between Popocatepetl and Iztactepetl, at Quauhtechcac. They gave [the Spaniards] golden banners, banners of precious feathers, and golden necklaces.

And when they had given the things to them, they seemed to smile, to rejoice and be very happy. Like monkeys they grabbed the gold. It was as though their hearts were put to rest, brightened, freshened. For gold was what they greatly thirsted for; they were gluttonous for it, starved for it, piggishly wanting it. They came lifting up the golden banners, waving them from side to side, showing them to each other. They seemed to babble; what they said to each other was in a babbling tongue.

And when they saw Tzihuacpopocatzin, they said, "Is this one then Moteucçoma?" They said it to the Tlaxcalans and Cempoalans, their lookouts, who came among them, questioning them secretly. They said, "It is not that one, o our lords. This is Tzihuacpopocatzin, who is representing Moteucçoma."

[The Spaniards] said to him, "Are you then Moteucçoma?" He said, "I am your agent Moteucçoma."

Then they told him, "Go on with you! Why do you lie to us? What do you take us for? You can't lie to us, you can't fool us, (turn our heads), flatter us, (make faces at us), trick us, confuse our vision, distort things for us, blind us, dazzle us, throw mud in our eyes, put muddy hands on our faces. It is not you. Moteucçoma exists; he will not be able to hide from us, he will not be able to find refuge. Where will he go? Is he a bird, will he fly? Or will he take an underground route, will he go somewhere into a mountain that is hollow inside? We will see him, we will not fail to gaze on his face and hear his words from his lips."

... Fourteenth chapter, where it is said how Moteucçoma gave orders for the roads to be closed so that the Spaniards could not get to Mexico here.

And in vain attempt Moteucçoma ordered that the roads and highways be closed off in various places. They planted magueys in the road coming straight to Mexico here, directing them [instead] onto the road going into Tezcoco.

And where they closed the road with a wall of maguey, [the Spaniards] immediately recognized it, they saw that they had just blocked it, and they disregarded it. They took the magueys, kicked them far away, sent them flying, hurled them far off to the side.

Figure 4. *Spaniards Dismiss Moctezuma's Envoys.*
Fray Bernardino de Sahagún, *The Florentine Codex: Historia general de las cosas de Nueva España*, Libro 12, f.18, 1577.

They spent the night at Amaquemecan, then came straight on along the road and reached Cuitlahuac, where they also spent the night. They assembled the rulers from each of the kingdoms among the chinampa people: Xochimilco, Cuitlahuac, Mizquic. They told them what they had told the rulers of Chalco. And the rulers of the chinampa people also submitted to them.

And when the Spaniards were satisfied, they moved on this way and made a halt in Itztapalapan. Then they summoned, had summoned the rulers there as well, called the Four Lords, of Itztapalapan, Mexicatzinco, Colhuacan, and Huitzilopochco. They talked with them in the same way they had spoken to [the chinampa people] (as was said). And they too peacefully submitted to the Spaniards.

Moteucçoma did not give orders for anyone to make war against them or for anyone to meet them in battle. No one was to meet them in battle. He just ordered that they be strictly obeyed and very well attended to.

And at this time there was silence here in Mexico. No one went out any more; mothers no longer let [their children] go out. The roads were as if swept clean, wide open, as if at dawn, with no one crossing. People assembled in the houses and did nothing but grieve. The people said, "Let it be that way; curses on it. What more can you do? For we are about to die and perish, we are awaiting our deaths."

14

Tlaxcalan Noblemen Greet Cortés
and
Massacre at Cholula

From the *Lienzo de Tlaxcala*

The content of the Lienzo, *like the history written by the Tlaxcalan author Diego Muñoz Camargo in the sixteenth century, demonstrates how history can be repurposed for different political ends.[1] The early battles between the Spaniards and Tlaxcalans described by Bernal Díaz, for instance,*

[1]Diego Muñoz Camargo, *Historia de Tlaxcala* (México: Oficina tip. de la Secretaría de fomento, 1892). http://archive.org/details/historiadetlaxca00muno.

were carefully omitted from Tlaxcalan historical narratives, which concentrated instead on later cooperation and alliance. Doña Marina (Malintzin) plays a central role in the rendering of the fall of the Mexica Empire and is repeatedly shown as a major figure next to Cortés.

The first scene has Cortés grabbing the wrist of a Tlaxcalan nobleman before the cross, while two other noblemen holding flowers look on; to the right, Malintzin and a Franciscan friar also bear witness to the encounter. The second scene is the massacre at Cholula. At left, Tlaxcalan and Spanish soldiers attack Cholulan priests at the Temple of Quetzalcoatl; two Tlaxcalan noblemen stand at center, apparently orchestrating the events. Malintzin, at right, is shown directing a Spanish horseman to strike residents of the city-state.

Tlaxcalan Noblemen Greet Cortés at Tlaxcala.
Lienzo de Tlaxcala, reconstruction, cell 5. Liza Bakewell and Byron E. Hamann, "Mesolore: Exploring Mesoamerican Culture." Prolarti Enterprise, LLC and Brown University.

Massacre at Cholula.

Lienzo de Tlaxcala, reconstruction, cell 9. Liza Bakewell and Byron E. Hamann, "Mesolore: Exploring Mesoamerican Culture." Prolarti Enterprise, LLC and Brown University.

5

Tenochtitlan

After the massacre at Cholula, Cortés's expedition continued on toward the Mexica capital, ignoring both the attempts to have them turn back and the hardships of the march. The entry of the Spaniards and their Tlaxcalan allies into Tenochtitlan on November 8, 1519, was a quintessential moment in world history. From the European side, it was a moment of marvel and wonder. "And some of our soldiers asked whether the things we saw were not a dream," wrote Bernal Díaz. Some Spaniards who had been to Rome or Venice could compare Tenochtitlan to those cities, but most like Díaz thought that what they were seeing compared to the fantasies, dreams, and dangers of popular books of chivalry. On the Mexica side, the Spanish–Tlaxcalan entry was just as unusual. Thousands of people lined the causeways, stood on the rooftops (*azoteas*), or took to the thousands of canoes that filled the lake to catch a glimpse of the strange "deer" and Spaniards brandishing gleaming swords. They also wondered and worried about the meaning of the thousands of Tlaxcalan soldiers and auxiliaries, their traditional enemies.

A ceremonial meeting took place between Moctezuma and Cortés at the entrance to the city, which both Spanish and Nahuatl accounts recorded, and then the Spaniards were lodged within the main temple complex at the heart of the city. Within a week, Cortés imprisoned Moctezuma in his own palaces. The seizure of the Mexica leader, even a hospitable one, was a treachery to be sure, but a tactic that had already been used effectively by Spaniards against other Indigenous leaders in the Caribbean. During the following eight months Spaniards and Tlaxcalans resided in Tenochtitlan as guests and invaders. While the city was restive, there was no overt resistance against them in the city. Both Spaniards and Mexica had an opportunity to observe each other closely during this time. Bernal Díaz's account is filled with details about Moctezuma and his court. But in reality, neither the Spanish nor the Nahua accounts provide much detail of their day-to-day interactions. The Spanish used this time to try to install Catholic images in the temples and to reconnoiter the city. They also discovered treasure in the palaces and seized it; their delight and greed caught the notice of the Mexica. This period of general uneasiness transitioned to open Mexica resistance (called rebellion by Cortés).

The Nahua accounts gathered by Sahagún describe the Spanish entry into the city. The observations about the panting of the Spanish war mastiffs, the sweating of the horses, and the strange weapons of the Spaniards contain both details and a sense of curiosity that convey the feel of eyewitness observation. The excerpts from Bernal Díaz are some of his most colorful writing and provide us with the sense of awe that he felt. Moreover, they are filled with ethnographic details that make his account so valuable as a window into Mexica life, especially that of the palace. Also included is his discussion of Moctezuma's reactions to the Spanish attempts at conversion, as well as Díaz's description of Moctezuma's personality and the unusual relationship that developed between the emperor and his captors.

15

FRAY BERNARDINO DE SAHAGÚN

From the *Florentine Codex*

The Nahua accounts concentrate on those things that were new and strange, like horses, but also seek to find parallels and comparisons between their own practices and customs and the ways of the strangers. Here, for example, Cortés is compared to the tlacatecatl *or military commander. The welcoming "speech" of Moctezuma is particularly revealing and raises questions about the nature of "polite" political discourse among Nahua elites, as well as the possibility of later interpretations and explanations being placed in the historical record after the conquest. The Spaniards approached Tenochtitlan from the south, crossing to the city along the causeway from Ixtapalapa (Map 2).*

James Lockhart, *We People Here: Nahuatl Accounts of the Conquest of Mexico,* Repertorium Columbianum, UCLA Center for Medieval and Renaissance Studies (Los Angeles: University of California Press, 1993), 108–118.

Figure 5. *Spaniards and Indian Allies Marching into Tenochtitlan.*
Fray Bernardino de Sahagún, *The Florentine Codex: Historia general de las cosas de Nueva España,* Libro 12, f.23v, 1577.

Fifteenth chapter, where it is said how the Spaniards came from Itztapalapan when they reached Mexico.

Then they set out in this direction, about to enter Mexico here. Then they all dressed and equipped themselves for war. They girded themselves, tying their battle gear tightly on themselves and then on their horses. Then they arranged themselves in rows, files, ranks.

Four horse [men] came ahead, going first, staying ahead, leading. They kept turning about as they went, facing people, looking this way and that, looking sideways, gazing everywhere between the houses, examining things, looking up at the roofs.

Also the dogs, their dogs, came ahead, sniffing at things and constantly panting.

By himself came marching ahead, all alone, the one who bore the standard on his shoulder. He came waving it about, making it spin, tossing it here and there. It came stiffening, rising up like a warrior, twisting and turning.

Following him came those with iron swords. Their iron swords came bare and gleaming. On their shoulders they bore their shields, of wood or leather.

The second contingent and file were horses carrying people, each with his cotton cuirass, his leather shield, his iron lance, and his iron sword hanging down from the horse's neck. They came with bells on, jingling or rattling. The horses, the deer, neighed, there was much neighing, and they would sweat a great deal; water seemed to fall from them. And their flecks of foam splattered on the ground, like soapsuds splatting. As they went they made a beating, throbbing, and hoof-pounding like throwing stones. Their hooves made holes, they dug holes in the ground wherever they placed them. Separate holes formed wherever they went placing their hindlegs and forelegs.

The third file were those with iron crossbows, the crossbowmen. As they came, the iron crossbows lay in their arms. They came along testing them out, brandishing them, (aiming them). But some carried them on their shoulders, came shouldering the crossbows. Their quivers went hanging at their sides, passed under their armpits, well filled, packed with arrows, with iron bolts. Their cotton upper armor reached to their knees, very thick, firmly sewn, and dense, like stone. And their heads were wrapped in the same cotton armor, and on their heads plumes stood up, parting and spreading.

The fourth file were likewise horse [men]; their outfits were the same as has been said.

The fifth group were those with harquebuses, the harquebusiers, shouldering their harquebuses; some held them [level]. And when they went into the great palace, the residence of the ruler, they repeatedly shot off their harquebuses. They exploded, sputtered, discharged, thundered, (disgorged). Smoke spread, it grew dark with smoke, everyplace filled with smoke. The fetid smell made people dizzy and faint.

And last, bringing up the rear, went the war leader, thought to be the ruler and director in battle, like [among us] a *tlacateccatl*. Gathered and massed about him, going at his side, accompanying him, enclosing him were his warriors, those with devices, his [aides], like [among us] those with scraped heads [*quaquachictin*] and the Otomí warriors, the strong and valiant ones of the altepetl, its buttress and support, its heart and foundation.

Then all those from the various altepetl on the other side of the mountains, the Tlaxcalans, the people of Tliliuhquitepec, of Huexotzinco, came following behind. They came outfitted for war with their cotton upper armor, shields, and bows, their quivers full and packed with feathered arrows, some barbed, some blunted, some with obsidian points. They went crouching, hitting their mouths with their hands and yelling, singing in Tocuillan style, whistling, shaking their heads.

Some bore burdens and provisions on their backs; some used [tumplines for] their foreheads, some [bands around] their chests, some carrying frames, some board cages, some deep baskets. Some made bundles, perhaps putting the bundles on their backs. Some dragged the large cannons, which went resting on wooden wheels, making a clamor as they came.

Sixteenth chapter, where it is said how Moteucçoma went in peace and quiet to meet the Spaniards at Xoloco, where the house of Alvarado is now, or at the place they call Huitzillan.

And when they [the Spaniards] had come as far as Xoloco, when they had stopped there, Moteucçoma dressed and prepared himself for a meeting, along with other great rulers and high nobles, his rulers and nobles. Then they went to the meeting. On gourd bases they set out different precious flowers, in the midst of the shield flowers and heart flowers stood popcorn flowers, yellow tobacco flowers, cacao flowers, [made into] wreaths for the head, wreaths to be girded around. And they carried golden necklaces, necklaces with pendants, wide necklaces.

And when Moteucçoma went out to meet them at Huitzillan, thereupon he gave various things to the war leader, the commander of the warriors; he gave him flowers, he put necklaces on him, he put flower necklaces on him, he girded him with flowers, he put flower wreaths on his head. Then he laid before him the golden necklaces, all the different things for greeting people. He ended by putting some of the necklaces on him.

Then [Cortés] said in reply to Moteucçoma, "Is it not you? Is it not you then? Moteucçoma?"

Moteucçoma said, "Yes, it is me." Thereupon he stood up straight, he stood up with their faces meeting. He bowed down deeply to him. He stretched as far as he could, standing stiffly. Addressing him, he said to him,

"O our lord, be doubly welcomed on your arrival in this land; you have come to satisfy your curiosity about your altepetl of Mexico, you have come to sit on your seat of authority, which I have kept a while for you, where I have been in charge for you, for your agents the rulers— Itzcoatzin, the elder Moteucçoma, Axayacatl, Tiçocic, and Ahuitzotl— have gone, who for a very short time came to be in charge for you, to govern the altepetl of Mexico. It is after them that your poor vassal [myself] came. Will they come back to the place of their absence? If only one of them could see and behold what has now happened in my time, what I now see after our lords are gone! For I am not just dreaming, not just sleepwalking, not just seeing it in my sleep. I am not just dreaming that I have seen you, have looked upon your face. For a time I have been concerned, looking toward the mysterious place from which you have come, among clouds and mist. It is so that the rulers on departing said that you would come in order to acquaint yourself with your altepetl and sit upon your seat of authority. And now it has come true, you have come. Be doubly welcomed, enter the land, go to enjoy your palace; rest your body. May our lords be arrived in the land."

And when the speech that Moteucçoma directed to the Marqués had concluded, Marina reported it to him, interpreting it for him. And when the Marqués had heard what Moteucçoma had said, he spoke to Marina in return, babbling back to them, replying in his babbling tongue,

"Let Moteucçoma be at ease, let him not be afraid, for we greatly esteem him. Now we are truly satisfied to see him in person and hear him, for until now we have greatly desired to see him and look upon his face. Well, now we have seen him, we have come to his homeland of Mexico. Bit by bit he will hear what we have to say."

Thereupon [the Spaniards] took [Moteucçoma] by the hand. They came along with him, stroking his hair to show their good feeling. And the Spaniards looked at him, each of them giving him a close look. They would start along walking, then mount, then dismount again in order to see him. . . .

Figure 6. *Spaniards Take Moctezuma Hostage.*
Fray Bernardino de Sahagún, *The Florentine Codex: Historia general de las cosas de Nueva España,* Libro 12, f.26v, 1577.

Moctezuma and Cortés Meet in Tenochtitlan
From the *Lienzo de Tlaxcala*

In this scene from the Lienzo de Tlaxcala, *Emperor Moctezuma greets Cortés and Malintzin at the palace of his forefather, Moctezuma I. Three Mexica noblemen stand behind him. The guests are presented with gifts like deer, birds, and maize, shown at bottom. Malintzin stands at right, translating for the two men, both seated on folding chairs.*

Moctezuma and Cortés Meet in Tenochtitlan.

Lienzo de Tlaxcala, reconstruction, cell 11. Liza Bakewell and Byron E. Hamann, "Mesolore: Exploring Mesoamerican Culture." Prolarti Enterprise, LLC and Brown University, http://mesolore.org.

BERNAL DÍAZ

From *The True History of the Conquest of New Spain*

Bernal Díaz provides an account of the court life of the Mexico tlahtoani
*and makes numerous observations about Moctezuma's personality
and wealth, as well as his political standing vis-à-vis noblemen
from the surrounding city-states. Díaz's description of Tenochtitlan's
infrastructure, commercial activity, and religious and cultural practices
conveys a combination of appreciation and aversion, but his report of
Moctezuma's defense of his religion and of the ruler's conversations with
Cortés are somewhat sympathetic.*

Early next day we left Iztapalapa with a large escort of those great
Caciques whom I have already mentioned. We proceeded along the
Causeway which is here eight paces in width and runs so straight to the
City of Mexico that it does not seem to me to turn either much or little,
but, broad as it is, it was so crowded with people that there was hardly
room for them all, some of them going to and others returning from
Mexico, besides those who had come out to see us, so that we were
hardly able to pass by the crowds of them that came; and the towers and
cues were full of people as well as the canoes from all parts of the lake.
It was not to be wondered at, for they had never before seen horses or
men such as we are.

Gazing on such wonderful sights, we did not know what to say, or
whether what appeared before us was real, for on one side, on the land,
there were great cities, and in the lake ever so many more, and the
lake itself was crowded with canoes, and in the Causeway were many
bridges at intervals, and in front of us stood the great City of Mexico,
and we,—we did not even number four hundred soldiers! and we well
remembered the words and warnings given us by the people of Huexot-
zingo and Tlaxcala and Tlamanalco, and the many other warnings that

Bernal Díaz del Castillo, *The True History of the Conquest of New Spain,* trans. Alfred
P. Maudslay, 2d series (London: Printed for the Hakluyt Society, 1908), 39–44, 53–83.

had been given that we should beware of entering Mexico, where they would kill us, as soon as they had us inside.

Let the curious readers consider whether there is not much to ponder over in this that I am writing. What men have there been in the world who have shown such daring? But let us get on, and march along the Causeway. When we arrived where another small causeway branches off (leading to Coyoacan, which is another city) where there were some buildings like towers, which are their oratories, many more chieftains and Caciques approached clad in very rich mantles, the brilliant liveries of one chieftain differing from those of another, and the causeways were crowded with them. The Great Montezuma had sent these great Caciques in advance to receive us, and when they came before Cortés they bade us welcome in their language, and as a sign of peace, they touched their hands against the ground, and kissed the ground with the hand.

There we halted for a good while, and Cacamatzin, the Lord of Texcoco, and the Lord of Iztapalapa and the Lord of Tacuba and the Lord of Coyoacan went on in advance to meet the Great Montezuma, who was approaching in a rich litter accompanied by other great Lords and Caciques, who owned vassals. When we arrived near to Mexico, where there were some other small towers, the Great Montezuma got down from his litter, and those great Caciques supported him with their arms beneath a marvelously rich canopy of green colored feathers with much gold and silver embroidery and with pearls and chalchihuites suspended from a sort of bordering, which was wonderful to look at.

The Great Montezuma was richly attired according to his usage, and he was shod with sandals, for so they call what they wear on their feet, the soles were of gold and the upper part adorned with precious stones. The four Chieftains who supported his arms were also richly clothed according to their usage, in garments which were apparently held ready for them on the road to enable them to accompany their prince, for they did not appear in such attire when they came to receive us. Besides these four Chieftains, there were four other great Caciques, who supported the canopy over their heads, and many other Lords who walked before the Great Montezuma, sweeping the ground where he would tread and spreading cloths on it, so that he should not tread on the earth. Not one of these chieftains dared even to think of looking him in the face, but kept their eyes lowered with great reverence, except those four relations, his nephews, who supported him with their arms.

When Cortés was told that the Great Montezuma was approaching, and he saw him coming, he dismounted from his horse, and when he was near Montezuma, they simultaneously paid great reverence to one another. Montezuma bade him welcome and our Cortés replied through Doña Marina wishing him very good health. And it seems to me that Cortés, through Doña Marina, offered him his right hand, and Montezuma did not wish to take it, but he did give his hand to Cortés and Cortés brought out a necklace which he had ready at hand, made of glass stones, which I have already said are called margaritas, which have within them many patterns of diverse colors, these were strung on a cord of gold and with musk so that it should have a sweet scent, and he placed it round the neck of the Great Montezuma and when he had so placed it he was going to embrace him, and those great Princes who accompanied Montezuma held back Cortés by the arm so that he should not embrace him, for they considered it an indignity.

Then Cortés through the mouth of Doña Marina told him that now his heart rejoiced at having seen such a great Prince, and that he took it as a great honor that he had come in person to meet him and had frequently shown him such favor.

Then Montezuma spoke other words of politeness to him, and told two of his nephews who supported his arms, the Lord of Texcoco and the Lord of Coyoacan, to go with us and show us to our quarters, and Montezuma with his other two relations, the Lord of Cuitlahuac and the Lord of Tacuba who accompanied him, returned to the city, and all those grand companies of Caciques and chieftains who had come with him returned in his train. As they turned back after their Prince we stood watching them and observed how they all marched with their eyes fixed on the ground without looking at him, keeping close to the wall, following him with great reverence.

Thus space was made for us to enter the streets of Mexico, without being so much crowded. But who could now count the multitude of men and women and boys who were in the streets and on the rooftops, and in canoes on the canals, who had come out to see us. It was indeed wonderful, and, now that I am writing about it, it all comes before my eyes as though it had happened but yesterday. Coming to think it over it seems to be a great mercy that our Lord Jesus Christ was pleased to give us grace and courage to dare to enter into such a city; and for the many times He has saved me from danger of death, as will be seen later on, I give Him sincere thanks, and in that He has preserved me to write about it, although I cannot do it as fully as is fitting or the subject needs. Let us make no words about it, for deeds are the best witnesses to what I say here and elsewhere.

Let us return to our entry to Mexico. They took us to lodge in some large houses, where there were apartments for all of us, for they had belonged to the father of the Great Montezuma, who was named Axayaca, and at that time Montezuma kept there the great oratories for his idols, and a secret chamber where he kept bars and jewels of gold, which was the treasure that he had inherited from his father Axayaca, and he never disturbed it. They took us to lodge in that house, because they called us Teules, and took us for such, so that we should be with the Idols or Teules which were kept there. However, for one reason or another, it was there they took us, where there were great halls and chambers canopied with the cloth of the country for our Captain, and for every one of us beds of matting with canopies above, and no better bed is given, however great the chief may be, for they are not used. And all these palaces were [coated] with shining cement and swept and garlanded.

As soon as we arrived and entered into the great court, the Great Montezuma took our Captain by the hand, for he was there awaiting him, and led him to the apartment and salon where he was to lodge, which was very richly adorned according to their usage, and he had at hand a very rich necklace made of golden crabs, a marvelous piece of work, and Montezuma himself placed it round the neck of our Captain Cortés, and greatly astonished his [own] Captains by the great honor that he was bestowing on him. When the necklace had been fastened, Cortés thanked Montezuma through our interpreters, and Montezuma replied — "Malinche you and your brethren are in your own house, rest awhile," and then he went to his palaces which were not far away, and we divided our lodgings by companies, and placed the artillery pointing in a convenient direction, and the order which we had to keep was clearly explained to us, and that we were to be much on the alert, both the cavalry and all of us soldiers. A sumptuous dinner was provided for us according to their use and custom, and we ate it at once. So this was our lucky and daring entry into the great city of Tenochtitlan Mexico on the 8th day of November the year of our Savior Jesus Christ 1519. . . .

When the Great Montezuma had dined and he knew that some time had passed since our Captain and all of us had done the same, he came in the greatest state to our quarters with a numerous company of chieftains, all of them his kinsmen. When Cortés was told that he was approaching he came out to the middle of the Hall to receive him, and Montezuma took him by the hand, and they brought some seats, made according to their usage and very richly decorated and embroidered with gold in many designs, and Montezuma asked our Captain to be seated, and both of them sat down each on his chair. Then Montezuma began a very good speech, saying that he was greatly rejoiced to have in his house and his kingdom such valiant gentlemen as were Cortés and all of us. That two years ago he had received news of another Captain who came to Chanpoton, and likewise last year they had brought him news of another Captain who came with four ships, and that each time he had wished to see them, and now that he had us with him he was at our service, and would give us of all that he possessed; that it must indeed be true that we were those of whom his ancestors in years long past had spoken, saying that men would come from where the sun rose to rule over these lands, and that we must be those men, as we had fought so valiantly in the affairs at Potonchan and Tabasco and against the Tlaxcalans; for they had brought him pictures of the battles true to life.

Cortés answered him through our interpreters who always accompanied him, especially Doña Marina, and said to him that he and all of us did not know how to repay him the great favors we received from him every day. It was true that we came from where the sun rose, and were the vassals and servants of a great Prince called the Emperor Don Carlos, who held beneath his sway many and great princes, and that the Emperor having heard of him and what a great prince he was, had sent us to these parts to see him, and to beg them to become Christians, the same as our Emperor and all of us, so that his soul and those of all his vassals might be saved. Later on he would further explain how and in what manner this should be done, and how we worship one only true God, and who He is, and many other good things which he should listen to, such as he had already told to his ambassadors Tendile, and Pitalpitoque and Quintalbor when we were on the sand dunes.

When this conference was over, the Great Montezuma had already at hand some very rich golden jewels, of many patterns, which he gave to our Captain, and in the same manner to each one of our Captains he gave trifles of gold, and three loads of mantles of rich feather work, and to the soldiers also he gave to each one two loads of mantles, and he did it cheerfully and in every way he seemed to be a great Prince. When these things had been distributed, he asked Cortés if we were all brethren and vassals of our great Emperor, and Cortés replied yes, we were brothers in affection and friendship, and persons of great distinction, and servants of our great King and Prince. Further polite speeches passed between Montezuma and Cortés, and as this was the first time he had come to visit us, and so as not to be wearisome, they ceased talking. Montezuma had ordered his stewards that, according to our own use and customs in all things, we should be provided with maize and [grinding] stones, and women to make bread, and fowls and fruit, and much fodder for the horses. Then Montezuma took leave of our Captain and all of us with the greatest courtesy, and we went out with him as far as the street. Cortés ordered us not to go far from our quarters for the present, until we knew better what was expedient. . . .

The next day Cortés decided to go to Montezuma's palace, and he first sent to find out what he intended doing and to let him know that we were coming. He took with him four captains . . . and five of us soldiers also went with him.

When Montezuma knew of our coming he advanced to the middle of the hall to receive us, accompanied by many of his nephews, for no other chiefs were permitted to enter or hold communication with Montezuma where he then was, unless it were on important business. Cortés and he paid the greatest reverence to each other and then they took one another by the hand and Montezuma made him sit down on his couch on his right hand, and he also bade all of us to be seated on seats which he ordered to be brought.

Then Cortés began to make an explanation through our interpreters Doña Marina and Aguilar, and said that he and all of us were rested, and that in coming to see and converse with such a great Prince as he was, we had completed the journey and fulfilled the command which our great King and prince had laid on us. But what he chiefly came to say on behalf of our Lord God had already been brought to his [Montezuma's] knowledge through his ambassadors, Tendile, Pitalpitoque and Quintalbor, at the time when he did us the favor to send the golden sun and moon to the sand dunes; for we told them then that we were Christians and worshipped one true and only God, named Jesus Christ, who suffered death and passion to save us, and we told them that a cross (when they asked us why we worshipped it) was a sign of the other Cross on which our Lord God was crucified for our salvation . . . and it is He who made the heavens and the earth, the sea and the sands, and created all the things there are in the world, and He sends the rain and the dew, and nothing happens in the world without His holy will. That we believe in Him and worship Him, but that those whom they look upon as gods are not so, but are devils, which are evil things, and if their looks are bad their deeds are worse, and they could see that they were evil and of little worth, for where we had set up crosses such as those his ambassadors had seen, they dared not appear before them, through fear of them, and that as time went on they would notice this.

The favor he now begged of him was his attention to the words that he now wished to tell him; then he explained to him very clearly about the creation of the world, and how we are all brothers, sons of one father and one mother who were called Adam and Eve, and how such a brother as our great Emperor, grieving for the perdition of so many souls, such as those which their idols were leading to Hell, where they burn in living flames, had sent us, so that after what he [Montezuma] had now heard he would put a stop to it and they would no longer adore these Idols or sacrifice Indian men and women to them, for we were all brethren, nor should they commit sodomy or thefts. He also told them that, in course of time, our Lord and King would send some men who among us lead very holy lives, much better than we do, who will explain to them all about it, for at present we merely came to give them due warning, and so he prayed him to do what he was asked and carry it into effect.

As Montezuma appeared to wish to reply, Cortés broke off his argument, and to all of us who were with him he said: "with this we have done our duty considering it is the first attempt."

Montezuma replied—"Señor Malinche,* I have understood your words and arguments very well before now, from what you said to my servants at the sand dunes, this about three Gods and the Cross, and all those things that you have preached in the towns through which you have come. We have not made any answer to it because here throughout all time we have worshipped our own gods, and thought they were good, as no doubt yours are, so do not trouble to speak to us any more about them at present. Regarding the creation of the world, we have held the same belief for ages past, and for this reason we take it for certain that you are those whom our ancestors predicted would come from the direction of the sunrise. As for your great King, I feel that I am indebted to him, and I will give him of what I possess, for as I have already said, two years ago I heard of the Captains who came in ships from the direction in which you came, and they said that they were the servants of this your great King, and I wish to know if you are all one and the same.

Cortés replied, Yes, that we were all brethren and servants of our Emperor, and that those men came to examine the way and the seas and the ports so as to know them well in order that we might follow as we had done. Montezuma was referring to the expeditions of Francisco Hernández de Córdova and of Grijalva, when we first came on voyages of discovery, and he said that ever since that time he had wished to capture some

---

*Malinche, a term of respect, refers to Cortés in this case, not to Doña Marina.

of those men who had come so as to keep them in his kingdoms and cities and to do them honor, and his gods had now fulfilled his desires, for now that we were in his home, which we might call our own, we should rejoice and take our rest for there we should be well treated. And if he had on other occasions sent to say that we should not enter his city, it was not of his free will, but because his vassals were afraid, for they said that we shot out flashes of lightning, and killed many Indians with our horses, and that we were angry Teules, and other childish stories, and now that he had seen our persons and knew we were of flesh and bone, and had sound sense, and that we were very valiant, for these reasons he held us in much higher regard than he did from their reports, and he would share his possessions with us.

Then Cortés and all of us answered that we thanked him sincerely for such signal good will, and Montezuma said, laughing, for he was very merry in his princely way of speaking: "Malinche, I know very well that these people of Tlaxcala with whom you are such good friends have told you that I am a sort of God or Teul, and that everything in my houses is made of gold and silver and precious stones, I know well enough that you are wise and did not believe it but took it as a joke. Behold now, Señor Malinche, my body is of flesh and bone like yours, my houses and palaces of stone and wood and lime; that I am a great king and inherit the riches of my ancestors is true, but not all the nonsense and lies that they have told you about me, although of course you treated it as a joke, as I did your thunder and lightning."

Cortés answered him, also laughing, and said that opponents and enemies always say evil things, without truth in them, of those whom they hate, and that he well knew that he could not hope to find another Prince more magnificent in these countries, and that not without reason had he been so vaunted to our Emperor. . . .

The Great Montezuma was about forty years old, of good height and well proportioned, slender, and spare of flesh, not very swarthy, but of the natural color and shade of an Indian. He did not wear his hair long, but so as just to cover his ears, his scanty black beard was well shaped and thin. His face was somewhat long, but cheerful, and he had good eyes and showed in his appearance and manner both tenderness and, when necessary, gravity. He was very neat and clean and bathed once every day in the afternoon. He had many women as mistresses, daughters of Chieftains, and he had two great Cacicas as his legitimate wives, and when he had intercourse with them it was so secretly that no one knew anything about it, except some of his servants. He was free from unnatural offences. The clothes that he wore one day, he did not put on again until four days later. He had over two hundred chieftains in his guard, in other rooms close to his own, not that all were meant to converse with him, but only one or another, and when they went to speak to him they were obliged to take off their rich mantles and put on others of little worth, but they had to be clean, and they had to enter barefoot with their eyes lowered to the ground, and not to look up in his face. And they made him three obeisances, and said: "Lord, my Lord, my Great Lord," before they came up to him, and then they made their report and with a few words he dismissed them, and on taking leave they did not turn their backs, but kept their faces toward him with their eyes to the ground, and they did not turn their backs until they left the room. I noticed another thing, that when other great chiefs came from distant lands about disputes or business, when they reached the apartments of the Great Montezuma, they had to come barefoot and with poor mantles, and they might not enter directly into the Palace, but had to loiter about a little on one side of the Palace door, for to enter hurriedly was considered to be disrespectful.

For each meal, over thirty different dishes were prepared by his cooks according to their ways and usage, and they placed small pottery braziers beneath the dishes so that they should not get cold. They prepared more than three hundred plates of the food that Montezuma was going to eat, and more than a thousand for the guard. When he was going to eat, Montezuma would sometimes go out with his chiefs and stewards, and they would point out to him which dish was best, and of what birds and other things it was composed, and as they advised him, so he would eat, but it was not often that he would go out to see the food, and then merely as a pastime.

I have heard it said that they were wont to cook for him the flesh of young boys, but as he had such a variety of dishes, made of so many things, we could not succeed in seeing if they were of human flesh or of other things, for they daily cooked fowls, turkeys, pheasants, native partridges, quail, tame and wild ducks, venison, wild boar, reed birds, pigeons, hares and rabbits, and many sorts of birds and other things which are bred in this country, and they are so numerous that I cannot finish naming them in a hurry; so we had no insight into it, but I know for certain that after our Captain censured the sacrifice of human beings, and the eating of their flesh, he ordered that such food should not be prepared for him thenceforth.

Let us cease speaking of this and return to the way things were served to him at meal times. It was in this way: if it was cold they made up a large fire of live coals of a firewood made from the bark of trees which did not give off any smoke, and the scent of the bark from which the fire was made was very fragrant, and so that it should not give off more heat than he required, they placed in front of it a sort of screen adorned with figures of idols worked in gold. He was seated on a low stool, soft and richly worked, and the table, which was also low, was made in the same style as the seats, and on it they placed the table cloths of white cloth and some rather long napkins of the same material. Four very beautiful cleanly women brought water for his hands in a sort of deep basin which they called xicales [*xicalli* = gourds] and they held others like plates below to catch the water, and they brought him towels. And two other women brought him tortilla bread, and as soon as he began to eat they placed before him a sort of wooden screen painted over with gold, so that no one should watch him eating. Then the four women stood aside, and four great chieftains who were old men came and stood beside them, and with these Montezuma now and then conversed, and asked them questions, and as a great favor he would give to each of these elders a dish of what to him tasted best. They say that these elders were his near relations, and were his counselors and judges of law suits, and the dishes and food which Montezuma gave them they ate standing up with much reverence and without looking at his face. He was served on Cholula earthenware either red or black. While he was at his meal the men of his guard who were in the rooms near to that of Montezuma, never dreamed of making any noise or speaking aloud. They brought him fruit of all the different kinds that the land produced, but he ate very little of it. From time to time they brought him, in cup-shaped vessels of pure gold, a certain drink made from cacao which they said he took when he was going to visit his wives, and at the time he took no heed of it, but what I did see was that they brought over fifty great jugs of good cacao frothed up, and he drank of that, and the women served this drink to him with great reverence.

Sometimes at meal-times there were present some very ugly humpbacks, very small of stature and their bodies almost broken in half, who are their jesters, and other Indians, who must have been buffoons, who told him witty sayings, and others who sang and danced, for Montezuma was fond of pleasure and song, and to these he ordered to be given what was left of the food and the jugs of cacao. Then the same four women removed the tablecloths and with much ceremony they brought water for his hands. And Montezuma talked with those four old chieftains about things that interested him, and they took leave of him with the great reverence in which they held him, and he remained to repose.

As soon as the Great Montezuma had dined, all the men of the Guard had their meal and as many more of the other house servants, and it seems to me that they brought out over a thousand dishes of the food of which I have spoken, and then over two thousand jugs of cacao all frothed up, as they make it in Mexico, and a limitless quantity of fruit, so that with his women and female servants and bread makers and cacao makers his expenses must have been very great.

Let us cease talking about the expenses and the food for his household and let us speak of the Stewards and the Treasurers and the stores and pantries and of those who had charge of the houses where the maize was stored. I say that there would be so much to write about, each thing by itself, that I should not know where to begin, but we stood astonished at the excellent arrangements and the great abundance of provisions that he had in all, but I must add what I had forgotten, for it is as well to go back and relate it, and that is, that while Montezuma was at table eating as I have described, there were waiting on him two other graceful women to bring him tortillas, kneaded with eggs and other sustaining ingredients, and these tortillas were very white, and they were brought on plates covered with clean napkins, and they also brought him another kind of bread, like long balls kneaded with other kinds of sustaining food, and "pan pachol" for so they call it in this country, which is a sort of wafer. There were also placed on the table three tubes much painted and gilded, which held liquidambar [aromatic resin] mixed with certain herbs which they call tabaco, and when he had finished eating, after they had danced before him and sung and the table was removed, he inhaled the smoke from one of those tubes, but he took very little of it and with that he fell asleep.

Let us cease speaking about the service of his table and go back to our story. I remember that at that time his steward was a great Cacique to whom we gave the name of Tápia, and he kept the accounts of all the revenue that was brought to Montezuma, in his books which were made of paper which they call Amal, and he had a great house full of these books. Now we must leave the books and the accounts for it is outside our story, and say how Montezuma had two houses full of every sort of arms, many of them richly adorned with gold and precious stones.

There were shields great and small, and a sort of broadswords, and others like twohanded swords set with stone knives which cut much better than our swords, and lances longer than ours are, with a fathom of blade with many knives set in it, which even when they are driven into a buckler or shield do not come out, in fact they cut like razors so that they can shave their heads with them. There were very good bows and arrows and double-pointed lances and others with one point, as well as their throwing sticks, and many slings and round stones shaped by hand, and some sort of artful shields which are so made that they can be rolled up, so as not to be in the way when they are not fighting, and when they are needed for fighting they let them fall down, and they cover the body from top to toe. There was also much quilted cotton armor, richly ornamented on the outside with many colored feathers, used as devices and distinguishing marks, and there were casques or helmets made of wood and bone, also highly decorated with feathers on the outside, and there were other arms of other makes which, so as to avoid prolixity, I will not describe, and there were artisans who were skilled in such things and worked at them, and stewards who had charge of the arms.

Let us leave this and proceed to the Aviary, and I am forced to abstain from enumerating every kind of bird that was there and its peculiarity, for there was everything from the Royal Eagle and other smaller eagles, and many other birds of great size, down to tiny birds of many-colored plumage, also birds from which they take the rich plumage which they use in their green feather work. The birds which have these feathers are about the size of the magpies in Spain, they are called in this country Quezales [*quetzal*], and there are other birds which have feathers of five colors—green, red, white, yellow and blue; I don't remember what they are called; then there were parrots of many different colors, and there are so many of them that I forget their names, not to mention the beautifully marked ducks and other larger ones like them. From all these birds they plucked the feathers when the time was right to do so, and the feathers grew again. All the birds that I have spoken about breed in these houses, and in the setting season certain Indian men and women who look after the birds, place the eggs under them and clean the nests and feed them, so that each kind of bird has its proper food. In this house that I have spoken of there is a great tank of fresh water and in it there are other sorts of birds with long stilted legs, with body, wings and tail all red; I don't know their names. . . .

Let us leave this and go on to another great house, where they keep many Idols, and they say that they are their fierce gods, and with them many kinds of carnivorous beasts of prey, tigers and two kinds of lions, and animals something like wolves which in this country they call jackals and foxes, and other smaller carnivorous animals, and all these carnivores they feed with flesh, and the greater number of them breed in the house. They give them as food deer and fowls, dogs and other things

which they are used to hunt, and I have heard it said that they feed them
on the bodies of the Indians who have been sacrificed. It is in this way:
you have already heard me say that when they sacrifice a wretched
Indian they saw open the chest with stone knives and hasten to tear out
the palpitating heart and blood, and offer it to their Idols in whose name
the sacrifice is made. Then they cut off the thighs, arms and head and eat
the former at feasts and banquets, and the head they hang up on some
beams, and the body of the man sacrificed is not eaten but given to these
fierce animals. They also have in that cursed house many vipers and
poisonous snakes which carry on their tails things that sound like bells.
These are the worst vipers of all, and they keep them in jars and great
pottery vessels with many feathers, and there they lay their eggs and
rear their young, and they give them to eat the bodies of the Indians who
have been sacrificed, and the flesh of dogs which they are in the habit
of breeding. We even knew for certain that when they drove us out of
Mexico and killed over eight hundred of our soldiers that they fed those
fierce animals and snakes for many days on their bodies, as I will relate
at the proper time and season. And those snakes and wild beasts were
dedicated to those savage Idols, so that they might keep them company.

Let me speak now of the infernal noise when the lions and tigers
roared and the jackals and the foxes howled and the serpents hissed, it
was horrible to listen to and it seemed like a hell. Let us go on and speak
of the skilled workmen he [Montezuma] employed in every craft that
was practiced among them. We will begin with lapidaries and workers in
gold and silver and all the hollow work, which even the great goldsmiths
in Spain were forced to admire, and of these there were a great number
of the best in a town named Azcapotzalco, a league from Mexico. Then
for working precious stones and chalchihuites, which are like emeralds,
there were other great artists. . . .

Let us go on to the Indian women who did the weaving and the washing,
who made such an immense quantity of fine fabrics with wonderful feather
work designs; the greater part of it was brought daily from some towns of
the province on the north coast near Vera Cruz called Cotaxtla, close by
San Juan de Ulua, where we disembarked when we came with Cortés.

In the house of the Great Montezuma himself, all the daughters of
chieftains whom he had as mistresses always wore beautiful things, and
there were many daughters of Mexican citizens who lived in retirement
and wished to appear to be like nuns, who also did weaving but it was
wholly of feather work. These nuns had their houses near the great Cue
of Huichilobos and out of devotion to it, or to another idol, that of a
woman who was said to be their mediator in the matter of marriage,

their fathers placed them in that religious retirement until they married, and they were [only] taken out thence to be married.

Let us go on and tell about the great number of dancers kept by the Great Montezuma for his amusement, and others who used stilts on their feet, and others who flew when they danced up in the air, and others like Merry-Andrews, and I may say that there was a district full of these people who had no other occupation.

Let us go on and speak of the workmen that he had as stone cutters, masons and carpenters, all of whom attended to the work of his houses, I say that he had as many as he wished for.

We must not forget the gardens of flowers and sweetscented trees, and the many kinds that there were of them, and the arrangement of them and the walks, and the ponds and tanks of fresh water where the water entered at one end and flowed out at the other; and the baths which he had there, and the variety of small birds that nested in the branches, and the medicinal and useful herbs that were in the gardens. It was a wonder to see, and to take care of it there were many gardeners. Everything was made in masonry and well cemented, baths and walks and closets, and apartments like summer houses where they danced and sang. There was as much to be seen in these gardens as there was everywhere else, and we could not tire of witnessing his great power. Thus as a consequence of so many crafts being practiced among them, a large number of skilled Indians were employed. . . .

As we had already been four days in Mexico and neither the Captain nor any of us had left our lodgings except to go to the houses and gardens, Cortés said to us that it would be well to go to the great Plaza and see the great Temple of Huichilobos, and that he wished to consult the Great Montezuma and have his approval. For this purpose he sent Jerónimo de Aguilar and the Doña Marina as messengers, and with them went our Captain's small page named Orteguilla, who already understood something of the language. When Montezuma knew his wishes he sent to say that we were welcome to go; on the other hand, as he was afraid that we might do some dishonor to his Idols, he determined to go with us himself with many of his chieftains. He came out from his Palace in his rich litter, but when half the distance had been traversed and he was near some oratories, he stepped out of the litter, for he thought it a great affront to his idols to go to their house and temple in that manner. Some of the great chieftains supported him with their arms, and the tribal lords went in front of him carrying two staves like scepters held on high, which was the sign that the Great Montezuma was coming. (When he went in his litter he carried a wand half of gold and half of wood, which was held up like a wand of justice.) So he went on and ascended the great Cue accompanied by many priests, and he began to burn incense and perform other ceremonies to Huichilobos.

Let us leave Montezuma, who had gone ahead as I have said, and return to Cortés and our captains and soldiers, who according to our custom both night and day were armed, and as Montezuma was used to see us so armed when we went to visit him, he did not look upon it as anything new. I say this because our captain and all those who had horses went to Tlaltelolco on horseback, and nearly all of us soldiers were fully equipped, and many Caciques whom Montezuma had sent for that purpose went in our company. When we arrived at the great market place, called Tlaltelolco, we were astonished at the number of people and the quantity of merchandise that it contained, and at the good order and control that was maintained, for we had never seen such a thing before.

The chieftains who accompanied us acted as guides. Each kind of merchandise was kept by itself and had its fixed place marked out. Let us begin with the dealers in gold, silver, and precious stones, feathers, mantles, and embroidered goods. Then there were other wares consisting of Indian slaves both men and women; and I say that they bring as many of them to that great market for sale as the Portuguese bring negroes from Guinea; and they brought them along tied to long poles, with collars round their necks so that they could not escape, and others they left free. Next there were other traders who sold great pieces of cloth and cotton, and articles of twisted thread, and there were cacahuateros who sold cacao. In this way one could see every sort of merchandise that is to be found in the whole of New Spain, placed in arrangement in the same manner as they do in my own country, which is Medina del Campo, where they hold the fairs, where each line of booths has its particular kind of merchandise, and so it is in this great market. There were those who sold cloths of henequen and ropes and the sandals with which they are shod, which are made from the same plant, and sweet cooked roots, and other tubers which they get from this plant, all were kept in one part of the market in the place assigned to them. In another part there were skins of tigers and lions, of otters and jackals, deer and other animals and badgers and mountain cats, some tanned and others untanned, and other classes of merchandise.

Let us go on and speak of those who sold beans and sage and other vegetables and herbs in another part, and to those who sold fowls, cocks with wattles, rabbits, hares, deer, mallards, young dogs and other things of that sort in their part of the market, and let us also mention the fruiterers, and the women who sold cooked food, dough and tripe in their own part of the market; then every sort of pottery made in a thousand different forms from great water jars to little jugs, these also had a place to themselves; then those who sold honey and honey paste and other dainties like nut paste, and those who sold lumber, boards, cradles, beams, blocks and benches, each article by itself, and the vendors of *ocote* firewood, and other things of a similar nature. I must furthermore mention, asking your pardon, that they also sold many canoes full of human excrement, and these were kept in the creeks near the market, and this they use to make salt or for tanning skins, for without it they say that they cannot be well prepared. I know well that some gentlemen laugh at this, but I say that it is so, and I may add that on all the roads it is a usual thing to have places made of reeds or straw or grass, so that they may be screened from the passers by, into these they retire when they wish to purge their bowels so that even that filth should not be lost.

But why do I waste so many words in recounting what they sell in that great market, for I shall never finish if I tell it all in detail. Paper, which in this country is called Amal [amatl], and reeds scented with liquidambar, and full of tobacco, and yellow ointments and things of that sort are sold by themselves, and much cochineal [insects for red dye] is sold under the arcades which are in that great market place, and there are many vendors of herbs and other sorts of trades. There are also buildings where three magistrates sit in judgment, and there are executive officers like Alguacils who inspect the merchandise. I am forgetting those who sell salt, and those who make the stone knives, and how they split them off the stone itself; and the fisherwomen and others who sell some small cakes made from a sort of ooze which they get out of the great lake, which curdles, and from this they make a bread having a flavor something like cheese. There are for sale axes of brass and copper and tin, and gourds and gaily painted jars made of wood. I could wish that I had finished telling of all the things which are sold there, but they are so numerous and of such different quality and the great market place with its surrounding arcades was so crowded with people, that one would not have been able to see and inquire about it all in two days.

Then we went to the great Cue, and when we were already approaching its great courts, before leaving the market place itself, there were many more merchants, who, as I was told, brought gold for sale in grains, just as it is taken from the mines. The gold is placed in thin quills of the geese of the country, white quills, so that the gold can be seen through, and according to the length and thickness of the quills they arrange their accounts with one another, how much so many mantles or so many gourds full of cacao were worth, or how many slaves, or whatever other thing they were exchanging.

Now let us leave the great market place, and not look at it again, and arrive at the great courts and walls where the great Cue stands. Before reaching the great Cue there is a great enclosure of courts, it seems to me larger than the plaza of Salamanca, with two walls of masonry surrounding it and the court itself all paved with very smooth great white flagstones. And where there were not these stones it was cemented and burnished and all very clean, so that one could not find any dust or a straw in the whole place. . . .

When we arrived there Montezuma came out of an oratory where his cursed idols were, at the summit of the great Cue, and two priests came with him, and after paying great reverence to Cortés and to all of us he said: "You must be tired, Señor Malinche, from ascending this our great Cue," and Cortés replied through our interpreters who were with us that he and his companions were never tired by anything. Then Montezuma took him by the hand and told him to look at his great city and all the other cities that were standing in the water, and the many other towns on the land round the lake, and that if he had not seen the great market place well, that from where they were they could see it better.

So we stood looking about us, for that huge and cursed temple stood so high that from it one could see over everything very well, and we saw the three causeways which led into Mexico, that is the causeway of Iztapalapa by which we had entered four days before, and that of Tacuba, along which later on we fled on the night of our great defeat, when Cuitlahuac the new prince drove us out of the city, as I shall tell later on, and that of Tepeaquilla, and we saw the fresh water that comes from Chapultepec which supplies the city, and we saw the bridges on the three causeways which were built at certain distances apart through which the water of the lake flowed in and out from one side to the other, and we beheld on that great lake a great multitude of canoes, some coming with supplies of food and others returning loaded with cargoes of merchandise; and we saw that from every house of that great city and of all the other cities that were built in the water it was impossible to pass from house to house, except by drawbridges which were made of wood or in canoes; and we saw in those cities Cues and oratories like towers and fortresses and all gleaming white, and it was a wonderful thing to behold; then the houses with flat roofs, and on the causeways other small towers and oratories which were like fortresses.

After having examined and considered all that we had seen we turned to look at the great market place and the crowds of people that were in it, some buying and others selling, so that the murmur and hum of their voices and words that they used could be heard more than a league off. Some of the soldiers among us who had been in many parts of the world, in Constantinople, and all over Italy, and in Rome, said that so large a market place and so full of people, and so well regulated and arranged, they had never beheld before.

Let us leave this, and return to our Captain, who said to Fray Bartolomé de Olmedo, who has often been mentioned by me, and who happened to be near by him: "It seems to me, Señor Padre, that it would be a good thing to throw out a feeler to Montezuma, as to whether he would allow us to build our church here"; and the Padre replied that it would be a good thing if it were successful, but it seemed to him that it was not quite a suitable time to speak about it, for Montezuma did not appear to be inclined to do such a thing.

Then our Cortés said to Montezuma through the interpreter Doña Marina: "Your Highness is indeed a very great prince and worthy of even greater things. We are rejoiced to see your cities, and as we are here in your temple, what I now beg as a favor is that you will show us your gods and Teules. Montezuma replied that he must first speak with his high priests, and when he had spoken to them he said that we might enter into a small tower and apartment, a sort of hall, where there were two altars, with very richly carved boardings on the top of the roof. On each altar were two figures, like giants with very tall bodies and very fat, and the first which stood on the right hand they said was the figure of Huichilobos their god of War; it had a very broad face and monstrous and terrible eyes, and the whole of his body was covered with precious stones, and gold and pearls, and with seed pearls stuck on with a paste that they make in this country out of a sort of root, and all the body and head was covered with it, and the body was girdled by great snakes made of gold and precious stones, and in one hand he held a bow and in the other some arrows. And another small idol that stood by him, they said was his page, and he held a short lance and a shield richly decorated with gold and stones. Huichilobos had round his neck some Indians' faces and other things like hearts of Indians, the former made of gold and the latter of silver, with many precious blue stones.

There were some braziers with incense which they call copal, and in them they were burning the hearts of the three Indians whom they had sacrificed that day, and they had made the sacrifice with smoke and copal. All the walls of the oratory were so splashed and encrusted with blood that they were black, the floor was the same and the whole place stank vilely. Then we saw on the other side on the left hand there stood the other great image the same height as Huichilobos, and it had a face like a bear and eyes that shone, made of their mirrors which they call Tezcat [*tezcatl*], and the body plastered with precious stones like that of Huichilobos, for they say that the two are brothers; and this Tezcatepuca was the god of Hell and had charge of the souls of the Mexicans, and his body was girt with figures like little devils with snakes' tails. The walls were so clotted with blood and the soil so bathed with it that in the slaughterhouses in Spain there is not such another stench.

They had offered to this Idol five hearts from that day's sacrifices. In the highest part of the Cue there was a recess of which the woodwork was very richly worked, and in it was another image half man and half lizard, with precious stones all over it, and half the body was covered with a mantle. They say that the body of this figure is full of all the seeds that there are in the world, and they say that it is the god of seed time and harvest, but I do not remember its name, and everything was covered with blood, both walls and altar, and the stench was such that we could hardly wait the moment to get out of it.

They had an exceedingly large drum there, and when they beat it the sound of it was so dismal and like, so to say, an instrument of the infernal regions, that one could hear it a distance of two leagues, and they said that the skins it was covered with were those of great snakes. In that small place there were many diabolical things to be seen, bugles and trumpets and knives, and many hearts of Indians that they had burned in fumigating their idols, and everything was so clotted with blood, and there was so much of it, that I curse the whole of it, and as it stank like a slaughter house we hastened to clear out of such a bad stench and worse sight.

Our Captain said to Montezuma through our interpreter, half laughing: "Señor Montezuma, I do not understand how such a great Prince and wise man as you are has not come to the conclusion, in your mind, that these idols of yours are not gods, but evil things that are called devils, and so that you may know it and all your priests may see it clearly, do me the favor to approve of my placing a cross here on the top of this tower, and that in one part of these oratories where your Huichilobos and Tezcatepuca stand we may divide off a space where we can set up an image of Our Lady (an image which Montezuma had already seen) and you will see by the fear in which these Idols hold it that they are deceiving you."

Montezuma replied half angrily, (and the two priests who were with him showed great annoyance,) and said: "Señor Malinche, if I had known that you would have said such defamatory things I would not have shown you my gods, we consider them to be very good, for they give us health and rains and good seed times and seasons and as many victories as we desire, and we are obliged to worship them and make sacrifices, and I pray you not to say another word to their dishonor."

When our Captain heard that and noted the angry looks he did not refer again to the subject, but said with a cheerful manner: "It is time for your Excellency and for us to return," and Montezuma replied that it was well, but that he had to pray and offer certain sacrifices on account of the great tatacul, that is to say sin, which he had committed in allowing us to ascend his great Cue, and being the cause of our being permitted to see his gods, and of our dishonoring them by speaking evil of them, so that before he left he must pray and worship.

Then Cortés said "I ask your pardon if it be so," and then we went down the steps, and as they numbered one hundred and fourteen, and as some of our soldiers were suffering from tumors and abscesses, their legs were tired by the descent.

I will leave off talking about the oratory, and I will give my impressions of its surroundings. . . . To go back to the facts, it seems to me that the circuit of the great Cue was equal to [that of] six large sites, [*solares*],* such as they measure in this country, and from below up to where a small tower stood, where they kept their idols, it narrowed, and in the middle of the lofty Cue up to its highest point, there were five hollows like barbicans, but open, without screens, and as there are many Cues painted on the banners of the conquerors, and on one which I possess, any one who has seen them can infer what they looked like from outside, better that I myself saw and understood it.

There was a report that at the time they began to build that great Cue, all the inhabitants of that mighty city had placed as offerings in the foundations, gold and silver and pearls and precious stones, and had bathed them with the blood of the many Indian prisoners of war who were sacrificed, and had placed there every sort and kind of seed that the land produces, so that their Idols should give them victories and riches, and large crops. Some of my inquisitive readers will ask, how could we come to know that into the foundations of that great Cue they cast gold and silver and precious chalchihuites and seeds, and watered them with the human blood of the Indians whom they sacrificed, when it was more

Solar is a town lot for house building.

than a thousand years ago that they built and made it? The answer I give to this is that after we took that great and strong city, and the sites were apportioned, it was then proposed that in [the place of] the great Cue we should build a church to our patron and guide Señor Santiago, and a great part of the site of the great temple of Huichilobos was occupied by the site of the holy church, and when they opened the foundations in order to strengthen them, they found much gold and silver and chalchihuites and pearls and seed pearls and other stones. . . .

Let us leave this and speak of the great and splendid Courts which were in front of the [temple of] Huichilobos, where now stands [the church of] Señor Santiago, which was called Tlaltelolco, for so they were accustomed to call it.

I have already said that there were two walls of masonry [which had to be passed] before entering, and that the court was paved with white stones, like flagstones, carefully whitewashed and burnished and clean, and it was as large and as broad as the plaza of Salamanca. A little way apart from the great Cue there was another small tower which was also an Idol house, or a true hell, for it had at the opening of one gate a most terrible mouth such as they depict, saying that such there are in hell. The mouth was open with great fangs to devour souls, and here too were some groups of devils and bodies of serpents close to the door, and a little way off was a place of sacrifice all blood-stained and black with smoke, and encrusted with blood, and there were many great ollas and cántaros and tinajas* of water inside the house, for it was here that they cooked the flesh of the unfortunate Indians who were sacrificed, which was eaten by the priests. There were also near the place of sacrifice many large knives and chopping blocks, such as those on which they cut up meat in the slaughterhouses. Then behind that cursed house, some distance away from it, were some great piles of firewood, and not far from them a large tank of water which rises and falls, the water coming through a tube from the covered channel which enters the city from Chapultepec. I always called that house "the Infernal Regions."

Let us go on beyond the court to another Cue where the great Mexican princes were buried, where also there were many Idols, and all was full of blood and smoke, and it had other doorways with hellish figures, and then near that Cue was another full of skulls and large bones arranged in perfect order, which one could look at but could not count, for there were too many of them. The skulls were by themselves and the bones in separate piles. In that place there were other Idols, and in every house or Cue or

*Names of various large pottery vessels for holding water and cooking.

oratory that I have mentioned there were priests with long robes of black cloth and long hoods like those of the Dominicans, and slightly resembling those of the Canons. The hair of these priests was very long and so matted that it could not be separated or disentangled, and most of them had their ears scarified, and their hair was clotted with blood. Let us go on; there were other Cues, a little way from where the skulls were, which contained other Idols and places of sacrifice [decorated] with other evil paintings. And they said that those idols were intercessors in the marriages of men. I do not want to delay any longer telling about idols, but will only add that all round that great court there were many houses, not lofty, used and occupied by the priests and other Indians who had charge of the Idols.

On one side of the great Cue there was another much larger pond or tank of very clear water dedicated solely to the service of Huichilobos and Tezcatepuca, and the water entered that pond through covered pipes which came from Chapultepec. Near to this were other large buildings such as a sort of nunnery where many of the daughters of the inhabitants of Mexico were sheltered like nuns up to the time they were married, and there stood two Idols with the figures of women, which were the intercessors in the marriages of women, and women made sacrifices to them and held festivals so that they should give them good husbands.

I have spent a long time talking about this great Cue of Tlaltelolco and its Courts, but I say that it was the greatest temple in the whole of Mexico although there were many others, very splendid. Four or five parishes or districts possessed, between them, an oratory with its Idols, and as they were very numerous I have not kept count of them all. I will go on and say that the great oratory that they had in Cholula was higher than that of Mexico, for it had one hundred and twenty steps, and according to what they say they held the Idol of Cholula to be good, and they went to it on pilgrimages from all parts of New Spain to obtain absolution, and for this reason they built for it such a splendid Cue; but it is of another form from that of Mexico although the courts are the same, very large with a double wall. I may add that the Cue in the City of Texcoco was very lofty, having one hundred and seventeen steps, and the Courts were broad and fine, shaped in a different form from the others. It is a laughable matter that every province had its Idols and those of one province or city were of no use to the others, thus they had an infinite number of Idols and they made sacrifices to them all.

After our Captain and all of us were tired of walking about and seeing such a diversity of Idols and their sacrifices, we returned to our quarters, all the time accompanied by many Caciques and chieftains whom Montezuma sent with us. I will stop here and go on to say what more we did.

6

Things Fall Apart:
Toxcatl and the *Noche triste*

The Spaniards settled into a routine in the days after their arrival in Tenochtitlan, living in Moctezuma's palace compound and exploring the city. The Spaniards also built a small chapel for their prayers and discovered a vault filled with treasure in one of the temple walls. It is not clear if all Tlaxcalan soldiers remained by their side, or if only a small retinue of Tlaxcalan noblemen remained. Relations with Moctezuma remained cordial, and visits between him and Cortés were done with considerable courtesy and formality.

Bernal Díaz tells of this period in some detail. He also claims that some of the Spanish captains and soldiers prevailed upon Cortés to place Moctezuma under arrest in order to forestall any attack against them. Plans were already under way for this move when justification for it arrived from the coast. A battle had taken place near Vera Cruz between Totonac soldiers (backed by Spaniards from the garrison) and a Mexica legionary force sent to restore the Totonacs to a tributary status. Cortés used the incident as an excuse to take Moctezuma hostage and to demand the execution of the Mexica captains responsible for the attack against his allies.

Cortés seized the initiative with an audacious and treacherous act. Barely a week after the expedition's entry into Tenochtitlan, he imprisoned Moctezuma in his own palace. There was no immediate retaliation. Cortés and Bernal Díaz both suggested that Moctezuma was secretly organizing an assault, but in his absence many noblemen were reluctant to act alone. That said, some leaders like Cacamatzin, ruler of Texcoco, advocated confronting and expelling the strangers. In the final analysis, the various factions inside Tenochtitlan and among the city-states allied with the Mexica hesitated to mount a joint affront against the Spaniards and their native allies for various dynastic, ethnic, and personal reasons.

At the end of April 1520, news arrived from Vera Cruz that Diego Velázquez, governor of Cuba, had sent a large expedition to arrest Cortés for his disobedience. Almost a thousand soldiers with artillery and horses arrived under the leadership of Pánfilo Narváez. Whereas divisions among the Mexica nobility had until this moment hindered their actions, rifts between the Spaniards now threatened Cortés's program. In response, Cortés decided to leave a small occupying force in Moctezuma's palace compound under Pedro de Alvarado, and he marched with about two hundred Spaniards and an untold number of Tlaxcalan soldiers to meet this new threat.

At first Cortés pretended that the newly arrived Spaniards were his friends, although Moctezuma's spies had probably informed him of the truth. Then, in a surprise attack, Cortés's men routed Narváez and his forces. He then offered to let Narváez's men return to Cuba (in disgrace) or to join him in the conquest of a great and wealthy empire. By this stroke of good luck, Cortés converted a potential disaster into reinforcements and marched back to Tenochtitlan with hundreds of new Spanish recruits. Notably, a division developed between the men of the original band and those later recruited from Narváez's forces, which plagued Spanish operations in the months ahead.

Meanwhile in Tenochtitlan, the situation had darkened. Alvarado was brave but impulsive. Spanish and Nahua accounts differ on what happened, but they agree on the horror. In Cortés's absence, Mexica noblemen and governors approached Alvarado and asked permission to celebrate the festival of Toxcatl in honor of the deities Tezcatlipoca and Huitzilopochtli. Permission was granted, but during the festival when "song was linked to song" as the Nahua accounts retell it, Alvarado staged a surprise attack on the unarmed celebrants. Hundreds of the leading nobles and warriors were brutally slain. This cowardly episode galvanized the city's inhabitants, who surrounded the Spaniards in the temple precinct and placed them under siege. Alvarado forced Moctezuma to try to stop the siege but the emperor's authority was weakening.

Learning of the crisis, Cortés marched back to Tenochtitlan and reentered the city on June 24, 1520. No crowds of curious Mexica awaited the Spaniards this time, but rather abandoned streets and a sullen population. Moctezuma was already dead. Spanish and Nahua accounts disagree on what had happened to the Mexica ruler. The Spanish versions claim that Moctezuma was struck by a stone while making a public appearance to dissuade his people from attacking the palace compound. The Nahua accounts state that Spaniards murdered him. Whatever the case, Moctezuma's brother Cuitlahuac, lord of Iztapalapa, reacted by organizing a military affront against the Spaniards, and he soon after ascended to the Mexica throne as the new *tlahtoani*. There is no dispute over what happened to the nobles who waited on Moctezuma during his captivity: the Spaniards simply killed them.

The Spanish position had become untenable, surrounded as they were in the heart of the city, besieged and cut off from food and water. Bernal Díaz describes the conditions and the discussions on a plan of action. On the rainy night of June 30, 1520, Cortés, his men, and allies stealthily broke out of the palace compound, which was surrounded by Mexica forces. Discovered, a savage battle ensued. Hundreds of Spaniards and Tlaxcalans were killed before they could reach the lakeshore. The survivors escaped, but the Spaniards thereafter remembered the event as the "Sad Night" (*Noche triste*).

The first selection in this chapter is from a Spanish chronicler, Francisco López de Gómora, who sought to justify the Toxcatl massacre. The second is a folio from the *Tovar Codex*, which illustrates the pageantry of Toxcatl ceremonies. The next two sections present an Indigenous reckoning of the massacre, from the *Florentine Codex* and the *Codex Aubin*. Bernal Díaz narrates the story from Narvaez's arrival in Vera Cruz and through the Spaniards' near escape from Tenochtitlan. The chapter ends with another selection from the *Florentine Codex* that comments on Moctezuma's death and describes how the Mexicas galvanized to expel the Spaniards and Tlaxcalans from their capital.

18

FRANCISCO LÓPEZ DE GÓMARA

From *History of the Conquest of Mexico*

A chapter from Istoria de la conquista de Mexico *(Zaragoza, 1552) by Francisco López de Gómara, Cortés's secretary and biographer, addresses the question of responsibility for the Toxcatl massacre. Gómara had access to Cortés's private papers and his biography was always favorable to the conqueror's interests. Neither Bernal Díaz nor Cortés were in*

Francisco López de Gómara, *The pleasant historie of the conquest of the West India, now called New Spaine, atchieued by the most woorthie prince Hernando Cortés* (London: Thomas Creede, 1596), 259–61. http://www.openlibrary.org/books/OL25126448M.

Tenochtitlan during the Toxcatl massacre, so their accounts are based on hearsay rather than on their own observations. López de Gómara's history of the conquest, published in 1552 and dedicated to Cortés's son, was essentially a defense and an apologia. It was also a glorification of Spain's growing empire. Yet, by this time Cortés was in disfavor with the crown because of his political ambitions, and so López de Gómara's book, like Cortés's letters, was banned. The selection here is from an Elizabethan translation of this work, which attests to sixteenth-century Europeans' fascination with the events in Mexico.

The Causes of the Rebellion

Cortés procured to know the principal cause of the insurrection of the Mexican Indians, and having a general day of hearing, the charge being laid against them, some said, that it was through the letters and persuasion of Narvaez, others answered [that] their desire and meaning was to expel the strangers, according to agreement made, for in their skirmishes they cried nothing but "Get you hence, get you hence." Others said, that they pretended the liberty of Mutezuma, for in their combats they would say, "Let go our god and king, if you list not to be slain." Others said, that they [the Spaniards] were thieves and had robbed their gold and plate [silver] from them which was in value more than seven hundred thousand *ducados* [a Spanish coin]. Others cried, "Here you shall leave the gold that you have taken from us." Others said that they could not abide the Tlaxcaltecas and other mortal enemies. Many believed that the mutiny was for throwing down their gods and idols. Each of these causes were sufficient to rebel, how much more altogether.

But the chiefest and most principal cause was, that after the departure of Cortés toward Narvaez, happened a solemn holiday which the Mexicans were wont to celebrate, and desiring to observe the same, as they were wont to do, they came and besought the captain Alvarado to grant them license and not to imagine that they were formed together to kill the Spaniards. Alvarado gave them license with such conditions that in their sacrifice there should be no blood spilt nor yet to wear [bear] any weapon.

At this feast five hundred Gentlemen and principal persons joined together in the great Temple: some do say that there were more than a thousand persons of great estate, but that night they made a marvelous great noise with cornets, shells, cloven bones, wherewith they made a strange music. They celebrated the feast, their naked bodies covered with tele [cloth] made and wrought with precious stones, collars, girdles, bracelets, and many other jewels of gold, silver and aliofar [mother of pearl] with gallant tufts of feathers on their heads. They danced a dance called Mazeualiztli [*macehualiztli*] which is to say desert [reward] with pain, and so they call [the term derived from] Mazauali a husbandman. This dance is like Netoriliztli [*nitoteliztli*] which is another dance. The manner is that they lay out mats in the Temple yard, and with the sound of their drums called atabals they dance around, hand in hand, some singing and others answer, which songs were in honor and praise of the god or saint whose feast it is, hoping for this service to have rain, corn, health, victory, peace, children or any other thing that they may wish or desire.

These Indian gentlemen being occupied in their dancing and ceremonies, it fortuned that Pedro de Alvarado went to the Temple of Uitzilopochtli to behold their doings, and whether his going was of his own accord or by the consent of his company I am not certain, although some say that he was advised how the mutiny was there conspired, as after did follow: others hold opinion that their only going to the Temple was to behold the marvelous and strange dance. And then seeing them so richly attired, they coveted their gold and jewels which they wore and besieged the Temple with ten Spaniards at each door, and the Captain entered in with fifty men, and without any Christian respect slew and murdered them all and took from them all their treasure. Although this fact seemed odious to Cortés, yet his own proceedings as time did them require, not knowing what need he might have of them [the culprits], but especially to avoid contention among his company.

19

JUAN DE TOVAR

Dance of the Nobles

From *History of the Arrival of Indians to Populate Mexico*

This selection from Juan de Tovar's manuscript underlines the importance of religious celebrations to affirm political power. In the context of the Toxcatl massacre, it is notable that Mexica elites were not armed during religious performances, which underlines the deceit of the Spanish soldiers who assailed the festival participants.

The folio depicts a Mexica dance, possibly the one performed at the festival of Toxcatl. The two drummers wear military insignia; circling them are priests wearing cloaks (tilmatli) *with sun imagery, as well as elite soldiers from the jaguar and eagle military orders. The dance's pageantry celebrated Mexica military prowess.*

Juan de Tovar. "Historia de la benida de los yndios a poblar a Mexico . . ." (Mexico City, 1585), f.119. Courtesy of the John Carter Brown Library at Brown University.

FRAY BERNARDINO DE SAHAGÚN

From the *Florentine Codex*

The late Mexican scholar Miguel León-Portilla assembled a number of postconquest Nahua texts on the Toxcatl incident in his volume Broken Spears. *Included here are his renditions of the* Florentine Codex *accounts, which give no indication that any "rebellion" was coordinated with the festival. The shock of the events is overtly clear.*

The Preparations for the Fiesta

The Aztecs begged permission of their king to hold the fiesta of Huitzilopochtli. The Spaniards wanted to see this fiesta to learn how it was celebrated. A delegation of the celebrants came to the palace where Motecuhzoma was a prisoner, and when their spokesman asked his permission, he granted it to them.

As soon as the delegation returned, the women began to grind seeds of the chicalote [*chicalotl*].[1] These women had fasted for a whole year. They ground the seeds in the patio of the temple.

The Spaniards came out of the palace together, dressed in armor and carrying their weapons with them. They stalked among the women and looked at them one by one; they stared into the faces of the women who were grinding seeds. After this cold inspection, they went back into the palace. It is said that they planned to kill the celebrants if the men entered the patio.

The Beginning of the Fiesta

Early the next morning, the statue's face was uncovered by those who had been chosen for that ceremony. They gathered in front of the idol in single file and offered it gifts of food, such as round seedcakes or perhaps human flesh. But they did not carry it up to its temple on top of the pyramid.

[1]*Argemone mexicana*, an edible plant, also used in medicines.

Miguel León Portilla, *The Broken Spears: The Aztec Account of the Conquest of Mexico*, trans. Lysander Kemp, Expanded ed. (Boston: Beacon Press, 1992), 71–78.

All the young warriors were eager for the fiesta to begin. They had sworn to dance and sing with all their hearts, so that the Spaniards would marvel at the beauty of the rituals.

The procession began, and the celebrants filed into the temple patio to dance the Dance of the Serpent. When they were all together in the patio, the songs and the dance began. Those who had fasted for twenty days and those who had fasted for a year were in command of the others; they kept the dancers in file with their pine wands. (If anyone wished to urinate, he did not stop dancing, but simply opened his clothing at the hips and separated his clusters of heron feathers.)

If anyone disobeyed the leaders or was not in his proper place they struck him on the hips and shoulders. Then they drove him out of the patio, beating him and shoving him from behind. They pushed him so hard that he sprawled to the ground, and they dragged him outside by the ears. No one dared to say a word about this punishment, for those who had fasted during the year were feared and venerated; they had earned the exclusive title "Brothers of Huitzilopochtli."

The great captains, the bravest warriors, danced at the head of the files to guide the others. The youths followed at a slight distance. Some of the youths wore their hair gathered into large locks, a sign that they had never taken any captives. Others carried their headdresses on their shoulders; they had taken captives, but only with help.

Then came the recruits, who were called "the young warriors." They had each captured an enemy or two. The others called to them: "Come, comrades, show us how brave you are! Dance with all your hearts!"

The Spaniards Attack the Celebrants

At this moment in the fiesta, when the dance was loveliest and when song was linked to song, the Spaniards were seized with an urge to kill the celebrants. They all ran forward, armed as if for battle. They closed the entrances and passageways, all the gates of the patio: the Eagle Gate in the lesser palace, the Gate of the Canestalk and the Gate of the Serpent of Mirrors. They posted guards so that no one could escape, and then rushed into the Sacred Patio to slaughter the celebrants. They came on foot, carrying their swords and their wooden or metal shields.

They ran in among the dancers, forcing their way to the place where the drums were played. They attacked the man who was drumming and cut off his arms. Then they cut off his head, and it rolled across the floor.

They attacked all the celebrants, stabbing them, spearing them, striking them with their swords. They attacked some of them from behind, and these fell instantly to the ground with their entrails hanging out. Others they beheaded: they cut off their heads, or split their heads to pieces.

They struck others in the shoulders, and their arms were torn from their bodies. They wounded some in the thigh and some in the calf. They slashed others in the abdomen, and their entrails all spilled to the ground. Some attempted to run away, but their intestines dragged as they ran; they seemed to tangle their feet in their own entrails. No matter how they tried to save themselves, they could find no escape.

Some attempted to force their way out, but the Spaniards murdered them at the gates. Others climbed the walls, but they could not save themselves. Those who ran into the communal houses were safe there for a while; so were those who lay down among the victims and pretended to be dead. But if they stood up again, the Spaniards saw them and killed them.

The blood of the warriors flowed like water and gathered into pools. The pools widened, and the stench of blood and entrails filled the air. The Spaniards ran into the communal houses to kill those who were hiding. They ran everywhere and searched everywhere; they invaded every room, hunting and killing.

The Aztecs Retaliate

When the news of this massacre was heard outside the Sacred Patio, a great cry went up: "Mexicanos, come running! Bring your spears and shields! The strangers have murdered our warriors!"

This cry was answered with a roar of grief and anger: the people shouted and wailed and beat their palms against their mouths. The captains assembled at once, as if the hour had been determined in advance. They all carried their spears and shields.

Then the battle began. The Aztecs attacked with javelins and arrows, even with the light spears that are used for hunting birds. They hurled their javelins with all their strength, and the cloud of missiles spread out over the Spaniards like a yellow cloak.

The Spaniards immediately took refuge in the palace. They began to shoot at the Mexicans with their iron arrows and to fire their cannons and harquebuses. And they shackled Motecuhzoma in chains.

The Lament for the Dead

The Mexicans who had died in the massacre were taken out of the patio one by one and inquiries were made to discover their names. The fathers and mothers of the dead wept and lamented.

Each victim was taken first to his own home and then to the Sacred Patio, where all the dead were brought together. Some of the bodies were later burned in the place called the Eagle Urn, and others in the House of the Young Men.

Motecuhzoma's Message

At sunset, Itzcuauhtzin climbed onto the roof of the palace and shouted this proclamation: "Mexicanos! Tlatelolcas! Your king, the lord Motecuhzoma, has sent me to speak for him. Mexicanos, hear me, for these are his words to you: 'We must not fight them. We are not their equals in battle. Put down your shields and arrows.'

"He tells you this because it is the aged who will suffer most, and they deserve your pity. The humblest classes will also suffer, and so will the innocent children who still crawl on all fours, who still sleep in their cradles.

"Therefore your king says: 'We are not strong enough to defeat them. Stop fighting, and return to your homes.' Mexicanos, they have put your king in chains; his feet are bound with chains."

When Itzcuauhtzin had finished speaking, there was a great uproar among the people. They shouted insults at him in their fury, and cried: "Who is Motecuhzoma to give us orders? We are no longer his slaves!" They shouted war cries and fired arrows at the azotea. The Spaniards quickly hid Motecuhzoma and Itzcuauhtzin behind their shields so that the arrows would not find them.

The Mexicans were enraged because the attack on the captains had been so treacherous: their warriors had been killed without the slightest warning. Now they refused to go away or to put down their arms.

The Massacre

Motecuhzoma said to La Malinche: "Please ask the god [Cortés] to hear me. It is almost time to celebrate the fiesta of Toxcatl. It will last for only ten days, and we beg his permission to hold it. We merely burn some incense and dance our dances. There will be a little noise because of the music, but that is all."

The Captain said: "Very well, tell him they may hold it." Then he left the city to meet another force of Spaniards who were marching in this direction. Pedro de Alvarado, called The Sun, was in command during his absence.

When the day of the fiesta arrived, Motecuhzoma said to The Sun: "Please hear me, my lord. We beg your permission to begin the fiesta of our god."

The Sun replied: "Let it begin. We shall be here to watch it."

The Aztec captains then called for their elder brothers, who were given this order: "You must celebrate the fiestaas grandly as possible."

The elder brothers replied: "We will dance with all our might."

Then Tecatzin, the chief of the armory, said: "Please remind the lord that he is here, not in Cholula. You know how they trapped the Cholultecas in their patio! They have already caused us enough trouble. We should hide our weapons close at hand!"

But Motecuhzoma said: "Are we at war with them? I tell you, we can trust them."

Tecatzin said: "Very well."

Then the songs and dances began. A young captain wearing a lip plug guided the dancers; he was Cuatlazol, from Tolnahuac.

But the songs had hardly begun when the Christians came out of the palace. They entered the patio and stationed four guards at each entrance. Then they attacked the captain who was guiding the dance. One of the Spaniards struck the idol in the face, and others attacked the three men who were playing the drums. After that there was a general slaughter until the patio was heaped with corpses.

A priest from the Place of the Canefields cried out in a loud voice: "Mexicanos! Who said we are not at war? Who said we could trust them?"

The Mexicans could only fight back with sticks of wood; they were cut to pieces by the swords. Finally the Spaniards retired to the palace where they were lodged.

21

"Here Motecuhzoma Died and the Marques Arrived"

From the *Codex Aubin*

*Written by several scribes from San Juan Moyotlan, an Indian neighborhood (sub-*altepetl*) of Tenochtitlan-Mexico City, the* Codex Aubin *is an annal that records events in Mexica history from circa 1168 to 1607. The selection is a pictorial account of Spanish arrival. As in other postcontact manuscripts, the* Codex *combines alphabetic and pictographic writing. The folios that follow contain a description of the Toxcatl massacre in prose.*

Histoire de la nation mexicaine . . . (Paris: E. Leroux, 1893). http://arks.princeton.edu/ark:/88435/mg74qn39s.

Text continued on page 150

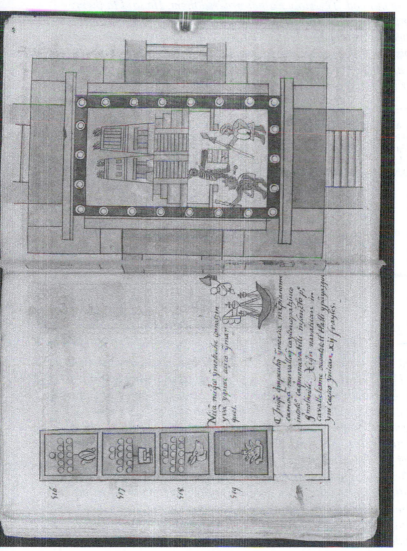

Histoire de la nation mexicaine depuis le départ d'Aztlan jusqu'à l'arrivée des conquérants espagnols (*et au dela 1607*) (Paris: E. Leroux, 1893).

Next to the date 1 Acatl (1519 in Mexica year-count), the text in Nahuatl reads: "Here Motecuhzoma died and the Marques arrived. It is when the Christians conquered the Mexica; not in vain, they came by revered orders of our god. The Holy Father ordered them. He said to them: 'Order the cavaliers to another land' [and] they went. With that, the XII [twelve] friars came to arrive here."[1] As in other postcontact manuscripts, the Codex combines alphabetic and pictographic writing. The painting on the right depicts a Mexica nobleman speaking with a Spanish soldier in front of a temple structure.

---

[1]We are grateful to Christopher M. Valesey for translating this entry from the original Nahuatl. For a Spanish translation, see Charles E. Dibble, ed., *Historia de la nación mexicana; reproducción a todo color del Códice de 1576 (Códice Aubin)* (Madrid: J. Porrúa Turanzas, 1963). Princeton University holds a digitized copy of the original, which is at the British Museum.

22

BERNAL DÍAZ

From *The True History of the Conquest of New Spain*

Bernal Díaz went with Cortés to deal with Narváez's expedition, so he missed the Toxcatl massacre. This selection expresses the Spaniards' surprise, on their return, at finding Tenochtitlan in an armed uprising against them. Cortés was furious with Alvarado, but also with Moctezuma, whom he suspected had been in contact with Narváez. The intercession of various Spanish captains in favor of the captive ruler did not pacify Cortés. It also quickly became clear that the Spaniards were besieged. Three excerpts are presented here: first, Díaz's account of the battle to control the main temple (templo mayor) *and pyramid of Huitzilopochtli; second, the death of Moctezuma; and lastly the escape of the Sad Night* (Noche triste) *and the disastrous (for the Spaniards and Tlaxcalans) fighting at the canal.*

Bernal Díaz del Castillo, *The True History of the Conquest of New Spain,* trans. Alfred P. Maudslay, 2d series (London: Printed for the Hakluyt Society, 1908), 230–48.

Battle For The Plaza Mayor

[A]s soon as it was dawn, our Captain decided that all of us and Narvaez' men should sally out to fight with them and that we should take the cannon and muskets and crossbows and endeavor to defeat them, [Mexica guarding the besieged palace], or at least to make them feel our strength and valor better than the day before. . . . We fought very well, but they were so strong, and had so many squadrons which relieved each other from time to time, that even if ten thousand Trojan Hectors and as many more Roldans had been there, they would not have been able to break through them. . . .

We noted [their] tenacity in fighting, but I declare that I do not know how to describe it, for neither cannon nor muskets nor crossbows availed, nor hand-to-hand fighting, nor killing thirty or forty of them every time we charged, for they still fought on in as close ranks and with more energy than in the beginning. Sometimes when we were gaining a little ground or a part of the street, they pretended to retreat, but it was [merely] to induce us to follow them and cut us off from our fortress and quarters, so as to fall on us in greater safety to themselves, believing that we could not return to our quarters alive, for they did us much damage when we were retreating.

Then, as to going out to burn their houses, I have already said . . . between one house and another, they have wooden drawbridges, and these they raised so that we could only pass through deep water. Then we could not endure the rocks and stones [hurled] from the roofs, in such a way that they damaged and wounded many of our men. I do not know why I write thus, so lukewarmly, for some three or four soldiers who were there with us and who had served in Italy, swore to God many times that they had never seen such fierce fights, not even when they had taken part in such between Christians, and against the artillery of the King of France, or of the Great Turk, nor had they seen men like those Indians with such courage in closing up their ranks.

. . . [W]ith great difficulty we withdrew to our quarters, many squadrons of warriors still pressing on us with loud yells and whistles, and trumpets and drums, calling us villains and cowards who did not dare to meet them all day in battle, but turned in flight.

On that day they killed ten or twelve more soldiers and we all returned badly wounded. What took place during the night was the arrangement that in two days' time all the soldiers in camp, as many as were able, should sally out with four engines like towers built of strong timber, in such a manner that five and twenty men could find shelter under each of them, and they were provided with apertures and loopholes through which to shoot, and musketeers and crossbowmen accompanied them, and close by them were to march the other soldiers, musketeers and crossbowmen and the guns, and all the rest, and the horsemen were to make charges.

When this plan was settled, as we spent all that day in carrying out the work and in strengthening many breaches that they had made in the walls, we did not go out to fight.

I do not know how to tell of the great squadrons of warriors who came to attack us in our quarters, not only in ten or twelve places, but in more than twenty, for we were distributed over them all and in many other places, and while we built up and fortified [ourselves], as I have related, many other squadrons openly endeavored to penetrate into our quarters, and neither with guns, crossbows nor muskets, nor with many charges and sword-thrusts could we force them back, for they said that not one of us should remain [alive] that day and they would sacrifice our hearts and blood to their gods, and would have enough to glut [their appetites] and hold feasts on our arms and legs, and would throw our bodies to the tigers, lions, vipers and snakes, which they kept caged, so that they might gorge on them, and for that reason they had ordered them not to be given food for the past two days. As for the gold we possessed, we would get little satisfaction from it or from all the cloths; and as for the Tlaxcalans who were with us, they said that they would place them in cages to fatten, and little by little they would offer their bodies in sacrifice; and, very tenderly, they said that we should give up to them their great Lord Montezuma, and they said other things. Night by night, in like manner, there were always many yells and whistles and showers of darts, stones and arrows.

As soon as dawn came, after commending ourselves to God, we sallied out from our quarters . . . with the cannon, muskets and crossbows in advance, and the horsemen making charges, but, as I have stated, although we killed many of them it availed nothing towards making them turn their backs, indeed if they had fought bravely on the two previous days, they proved themselves far more vigorous and displayed much greater forces and squadrons on this day. Nevertheless, we determined, although it should cost the lives of all of us, to push on with our towers and engines as far as the great Cue of Huichilobos.

I will not relate at length, the fights we had with them in a fortified house, nor will I tell how they wounded the horses, nor were they [the horses] of any use to us, because although they charged the squadrons to break through them, so many arrows, darts and stones were hurled at them, that they, well protected by armour though they were, could not prevail against them [the enemy], and if they pursued and overtook them, the Mexicans promptly dropped for safety into the canals and lagoons where they had raised other walls against the horsemen, and many other Indians were stationed with very long lances to finish killing them.

Thus it benefited us nothing to turn aside to burn or demolish a house, it was quite useless, for, as I have said, they all stood in the water, and between house and house there was a movable bridge, and to cross by swimming was very dangerous, for on the roofs they had such store of rocks and stones and such defenses, that it was certain destruction to risk it. In addition to this, where we did set fire to some houses, a single house took a whole day to burn, and the houses did not catch fire one from the other, as, for one reason, they stood apart with the water between; and, for the other, were provided with flat roofs thus it was useless toil to risk our persons in the attempt, so we went towards the great Cue of their Idols.

Then, all of a sudden, more than four thousand Mexicans ascended it, not counting other Companies that were posted on it with long lances and stones and darts, and placed themselves on the defensive, and resisted our ascent for a good while, and neither the towers nor the cannon or crossbows, nor the muskets were of any avail, nor the horsemen, for, although they wished to charge [with] their horses, the whole of the courtyard was paved with very large flagstones, so that the horses lost their foothold, and they [the stones] were so slippery that they [the horses] fell. While from the steps of the lofty Cue they forbade our advance, we had so many enemies both on one side and the other that although our cannon [shots] carried off ten or fifteen of them and we slew many others by sword-thrusts and charges, so many men attacked us that we were not able to ascend the lofty Cue. However with great unanimity . . . we made our way to the summit.

Here Cortés showed himself very much of a man, as he always was. Oh! what a fight and what a fierce battle it was that took place; it was a memorable thing to see us all streaming with blood, and covered with wounds and others slain. . . .

We set fire to their Idols and a good part of the chamber with the Idols Huichilobos and Tezcatepuca was burned. On that occasion the Tlaxcalans helped us very greatly. After this was accomplished, while some of us were fighting and others kindling the fire, as I have related, oh! to see the priests who were stationed on this great Cue, and the three or four thousand Indians, all men of importance. While we descended, oh! how they made us tumble down six or even ten steps at a time! And so much more there is to tell of the other squadrons posted on the battlements and recesses of the great Cue discharging so many darts and arrows that we could face neither one group of squadrons nor the other. We resolved to return, with much toil and risk to ourselves, to our quarters, our castles being destroyed, all of us wounded and sixteen slain, with the Indians constantly pressing on us and other squadrons on our flanks.

. . . In this battle, we captured two of the chief priests, whom Cortés ordered us to convey with great care.

Many times I have seen among the Mexicans and Tlaxcalans, paintings of this battle, and the ascent that we made of the great Cue, as they look upon it as a very heroic deed. And although in the pictures that they have made of it, they depict all of us as badly wounded and streaming with blood and many of us dead they considered it a great feat, this setting fire to the Cue, when so many warriors were guarding it both on the battlements and recesses, and many more Indians were below on the ground and the Courts were full of them and there were many more on the sides . . .

Death of Moctezuma

Let us return to the great attacks they made on us; Montezuma was placed by a battlement of the roof with many of us soldiers guarding him, and he began to speak to them [his people], with very affectionate expressions [telling them] to desist from the war, and that we would leave Mexico. Many of the Mexican Chieftains and Captains knew him well and at once ordered their people to be silent and not to discharge darts, stones or arrows, and four of them reached a spot where Montezuma could speak to them, and they to him, and with tears they said to him: "Oh! Señor, and our great Lord, how all your misfortune and injury and that of your children and relations afflicts us, we make known to you that we have already raised one of your kinsmen to be our Lord," and there he stated his name, that he was called Cuitlahuac, the Lord of Ixtapalapa, (for it was not Guatemoc, he who was Lord soon after,) and moreover they said that the war must be carried through, and that they had vowed to their Idols not to relax it until we were all dead, and that they prayed every day to their Huichilobos and Texcatepuca to guard him free and safe from our power, and that should it end as they desired, they would not fail to hold him in higher regard as their Lord than they did before, and they begged him to forgive them.

They had hardly finished this speech when suddenly such a shower of stones and darts was discharged that (our men who were shielding him having neglected their duty [to shield him] for a moment, because they saw how the attack ceased while he spoke to them) he was hit by three stones, one on the head, another on the arm and another on the leg, and although they begged him to have the wounds dressed and to take food, and spoke kind words to him about it, he would not. Indeed, when we least expected it, they came to say that he was dead. Cortés wept for him, and all of us Captains and soldiers, and there was no man among us who knew him and was intimate with him, who did not bemoan him as though he were our father, and it is not to be wondered at, considering how good he was. It was stated that he had reigned for seventeen years and that he was the best king there had ever been in Mexico, and that he had conquered in person, in three wars which he had carried on in the countries he had subjugated.

. . . At the end of much discussion Cortés ordered a priest and a chief from among the prisoners to go and tell the Cacique whom they had chosen for Lord, who was named Cuitlahuac [Cuahtémoc], and his Captains, that the great Montezuma was dead, and they had seen him die, and about the manner of his death and the wounds his own people had inflicted on him, and they should say how grieved we all were about it, and that they should bury him as the great king that he was, and they should raise the cousin of Montezuma who was with us, to be king, for the inheritance was his, or one of his (Montezuma's) other sons, and that he whom they had raised to be king was not so by right, and they should negotiate a peace so that we could leave Mexico; and if they did not do so, now that Montezuma was dead, whom we held in respect and for that reason had not destroyed their city, we should sally out to make war on them and burn all their houses and do them much damage.

So as to convince them that Montezuma was dead, he ordered six Mexicans who were high chieftains, and the priests whom we held as prisoners, to carry him out on their shoulders and to hand him [the body] over to the Mexican Captains, and to tell them what Montezuma had commanded at the time of his death, for those who carried him out on their backs were present at his death; and they told Cuitlahuac the whole truth, how his own people killed him with blows from three stones.

When they beheld him thus dead, we saw that they were in floods of tears and we clearly heard the shrieks and cries of distress that they gave for him, but for all this, the fierce assault they made on us with darts, stones and arrows never ceased, and then they came on us again with greater force and fury, and said to us: "Now for certain you will pay for the death of our King and Lord, and the dishonor to our Idols; and as for the peace you sent to beg for, come out here and we will settle how and in what way it is to be made," and they said many things about this and other matters that I cannot now remember and I will leave them unreported, and [they said] that they had already chosen a good king, and he would not be so fainthearted as to be deceived with false speeches like their good Montezuma, and as for the burial, we need not trouble about that, but about our own lives, for in two days there would not be one of us left;—so much for the messages we had sent them. With these words [they fell on us] with loud yells and whistles and showers of stones, darts and arrows, while other squadrons were still attempting to set fire to our quarters in many places.

When Cortés and all of us observed this, we agreed that next day we would all of us sally out from our camp and attack in another direction, where there were many houses on dry land, and we would do all the damage we were able and go towards the causeway, and that all the horsemen should break through the squadrons and spear them with their lances or drive them into the water, even though they [the enemy] should kill the horses. This was decided on in order to find out if by chance, with the damage and slaughter that we should inflict on them, they would abandon their attack and arrange some sort of peace, so that we could go free without more deaths and damage.

Although the next day we all bore ourselves very manfully and killed many of the enemy and burned a matter of twenty houses and almost reached dry land, it was all of no use, because of the great damage and deaths and wounds they inflicted on us, and we could not hold a single bridge, for they were all of them half broken down. Many Mexicans charged down on us, and they had set up walls and barricades in places which they thought could be reached by the horses, so that if we had met with many difficulties up to this time, we found much greater ones ahead of us.

Let us leave it here, and go back to say that we determined to get out of Mexico. . . .

Sad Night

Now we saw our forces diminishing every day and those of the Mexicans increasing, and many of our men were dead and all the rest wounded, and although we fought like brave men we could not drive back nor even get free from the many squadrons which attacked us both by day and night, and the powder was giving out, and the same was happening with the food and water, and the great Montezuma being dead, they were unwilling to grant the peace and truce which we had sent to demand of them. In fact we were staring death in the face, and the bridges had been raised.

It was decided by Cortés and all of us captains and soldiers that we should set out during the night, when we could see that the squadrons of warriors were most off their guard. In order to put them all the more off their guard, that very afternoon we sent to tell them, through one of their priests whom we held prisoner and who was a man of great importance among them and through some other prisoners, that they should let us go in peace within eight days and we would give up to them all the gold; and this [was done] to put them off their guard so that we might get out that night.

. . . I will relate how the order was given to make a bridge of very strong beams and planks, so that we could carry it with us and place it where the bridges were broken. Four hundred Tlaxcalan Indians and one hundred and fifty soldiers were told off to carry this bridge and place it in position and guard the passage until the army and all the baggage had crossed. Two hundred Tlaxcalan Indians and fifty soldiers were told off to carry the cannon, and Gonzalo de Sandoval, Diego de Ordás, Francisco de Sauzedo, Francisco de Lugo and a company of one hundred young and active soldiers were selected to go in the van to do the fighting. It was agreed that Cortés himself, Alonso de Ávila, Cristóbal de Olid, and other Captains should go in the middle and support the party that most needed help in fighting. Pedro de Alvarado and Juan Velázquez de Leon were with the rearguard, and placed in the middle between them [and the preceding section] were two captains and the soldiers of Narvaez, and three hundred Tlaxcalans, and thirty soldiers were told off to take charge of the prisoners and of Doña Marina and Doña Luisa; by the time this arrangement was made, it was already night.

In order to bring out the gold and divide it up and carry it, Cortés ordered his steward named Cristóbal de Guzman and other soldiers who were his servants to bring out all the gold and jewels and silver, and he gave them many Tlaxcalan Indians for the purpose, and they placed it in the Hall. Then Cortés told the King's officers named Alonso Dávila and Gonzalo Mejía to take charge of the gold belonging to His Majesty, and he gave them seven wounded and lame horses and one mare, and many friendly Tlaxcalans, more than eighty in number, and they loaded them with parcels of it, as much as they could carry, for it was put up into very broad ingots, as I have already said in the chapter that treats of it, and much gold still remained in the Hall piled up in heaps. Then Cortés called his secretary and the others who were King's Notaries, and said: "Bear witness for me that I can do no more with this gold. We have here in this apartment and Hall over seven hundred thousand pesos in gold, and, as you have seen, it cannot be weighed nor placed in safety. I now give it up to any of the soldiers who care to take it, otherwise it will be lost among these dogs."

When they heard this, many of the soldiers of Narvaez and some of our people loaded themselves with it. I declare that I had no other desire but the desire to save my life, but I did not fail to carry off from some small boxes that were there, four chalchihuites, which are stones very highly prized among the Indians, and I quickly placed them in my bosom under my armor, and, later on, the price of them served me well in healing my wounds and getting me food.

After we had learnt the plans that Cortés had made about the way in which we were to escape that night and get to the bridges, as it was somewhat dark and cloudy and rainy, we began before midnight to bring along the bridge and the baggage, and the horses and mare began their march, and the Tlaxcalans who were laden with the gold. Then the bridge was quickly put in place, and Cortés and the others whom he took with him in the first [detachment], and many of the horsemen, crossed over it.

While this was happening, the voices, trumpets, cries and whistles of the Mexicans began to sound and they called out in their language to the people of Tlaltelolco, "Come out at once with your canoes for the Teules are leaving; cut them off so that not one of them may be left alive." When I least expected it, we saw so many squadrons of warriors bearing down on us, and the lake so crowded with canoes that we could not defend ourselves. Many of our soldiers had already crossed [the bridge] and while we were in this position, a great multitude of Mexicans charged down on us [with the intention of] removing the bridge and wounding and killing our men who were unable to assist each other; and as misfortune is perverse at such times, one mischance followed another, and as it was raining, two of the horses slipped and fell into the lake. When I and others of Cortés's Company saw that, we got safely to the other side of the bridge, and so many warriors charged on us, that despite all our good fighting, no further use could be made of the bridge, so that the passage or water opening was soon filled up with dead horses, Indian men and women, servants, baggage and boxes.

Fearing that they would not fail to kill us, we thrust ourselves ahead along the causeway, and we met many squadrons armed with long lances waiting for us, and they used abusive words to us, and among them they cried "Oh! villains, are you still alive?" and with the cuts and thrusts we gave them, we got through, although they then wounded six of those who were going along [with me]. Then if there was some sort of plan such as we had agreed upon it was an accursed one; for Cortés and the captains and soldiers who passed first on horseback, so as to save themselves and reach dry land and make sure of their lives, spurred on along the causeway, and they did not fail to attain their object, and the horses with the gold and the Tlaxcalans also got out in safety. I assert that if we had waited, (the horsemen and the soldiers, one for the other,) at the bridges, we should all have been put an end to, and not one of us would have been left alive; the reason was this, that as we went along the causeway, charging the Mexican squadrons, on one side of us was water and on the other azoteas, and the lake was full of canoes so that we could do nothing. Moreover the muskets and crossbows were all left behind at the bridge, and as it was nighttime, what could we do beyond what we accomplished? which was to charge and give some swordthrusts to those who tried to lay hands on us, and to march and get on ahead so as to get off the causeway.

Had it been in the daytime, it would have been far worse, and we who escaped did so only by the Grace of God. To one who saw the hosts of warriors who fell on us that night and the canoes [full] of them coming along to carry off our soldiers, it was terrifying. So we went ahead along the causeway in order to get to the town of Tacuba where Cortés was already stationed with all the Captains. Gonzalo de Sandoval, Cristóbal de Olid and others of those horsemen who had gone on ahead were crying out: "Señor Capitan, let us halt, for they say that we are fleeing and leaving them to die at the bridges; let us go back and help them, if any of them survive"; but not one of them came out or escaped. Cortés's reply was that it was a miracle that any of us escaped. . . .

While Cortés was on the causeway with the rest of the captains, we repaired to the courtyard in Tacuba. Many squadrons had already arrived from Mexico, shouting out orders to Tacuba and to the other town named Azcapotzalco, and they began to hurl darts, stones, and arrows [and attack] with their long lances. We made some charges and both attacked [them] and defended ourselves. . . .

[W]hen we were waiting in Tacuba, many Mexican warriors came together from all those towns and they killed three of our soldiers, so we agreed to get out of that town as quickly as we could, and five Tlaxcalan Indians, who found out a way towards Tlaxcala without following the [main] road, guided us with great precaution until we reached some small houses placed on a hill, and near to them a Cue or Oratory [built] like a fort, where we halted. . . .

FRAY BERNARDINO DE SAHAGÚN

From the *Florentine Codex*

This selection reports the death of Moctezuma and the ensuing fighting that broke out in Tenochtitlan as residents organized to expel Spaniards and their allies from their city. The descriptions convey the intensity of the battles from the Mexica point of view. It should be remembered that many of Sahagún's informants were Tlatelolcans, who had their own complaints against Moctezuma's leadership.

Twenty-third chapter, where it is said how Moteucçoma and a great nobleman of Tlatelolco died, and the Spaniards threw their bodies out at the entryway of the house where they were.

Four days after people had been cast down from the temple, [the Spaniards] removed [the bodies of] Moteucçoma and Itzquauhtzin, who had died, to a place at the water's edge called Teoayoc [Place of the Divine Turtle], for an image of a turtle was there, carved in stone; the stone represented a turtle.

And when they were seen and recognized as Moteucçoma and Itzquauhtzin, they hastened to take Moteucçoma up in their arms and brought him to the place called Copolco. Then they placed him on a pile of wood and set fire to it, ignited it. Then the fire crackled and roared, with many tongues of flame, tongues of flame like tassels, rising up. And Moteucçoma's body lay sizzling, and it let off a stench as it burned.

And when it was burning, some people, enraged and no longer with goodwill, scolded at him, saying, "This miserable fellow made the whole world fear him, in the whole world he was dreaded, in the whole world he inspired respect and fright. If someone offended him only in some small way, he immediately disposed of him. He punished many for imagined things, not true, but just fabricated tales." And there were many others who scolded him, moaning, lamenting, shaking their heads.

James Lockhart, *We People Here: Nahuatl Accounts of the Conquest of Mexico*, Repertorium Columbianum, UCLA Center for Medieval and Renaissance Studies (Los Angeles: University of California Press, 1993), 150–56.

Figure 7. *Moctezuma's Funeral.*
Fray Bernardino de Sahagún, *The Florentine Codex: Historia general de las cosas de Nueva España*, Libro 12, f.40v, 1577.

But Itzquauhtzin they put in a boat; they took his body in a boat until they got him here to Tlatelolco. They grieved greatly, their hearts were desolate; the tears flowed down. Not a soul scolded him or cursed him. They said, "The lord Tlacochcalcatl Itzquauhtzin has suffered travail, for he suffered and was afflicted along with Moteucçoma. What tribulations he endured on our behalf in the past, during all of Moteucçoma's time!" Then they outfitted him, equipping him with the lordly banner and other items of paper, and they gave him provisions. Then they took him and burned him in the temple courtyard at the place called Quauhxicalco. It was with great splendor that his body was burned.

After four days of fighting, for seven days the Spaniards were just enclosed in the house. But when the seven days were past, they came back out for a while to take a look, looking around here and there; they went as far as Maçatzintamalco. They gathered stalks of green maize, beginning to form ears. They just gathered the maize leaves as one does in war, going in great haste. Hardly had they got where they were going when they quickly went back into the building. When they had come out the sun was already off to one side, about to set.

Twenty-fourth chapter, where it is said how the Spaniards and Tlaxcalans came out and fled from Mexico by night.

When night had fallen and midnight had come, the Spaniards came out. They formed up, along with all the Tlaxcalans. The Spaniards went ahead, and the Tlaxcalans went following, bringing up the rear, like their wall of protection. [The Spaniards] went carrying a wooden platform [or platforms]; they laid it down at a canal and crossed over on it.

At this time it was drizzling and sprinkling, the rain was gently dripping down. They were able to cross some other canals, at Tecpantzinco, Tzapotla, and Atenchicalco. But when they got to Mixcoatechialtitlan, at the fourth canal, there they were seen coming out. It was a woman fetching water who saw them; then she shouted, saying, "O Mexica, come running, your enemies have come out, they have emerged secretly!" Then another person shouted, on top of [the temple of] Huitzilopochtli; his crying spread everywhere, everyone heard it. He said, "O warriors, o Mexica, your enemies are coming out, let everyone hasten with the war boats and on the roads!"

When it was heard, there was a clamor. Everyone scrambled; the operators of the war boats hastened and paddled hard, hitting one another's boats as they went in the direction of Mictlantonco and Macuilcuitlapilco. The war boats came upon them from both directions; the war boats of the Tenochca and the war boats of the Tlatelolca converged on them. And some people went on foot, going straight to

Nonoalco, heading toward Tlacopan to try to cut them off there. Then the war-boat people hurled barbed darts at the Spaniards; from both sides the darts fell on them. But the Spaniards also shot at the Mexica, shooting back with iron bolts and guns. There were deaths on both sides. Spaniards and Tlaxcalans were hit, and Mexica were hit.

When the Spaniards reached Tlaltecayoacan, where the Tolteca canal is, it was as though they had fallen off a precipice; they all fell and dropped in, the Tlaxcalans, the people of Tliliuhquitepec, and the Spaniards, along with the horses, and some women. The canal was completely full of them, full to the very top. And those who came last just passed and crossed over on people, on bodies.

When they reached Petlacalco, where there was yet another canal, they passed gently, slowly, gradually, with caution, on the wooden platform. There they restored themselves, took their breath, regained their vigor. When they reached Popotlan, it dawned, light came. They began to go along with spirit, they went heading into the distance.

Then the Mexica went shouting at them, surrounding them, hovering about them. They captured some Tlaxcalans as they went, and some Spaniards died. Also Mexica and Tlatelolca were killed; there was death on both sides. They drove and pursued [the Spaniards] to Tlacopan. And when they had driven them to Tiliuhcan, to Xocotliiyohuican, at Xoxocotla, Chimalpopoca, son of Moteucçoma, died in battle. They came upon him lying hit by a barbed dart and struck [by some hand weapon]. At the same place died Tlaltecatzin, a Tepaneca lord who had been guiding the Spaniards, pointing out the way for them, conducting them, showing them the road.

Then they crossed the Tepçolatl (a small river); they forded and went over the water at Tepçolac. Then they went up to Acueco and stopped at Otoncalpolco, [where] wooden walls or barricades were in the courtyard. There they all took a rest and caught their breath, there they restored themselves. There the people of Teocalhueyacan came to meet them and guide them.

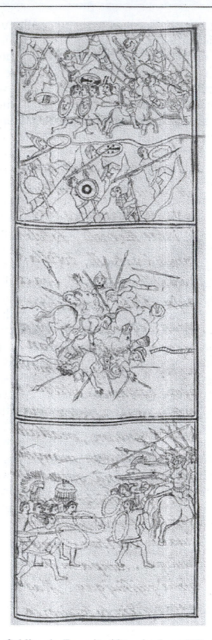

Figure 8. *Mexica Soldiers in Pursuit of Spaniards and Their Allies.*
Fray Bernardino de Sahagún, *The Florentine Codex: Historia general de las cosas de Nueva España*, Libro 12, f.43, 1577.

7

The Siege and Fall of Tenochtitlan

The final stage of the military conquest of Tenochtitlan took roughly over a year, beginning with the arrival of the Spaniards and their native allies in Tlaxcala on July 11, 1520 (after fleeing Tenochtitlan); continuing through their return to the Mexica capital; and ending with the surrender of the last Mexica emperor Cuahtémoc on August 13, 1521. During the first ten of those thirteen months, both the Mexica and the Spaniards maneuvered to secure allies and to muster their forces. These months were also filled with campaigns and battles around the valley of Mexico. The final siege of Tenochtitlan lasted about three months (Bernal Díaz says ninety-three days). It ended with the fall of the Mexica Empire.

The fighting in the last few months was bitter, and at the end it was often house-by-house combat. The Mexica had to contend with hundreds of Spanish troops and the thousands of Indigenous soldiers who accompanied them, as well as with another enemy: epidemic disease in the form of smallpox. The Nahua accounts mention the effects of the disease that decimated the population and devastated their leadership. Cuitlahuac, the brother of Moctezuma who became the *tlahtoani* when the latter died and who directed the attacks of the *Noche triste,* lived for only three months before succumbing to smallpox. Cuahtémoc, who replaced him, directed the final defense of the capital. Historian Ross Hassig has argued that the plague strengthened the Spanish position, although the Indigenous allies of the Spanish also suffered from its effects.

Meanwhile, Cuauhtémoc tried to win support by lowering the tribute demands on the Mexica dependents, but his attempts only made Tenochtitlan seem weak. This loss of face and the Mexica's dwindling military force encouraged other city-states to collaborate with the

Spaniards and Tlaxcalans in order to topple the regime. As the Spaniards consolidated their position and more soldiers arrived on the coast from Cuba and elsewhere, Cortés demonstrated considerable political ability in persuading various city-states into joining him for the final effort against Tenochtitlan. Key in this effort was the continued allegiance of Tlaxcala, which, even after the *Noche triste* when the Spaniards were at their weakest, maintained its loyalty.

The final battle for Tenochtitlan was a combined naval and land operation. First Cortés sought to isolate the city from its support. Texcoco, another major city-state on the shores of the lake system and a traditional ally of Tenochtitlan, was in the midst of a dynastic crisis and civil war. Cortés was able to gain its loyalty by supporting Tecocoltzin—one of the contenders for the *tlahtoani* position. By contrast, Iztapalapa remained loyal to the Mexica, and they forced out the Spaniards and their allies who tried to seize the city-state. Eventually, however, the Spaniards and their growing number of allies were able to neutralize many of the towns and city-states in the Valley of Mexico or to convince their leadership to join them (Map 2). By this strategy, Cortés's combined Spanish and Indian forces systematically defeated Mexica troops operating outside the lakes area. In the final battles, Tenochtitlan and its subdivision Tlatelolco were effectively left to fight on their own.

The city's location on an island in the midst of a lake had defensive advantages as long as the Mexica could control access across the lake. To mitigate this situation, Cortés ordered the construction of thirteen small (about forty feet long) shallow-draught ships or brigantines (also called launches). The ships were assembled at the shore of the lake and then outfitted with small cannon, sails, and rigging. The brigantines joined hundreds of war canoes provided by native allies, forming an awesome naval operation that took control of the lake system and tightened a noose around the throat of the city.

Meanwhile, the Mexica took advantage of the structure of Tenochtitlan with its many canals and its streets intersected by bridges. They would draw their attackers into the city and then cut off retreat by removing the bridges over which they had crossed. The Spanish and their allies eventually avoided these situations by not advancing beyond secured areas, or by carrying small portable bridges along with their forces. On a number of occasions, Mexica soldiers routed the invading forces. The spirited Mexica defense, however, was overwhelmed by the dogged assault of Spanish and Indigenous troops, who streamed into the city aboard the small ships and canoes.

In the final days of fighting, the Spaniards and their allies systematically demolished Tenochtitlan's buildings, leveling large parts of the city. Even

Cortés regretted the loss. In a moment of explanation and self-justification he told his king why he had burned many of the palaces and great houses in an attempt to bring the Mexica to submission: "I was much grieved to do this," he wrote, "but since it was still more grievous to them I determined on burning them." Such tactics had little effect on the Mexica will to fight. The admiration of Cortés and Bernal Díaz for the bravery and resilience of the Mexica defenders is evident throughout their accounts.

The selections in this chapter primarily reflect an Indigenous perspective. First are two pictorial representations from the *Lienzo de Tlaxcala*, which emphasize the centrality of the city-state in preparing for and carrying out the final siege of Tenochtitlan. An excerpt from Fernando de Alva Ixtlilxochitl's *Account of the Conquest of New Spain* describes events that took place in the lead up to the assault of the city, when Cortés garnered allies like Texcoco to fight the Mexica. Other perspectives come from the eyes of the Mexica's Purépecha neighbors (*Chronicles of Michoacán*), Nahua accounts drawn from the *Florentine Codex*, and some elegies preserved in Nahuatl after the fall of the city. An excerpt from Bernal Díaz presents Spanish viewpoints.

24

New Sun in Tlaxcala
and
Joint Spanish-Nahua Assault at Copolco

From the *Lienzo de Tlaxcala*

These two scenes from the Lienzo *place Tlaxcalans at the center of the narrative. The first illustration depicts events after the* Noche triste, *when Tlaxcalans and Spaniards returned to the city-state in order to regroup. The second scene depicts the joint assault of Tenochtitlan in June 1521.*

In the first cell, Cortés and a Tlaxcalan nobleman are shown discussing military strategy under a sign for a new sun, which is meant to evoke the coming of a new order. Malintzin is shown translating for the men; in front are provisions for the campaigns ahead.

Lienzo de Tlaxcala, reconstruction, cells 29 and 47. Liza Bakewell and Byron E. Hamann, "Mesolore: Exploring Mesoamerican Culture." Prolarti Enterprise, LLC and Brown University.

The second cell depicts the fighting that took place on the causeways to the city. Tlaxacalan and Spanish soldiers are under attack from Mexica forces shown on canoes. At left, Cortés falls back, struck by a Mexica soldier; at right, Cortés is held up by his native allies, saved from further injury.

New Sun in Tlaxcala.
Lienzo de Tlaxcala, reconstruction, cell 29. Liza Bakewell and Byron E. Hamann. "Mesolore: Exploring Mesoamerican Culture." Prolarti Enterprise, LLC and Brown University.

Joint Spanish-Nahua Assault at Copolco.
Lienzo de Tlaxcala, reconstruction, cell 47. Liza Bakewell and Byron E. Hamann, *Mesolore: Exploring Mesoamerican Culture*. Prolarti Enterprise, LLC and Brown University.

25

FERNANDO DE ALVA IXTLILXOCHITL

From the *Account of the Conquest of New Spain*

In this selection from Alva Ixtlilxochitl's Account of the Conquest of
New Spain, *we get the perspective of Texcoco noblemen who sided with
Cortés in 1520. The reading begins with the accession of Tecocoltzin
as Lord of Texcoco and accounts for his military contributions to the*

Fernando de Alva Ixtlilxóchitl, *The Native Conquistador: Alva Ixtlilxochitl's Account of the Conquest of New Spain*. Eds. and trans. Amber Brian, Bradley Benton, and Pablo García Loaeza (State College: Penn State University Press, 2015), 28–31, 59.

campaign against the Mexica. The narrative reveals some divisions among the Texcoco elite over this alliance and the need for them to hedge their bets in case the Spaniards lost. It also shows Cortés's dependence on cementing relationships with key allies to garner the necessary intelligence, manpower, and provisions to move forward against Cuauhtémoc. The reading continues with a summation of the losses sustained by Texcoco during the capture of Tenochtitlan.

Texcoco Alliance

When Cortés was nearing Tezcuco, some nobles came out to greet him, including Prince Ixtlixochitl and the rest of his brothers who were there. Cortés was pleased to see them. They told him about all that was happening and how their brother Cohuanacoch had gone to Mexico [Tenochtitlan]. Once in the city, they housed the Spaniards in King Nezahualcoyotl's palaces, where there was ample room for the whole army. Every day they spent in this city they were given everything they needed. On the very day that Cortés arrived in Tezcuco, he was informed how the residents were leaving and going to Mexico in canoes. Cortés ordered some nobles to call to them and make them come back and to tell them not to worry about Cohuanacoch because the rest of their lords, the princes of Tezcuco, were with Cortés, and Cortés would crown as their king and natural lord the one who had the most right to the title, or whomever they pleased. This was agreeable to everyone, and soon almost all the residents came back to their houses and city. Everyone agreed to make Tecocoltzin their lord, even though he was King Nezahualpilli's illegitimate son, because they did not dare nominate the legitimate ones until they saw how these things would turn out.

Tecocoltzin began his rule with good judgment. He sent his messengers to all the kingdoms of Tezcuco, especially to those that he knew had not sided with the Mexica, and spent the following eight days fortifying the city in case the enemies should want to besiege them. At the end of this period, Cortés wanted to see if he could take Iztapalapan, a well-fortified place that would be strategically valuable. So he left with as many as fifteen horsemen, two hundred Spaniards, and six thousand Aculhua [people from Aculhuacan, the region around Texcoco], Tlaxcalteca, and other allied nations. When they reached Iztapalapan, the Mexica, who already knew about the attack, came out to meet them. They had a fierce and hard-fought battle on that day. But, because the people of Iztapalapan had their houses on small islands on the water, the Spaniards could not take them or do them harm. They wanted to remain there that night, but the Mexica prevented it by breaking up the causeway that held back much water.* If the Spaniards had not left in a hurry they would have all drowned there. The Mexica followed them as they retreated, killing many of the allies because they were protecting the Christians. Only one Spaniard died, because he was more reckless than the others.

Here, Ixtlilxochitl, who was leading the Aculhua, greatly distinguished himself. He single-handedly killed many enemy captains. It pained Quauhtemoc to find out that one of the legitimate princes of Tezcuco had distinguished himself so much, considering that it was to the advantage of the Christians and damaging to the Mexica. Furthermore, Ixtlilxochitl had opposed them in Otumpan, Atenco, Cohuatlichan, and other places that the Mexica wanted to punish for their support of the Christians, gallantly defending these places. And for the reasons mentioned earlier, King Quauhtemoc and Cohuanacoch sent their bravest captains, offering to reward greatly the one who could capture or kill Ixtlilxochitl. . . .

Tecocoltzin ordered many quilts,** shields, arrows, clubs, throwing spears, and other types of weapons and ammunition to be made for his own people as well as for the Spaniards. He also commanded that maize, chickens, and other necessities for the army's sustenance be gathered in great amounts. Likewise, he readied all his vassals so that they would be ready when called. . . .

While these things were happening, Tecocoltzin, who had been baptized and given the name don Fernando—and was the first of this name in Tezcuco—died, to the great sorrow of the Spaniards, because he was extremely noble and loved them very much. Don Fernando Tecocoltzin was handsome, tall, and very white, as white as the whitest Spaniard; his person and stature reflected his exalted lineage. He spoke the Castilian language, and so, on most nights, after dinner Tecocoltzin and Cortés discussed everything that should be done regarding the wars. Owing to his sound judgment and diligence, they readily agreed on all matters. . . .

According to the histories, paintings, and accounts, especially the one by don Alonso Axayaca, the siege of Mexico lasted a full eighty days, and 30,000 of Ixtlilxochitl's Tezcuca warriors died, besides the 200,000 that were fighting alongside the Spaniards, as we have seen.

---

*Mexico was connected to the lakeshore by a system of causeways that also functioned as dikes.

**Nahua warriors used stiff quilted-cotton shirts as armor.

On the Mexica side more than 240,000 men died, among them nearly all the Mexica nobility. Only a few lords and gentlemen remained, most of them young children. This day, after having sacked the city, the Spaniards took the gold and silver for themselves, while the lords took the jewels and precious feathers. The soldiers took the blankets and everything else. Then they spent another four days burying the dead and in joyful celebration. They took many men and women as slaves. Then they went to Culhuacan with the whole army, where all the lords said goodbye to Ixtlilxochitl and went back to their lands, promising to support him in all his endeavors. Cortés thanked them profusely. The Tlaxcalteca, Huexotzinca, and Cholulteca said goodbye to him and likewise went back to their lands, wealthy and content. On the way the Tlaxcalteca plundered the city of Tezcuco and other places, stealing at night when the inhabitants could not hear them or protect their belongings from them. Afterward, the Spaniards settled in Coyohuacan.

26

FRAY MARTÍN DE JESÚS DE LA CORUÑA

From the *Chronicles of Michoacán*

This selection from the Chronicles of Michoacán *describes a Mexica appeal to the cazonci, the ruler of their traditional enemies, the Purépecha of Michoacán, in a desperate search for allies. Purépecha leaders had already turned down such approaches, and the failure of this embassy underlines the way in which regional politics tipped the balance against the Mexica. From the text it appears that the Purépecha conflated a number of delegations from the Mexica into the narrative of a single embassy.*

The Arrival of the Spaniards

According to Don Pedro, who is now governor, Montezuma sent ten messengers from Mexico City to Taximaroa [Purépecha capital]. They brought a message for the Cazonci [Purépecha ruler] called Zuangua,

Eugene R. Crane and Reginald C. Reindorp, trans. and eds., *Chronicles of Michoacán* (Norman: University of Oklahoma Press, 1970), 60–63, 65–67.

father of the one who had just died, who was very old and who had been the Master of Taximaroa. When asked what they wanted they answered that they brought a message from Montezuma for the Cazonci in Mechuacán and for him alone. The Master of Taximaroa reported this to the Cazonci who ordered that they be received well but that they should not come at once. When they came before Zuangua they delivered gifts of turquoise, jerky, green feathers, ten round shields with golden rims, rich blankets, belts, and large mirrors. All the lords and sons of the Cazonci disguised themselves and put on some old blankets so that they would not be recognized, for they had heard that the Mexicans had come for them. The Mexicans sat down and the Cazonci called in an interpreter of the Mexican language, by the name of Nuritan, who was his Nahuatl interpreter. The Cazonci asked him what the Mexicans wanted and why they came.

The Cazonci was calm, holding an arrow in his hand with which he struck the ground repeatedly. The Mexicans repeated their message. "The Master of Mexico, called Montezuma, sends us and some other Lords with orders to report to our brother the Cazonci about the strange people who have come and taken us by surprise. We have met them in battle and killed some two hundred of those who came riding deer and two hundred of those who were not mounted. Those deer wore coats of mail and carried something that sounds like the clouds, makes a great thundering noise and kills all those it meets leaving not one. They completely broke up our formation and killed many of us. They are accompanied by people from Tlaxcala, because these people have turned against us. We should have killed the people of Tezaico if it had not been for those who help them to keep us besieged and isolated in this city. If your sons had not come to help us, the ones called Tirimarasco, Anini, and Acuiche, bringing their people and defending us, we should have all died there."

Having heard the message Zuangua replied: "It is well, you are welcome. You have made your message known to our Gods Curicaveri and Xaratanga. At the moment I cannot send people because I have need of those whom you have named for they are busy conquering in the Four Quarters.* Rest here a day or so and these my interpreters, Nuritan and Pivo, and two others will go with you. They shall confer with the people of whom you speak as soon as everyone has returned from the conquest."

The messengers went out and were given quarters, food, belts, blankets, leather war jackets, and cloverleaf wreaths. The Cazonci called his advisors and said to them: "What shall we do? This message they have

---

*A region of the Purépecha state.

brought me is serious. What has happened to us for the sun used to look with favor upon these two Kingdoms, Mexico and ours, and we never knew that there were any other people for we all served the same gods. What purpose would I have in sending people to Mexico for we are always at war when we approach each other and there is rancor between us. Remember that the Mexicans are very astute when they talk and very artful with the truth—I have no need of them as I said. Take heed lest it be a trick. Since they have not been able to conquer some villages, they want to take out their vengeance on us by killing us through treachery. They want to destroy us. As I said, let the Nahuatls and interpreters go for they are not boys to do boyish things and they will learn what it is all about." His advisors replied: "Sire, let it be as ordered by you who are King and Master. How can we contradict you? Let those whom you mention go at once."

He sent for rich blankets, gourd dishes, leather war jackets, for the bloody skirts and blankets of their gods and for some of everything produced in Mechuacán. These gifts he gave to the messengers to give to Montezuma just as Montezuma had sent similar gifts from Mexico for the local gods. The Nahuatls went with them to learn the truth, and the Cazonci sent war people by another road who captured three Otomis and asked them whether they had any news from Mexico. The Otomis replied: "The Mexicans have been conquered; we do not know who the conquerors are, but all Mexico City is foul with the odor of dead bodies. For this reason they are looking for allies who will free and defend them. We know how they have sent throughout the villages for help. It is true that they have gone for we know it. Take us to Mechuacán so they will give us blankets for we are freezing to death and we want to be subjects of the Cazonci."

The capture of the three Otomis and the news they brought were reported to the Cazonci: "Sire, it is true. The Mexicans have been destroyed and the entire village smells of dead bodies. They are petitioning all the villages for help. This is what was reported also in Taximaroa for the chief *Capacapecho* verified it." Then the Cazonci spoke, saying: "Welcome; we do not know what may become of the poor fellows we sent to Mexico. Let us wait for their return to learn the truth."

News from Mexico City and the Death of Zuangua

The messengers who had been sent to Mexico City returned, appeared before the Cazonci, greeted him and showed him more gifts of rich blankets and belts sent by Montezuma. Zuangua returned their greeting, saying that it was good to see them again and telling them that "long ago, on another occasion, our ancient ancestors went to Mexico City."

Then he asked them about their journey and the messengers replied: "Sire, during the night we arrived by canoe in Mexico City and showed the gift you sent to Montezuma, who welcomed us. We explained your orders that we should go with his messengers, we told him that you had sent your people to the Four Quarters and that we came ahead against the day when the war people could come. We told him that we came to learn about these strange people who have come to our land, in order to be better advised. He welcomed us and said: 'Look at that mountain range over there. Behind it are the people who have come from Taxcala [Tlaxcala].' Then they took us by canoe to show us. We landed in Texcuco [Texcoco] and climbed to the top of a mountain. From there they pointed to a long, flat clearing occupied by the strangers and outlined a plan to us: 'You people from Mechuacán will come from that way over there and we shall go this other way to catch them between us and thus kill them all. Why should we not be successful since everyone flees from you people of Mechuacán, who are such great archers? You have seen them, now take this information to your Master and tell him that we plead with him not to break our agreement. This is what we say to him, our gods have told us that Mexico City will never be destroyed, nor will our houses be burned. Two Kingdoms only are appointed, Mexico and Mechuacán. Take heed for there is much work.'

We answered: 'Let us return to Mexico City.' We returned, the lords came out to receive us and we took our leave from Montezuma who said to us: 'Return to Mechuacán for you have seen the land. Let us not desert the land which we wish to give to you. This matter which we beg of your Master, what answer can he give except that you will all come? Are we peradventure to be slaves? Are they to conquer Mechuacán? Let us all die here first and not let them go to your land. This is what you shall say to your Master. May you all come; there is plenty of food so that the people may have strength for the war: do not pity the people. Let us die quickly, if we do not win, and we shall make our dais of the people who die supposing the cowardly gods do not favor us. It has been a long time since they told our god that no one would destroy his Kingdom, and we have heard of no other Kingdom but this one and Mechuacán. So, return.' We departed and the Mexicans came some distance with us before saying goodbye. This is the report we bring back."

Then the Cazonci, Zuangua, spoke: "Welcome back. It has been a long time since our old ancestors went to Mexico City and while I know not why they went, the reason for your going now is important. What the Mexicans said is serious business. For what purpose are we to go to Mexico? Each one of us might go only to die and we know not what they will say about us afterwards. Perchance they will sell us out to these people who are coming and will be the cause of our being killed. Let the Mexicans do their own conquering or let them all come join us with their captaincies. Let the strangers kill the Mexicans because for many days they have not lived right for they do not bring wood to the temples but instead, we have heard, they honor their gods only with songs. What good are songs alone? How are the gods to favor them if they only sing songs? We work much more than is customarily required for the needs of the gods. Now let us do a little better, nay more, bring in wood for the temples, perhaps they will forgive us, for the gods of the heavens have become angry with us. Why would the strangers come without cause? A god has sent them, that is why they came! The people must know their sins; recall them to their memory even though they may lay the blame for their sins on me, the King. The common people do not want to listen to me for I tell them to bring wood for the temples. They heed not my words and they lose count of the war people. Why should not our God Curicaveri and the Goddess Xaratanga become angry with us? Since Curicaveri has no children and Xaratanga has not given birth to any, they complain to Mother Cueravaperi. I shall admonish the people to try to do better because they will not forgive us if we have failed in anything." The lords answered: "You have spoken well, Sire; we shall tell the people this which you order." And they went to their houses and nothing more was learned.

At this time a plague of smallpox and hemorrhaging from the bowels struck all the people in the entire province. The bishop of the temples died, as did the old Cazonci Zuanga [Zuangua], leaving his sons Tangaxoan, otherwise known as Zincicha, [Tzintzicha Tangaxoan], the oldest, Tirimarasco, Azinche, and Anini.

Another embassy of ten Mexicans came to ask for help. Unfortunately, for their purpose, they arrived at a time when the people were mourning the death of the old Cazonci. The arrival of the Mexicans was reported to Zincicha [Tangaxoan], the oldest son of the deceased Cazonci who ordered them taken to his father's houses where they were welcomed. It was explained to the Mexicans that the Cazonci was not there, that he had gone to rest. The oldest son called the old men into consultation and asked what should be done about the petition which the Mexicans brought. "We know not what their real intent is. Let them follow my Father to the Inferno and present him with the petition there. Tell them to prepare themselves because this is the custom." The Mexicans were so informed, and they replied that as the Master had ordered it, it should be done, and they asked that it be done quickly, adding that there was nowhere for them to go; they had voluntarily come to their death. The Mexicans were made ready in the customary manner, after being informed that they were taking their message to the dead Cazonci, and were sacrificed in the temple of Curicaveri and Xaratanga. . . .

27

FRAY BERNARDINO DE SAHAGÚN

From the *Florentine Codex*

These excerpts make the agonies of defeat quite apparent, beginning with the report of the smallpox epidemic that was spreading through the city. Particular attention is paid to the places where the battles took place and the specific conditions of the combat. Sometimes the text identifies the military exploits and strategies of individual Mexicas, such as Tzilacatzin. Another excerpt describes the capture and sacrifice of a number of Spaniards in great detail. Sahagún's informants for these accounts were men from Tlatelolco, the quarter of Tenochtitlan that had once been a separate city and was politically subordinate. The excerpts indicate the strength of local pride and perhaps a Tlatelolcan bias against the political and military failure of Tenochtitlan. Just as supernatural signs accompanied the first arrival of the Spaniards in the Nahua accounts, the final defeat is also presaged by an omen, a blood-colored sky. The Nahua texts mention in matter-of-fact directness the Spanish actions after the surrender: the search for gold, and the taking of women and of slaves.

Twenty-ninth chapter, where it is said how, at the time the Spaniards left Mexico, there came an illness of pustules of which many local people died; it was called "the great rash" [smallpox].

Before the Spaniards appeared to us, first an epidemic broke out, a sickness of pustules. It began in Tepeilhuitl. Large bumps spread on people; some were entirely covered. They spread everywhere, on the face, the head, the chest, etc. [The disease] brought great desolation; a great many died of it. They could no longer walk about, but lay in their

James Lockhart, *We People Here: Nahuatl Accounts of the Conquest of Mexico.* Repertorium Columbianum, UCLA Center for Medieval and Renaissance Studies (Los Angeles: University of California Press, 1993), 180–84, 192–94, 198–200, 214–18, 242–44, 246–48.

dwellings and sleeping places, no longer able to move or stir. They were unable to change position, to stretch out on their sides or face down, or raise their heads. And when they made a motion, they called out loudly. The pustules that covered people caused great desolation; very many people died of them, and many just starved to death; starvation reigned, and no one took care of others any longer.

On some people, the pustules appeared only far apart, and they did not suffer greatly, nor did many of them die of it. But many people's faces were spoiled by it, their faces and noses were made rough. Some lost an eye or were blinded.

This disease of pustules lasted a full sixty days; after sixty days it abated and ended. When people were convalescing and reviving, the pustules disease began to move in the direction of Chalco. And many were disabled or paralyzed by it, but they were not disabled forever. It broke out in Teotleco, and it abated in Panquetzaliztli. The Mexica warriors were greatly weakened by it.

And when things were in this state, the Spaniards came, moving toward us from Tetzcoco. They appeared from the direction of Quauhtitlan and made a halt at Tlacopan. There they gave one another assignments and divided themselves. Pedro de Alvarado was made responsible for the road coming to Tlatelolco. The Marqués considered the Tenochca great and valiant warriors.

And it was right in Nextlatilco, or in Ilyacac, that war first began. Then [the Spaniards] quickly reached Nonoalco, and the warriors came pursuing them. None of the Mexica died; then the Spaniards retreated. The warriors fought in boats; the war-boat people shot at the Spaniards, and their arrows sprinkled down on them. Then [the main force of the Mexica] entered [Nonoalco]. Thereupon the Marqués sent [his men] toward the Tenochca, following the Acachinanco road. Many times they skirmished, and the Mexica went out to face them.

Thirty-first chapter, where it is said how the Spaniards came with the brigantines, pursuing those who were in boats. When they were done contending with them, they drew close and reached all the houses.

And when they had finished adjusting [the guns], they shot at the wall. The wall then ripped and broke open. The second time it was hit, the wall went to the ground; it was knocked down in places, perforated, holes were blown in it. Then, like the other time, the road stood clear. And the warriors who had been lying at the wall dispersed and came fleeing; everyone escaped in fear. And then all the different people [who were on the side of the Spaniards] quickly went filling in the canals and making them level with stones, adobes, and some logs, with which they closed off the water.

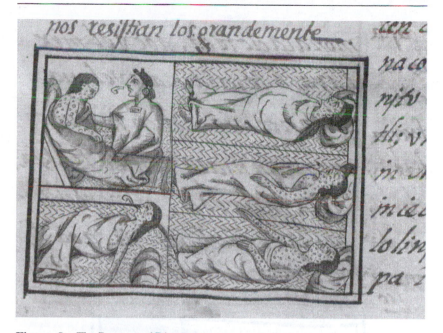

Figure 9. *The Ravages of Disease.*
Fray Bernardino de Sahagún, *The Florentine Codex: Historia general de las cosas de Nueva España*, Libro 12, f.53v, 1577.

And when the canals were stopped up, some horse[men] came, perhaps ten of them; they came going in circles, spinning, turning, twisting. Another group of horse[men] came following behind them. And some Tlatelolca who had quickly entered the palace that had been Moteucçoma's residence came back out in alarm to contend with the horse[men]. They lanced one of the Tlatclolca, but when they had lanced him, he was able to take hold of [the Spaniard's] iron lance. Then his companions took it from [the Spaniard's] hands, throwing him on his back and unhorsing him. When he fell to the ground, they struck him repeatedly on the back of the neck, and he died there.

Then the Spaniards sent everyone, they all moved together; they reached Quauhquiahuac [Eagle Gate]. As they went they took the cannon and its gear and set it down at Quauhquiahuac. (The reason it is so called is that an eagle stood there, carved of stone, some seven feet tall, and enclosing it were a jaguar standing on one side, and a wolf standing

Figure 10. *Naval Conflict on Lake Texcoco.*
Fray Bernardino de Sahagún, *The Florentine Codex: Historia general de las cosas de Nueva España*, Libro 12, f.56, 1577.

on the other, likewise carved in stone.) And when things were in this state the great warriors tried to take shelter behind the stone pillars; there were two rows of them, eight altogether. And the roof of the Coacalli was also full of warriors. None of them ventured to cross into the open.

And the Spaniards did not move at all; when they fired the cannon, it grew very dark, and smoke spread. Those who had been taking shelter behind the stone pillars fled; all who had been lying on the roof jumped down and ran far away. Then they brought the cannon up and set it down at the round stone [of gladiatorial sacrifice]. On top of [the temple of] Huitzilopochtli they were still trying to keep watch, beating the log drums, as though the air were full of them. Then two Spaniards climbed up and struck [the drummers]; after they had struck them they cast them aside, threw them down.

And those with scraped heads, all the warriors who were fighting in boats, came onto dry land, and only the youths who poled the others conducted the boats. And at this point the warriors inspected the passageways, with much running and shouting, saying "O warriors, let everyone come running!" . . .

Thirty-second chapter, where it is said how the Mexica left their altepetl in fear and came here when they dreaded the Spaniards.

And at this time the Tenochca came entering into Tlatelolco here, weeping and shouting. Many were the tears of the women; the men came accompanying their women, and some of them carried their children on their shoulders. In just one day they abandoned their altepetl. But the Tlatelolca still went to Tenochtitlan to fight.

And at this point Pedro de Alvarado hurled his forces at Ilyacac, toward Nonoalco, but they could do nothing; it was as though they had hit against a stone, because the Tlatelolca made great efforts. There was fighting on both sides of the road and in the water with war boats. When Alvarado tired, he returned and established himself in Tlacopan. But just two days later they sent out all the boats; at first only two came, then afterward all of them, and formed beside the houses in Nonoalco. Then they came onto dry land, and then they began to follow the narrow road between the houses; they came toward the center of them.

When the Spaniards landed it fell silent; not one of the people came out. But then Tzilacatzin, who was a great warrior and very valorous, hurled three stones he was carrying, huge round stones, wall stones or white stones; he had one in his hand and two on his shield. Then he went pursuing the Spaniards, scattering them, forcing them into the water. They went right into the water; those who went down in the water got thoroughly wetted.

This Tzilacatzin had the warrior [rank] of Otomí, for which reason he wore the Otomí hairstyle, so he looked down on his enemies, even though they be Spaniards, thinking nothing of them. He inspired general fear. When our enemies saw Tzilacatzin, they would hunch down. They strove greatly to kill him, whether shooting him with iron bolts or with guns. But Tzilacatzin disguised himself in order not to be recognized. Sometimes he would put on [his own] device, with his lip pendant and his golden earplugs, and he would put on his shell necklace. He would go with his head uncovered, showing that he was an Otomí. But sometimes he put on only cotton upper armor and covered his forehead with a little narrow cloth. Sometimes to disguise himself he put on a feather hairpiece or wig, with eagle feathers tied at the back of the neck. This was the way in which those who threw people in the fire were attired; he went about looking like one of them, imitating them. He had golden arm bands on both sides, on both arms, shimmering, and he also had shining golden bands on the calves of his legs.

Thirty-fifth chapter, where it is told how the Mexica took captives again—according to the count of the Spaniards they captured, there were fifty-three, as well as many Tlaxcalans and people of Tetzcoco, Chalco, and Xochimilco—and how they killed all of them before their former gods.

And at this point they let loose with all the warriors who had been crouching there; they came out and chased [the Spaniards] in the passageways, and when the Spaniards saw it they [the Mexica] seemed to be intoxicated. Then captives were taken. Many Tlaxcalans, and people of Acolhuacan, Chalco, Xochimilco, etc., were captured. A great abundance were captured and killed. They made the Spaniards and all the others go right into the water. And the road became very slippery; one could no longer walk on it, but would slip and slide. . . .

Then they took the captives to Yacacolco, hurrying them along, going along herding their captives together. Some went weeping, some singing, some went shouting while hitting their hands against their mouths. When they got them to Yacacolco, they lined them all up. Each one went to the altar platform, where the sacrifice was performed. The Spaniards went first, going in the lead; the people of all the different altepetl just followed, coming last. And when the sacrifice was over, they strung the Spaniards' heads on poles [on the skull rack or *tzompantli*]; they also strung up the horses' heads. They placed them below, and the Spaniards' heads were above them, strung up facing east. But they did not string up the heads of all the various [other] people from far away. There were fifty-three of the Spaniards they captured, along with four horses.

Figure 11. *Valiant Soldiers from Tlatelolco.*

Fray Bernardino de Sahagún, *The Florentine Codex: Historia general de las cosas de Nueva España*, Libro 12, f.61, 1577.

Nevertheless, watch was kept everywhere, and there was fighting. They did not stop keeping watch because of [what had happened]. The people of Xochimilco went about in boats surrounding us on all sides; there were deaths and captives taken on both sides.

And all the common people suffered greatly. There was famine; many died of hunger. They no longer drank good, pure water, but the water they drank was salty. Many people died of it, and because of it many got dysentery and died. Everything was eaten: lizards, swallows, maize straw, grass that grows on salt flats. And they chewed at colorin wood, glue flowers, plaster, leather, and deerskin, which they roasted, baked, and toasted so that they could eat them, and they ground up medicinal herbs and adobe bricks. There had never been the like of such suffering. The siege was frightening, and great numbers died of hunger. And bit by bit they came pressing us back against the wall, herding us together. . . .

Thirty-ninth chapter, where it is said how when [the Spaniards] had forced the Mexica to the very wall, there appeared and was seen a bloodcolored fire that seemed to come from the sky. It appeared like a great blazing coal as it came.

When night came, it rained and sprinkled off and on. It was very dark when a fire appeared. It looked and appeared as if it was coming from the sky, like a whirlwind. It went spinning around and around, turning on itself; as it went it seemed to explode into coals, some large, some small, some just like sparks. It seemed to take on the aspect of a "wind-axe." It sputtered, crackled, and snapped. It circled the walls at the water, heading toward Coyonacazco, then it went into the midst of the water and disappeared there. No one struck his hand against his mouth, no one uttered a sound.

And the next day, again nothing happened. Everyone just lay still, and so did our enemies. And the Captain was looking down from a rooftop in Amaxac, the roof of Aztahuatzin. From a varicolored canopy he was looking out at the people. The Spaniards crowded about him, consulting with one another.

And Quauhtemoctzin and the other rulers—. . . the Achcauhtli Teuctlamacazqui [chief lordly priest], and then the rulers of Tlatelolco . . . all of them rulers were gathered at Tolmayeccan consulting about what was to be done, what our tribute duty should be, and how we should submit to them.

Then they took Quauhtemoctzin in a boat. In it were only two people accompanying him, going with him: Tepotzitoloc, a seasoned warrior, and Iaztachimal, Quauhtemoctzin's page, with one person who poled them along, named Cenyaotl. When they were about to take Quauhtemoctzin, all the people wept, saying, "There goes the lord Quauhtemoctzin, going to give himself to the gods, the Spaniards."

Fortieth chapter, where it is said how the Tlatelolca and Tenochca and their ruler submitted to the Spaniards, and what happened when they were among them.

And when they had gotten him there and put him on land, all the Spaniards were waiting. They came to take him; the Spaniards grasped him by the hand, took him up to the roof, and stood him before the Captain, the war leader. When they stood him before him, he looked at Quauhtemoctzin, took a good look at him, stroked his hair; then they seated him next to him. And they fired off the guns; they hit no one, but they aimed over the people, the [shots] just went over their heads. Then they took a [cannon], put it in a boat, and took it to the home of Coyohuehuetzin. When they got there, they took it up on the roof. Then again they killed people; many died there. But [the Mexica] just fled, and the war came to an end.

Then everyone shouted, saying, "It's over! Let everyone leave! Go eat greens!" When they heard this, the people departed; they just went into the water. But when they went out on the highway, again they killed some people, which angered the Spaniards; a few of them were carrying their shields and war clubs. Those who lived in houses went straight to Amaxac, where the road forks. There the people divided, some going toward Tepeyacac, some toward Xoxohuiltitlan, some toward Nonoalco. But no one went toward Xoloco and Maçatzintamalco.

And all who lived in boats and on platforms [in the water] and those at Tolmayeccan just went into the water. The water came to the stomachs of some, to the chests of others, to the necks of others, and some sank entirely into the deep water. The little children were carried on people's backs. There was a general wail; but some rejoicing and amusing themselves as they went along the road. Most of the owners of boats left at night, though some left by day. They seemed to knock against one another as they went.

And along every stretch [of road] the Spaniards took things from people by force. They were looking for gold; they cared nothing for green-stone, precious feathers, or turquoise. They looked everywhere with the women, on their abdomens, under their skirts. And they looked everywhere with the men, under their loincloths and in their mouths. And [the Spaniards] took, picked out the beautiful women, with yellow bodies. And how some women got loose was that they covered their faces with mud and put on ragged blouses and skirts, clothing themselves in rags. And some men were picked out, those who were strong and in the prime of life, and those who were barely youths, to run errands for them and be their errand boys, called their *tlamacazque* [priests, acolytes]. Then they burned some of them on the mouth [branded them]; some they branded on the cheeks, some on the mouth.

And when the weapons were laid down and we collapsed, the year count was Three House, and the day count was One Serpent. . . .

28

BERNAL DÍAZ

From *The True History of the Conquest of New Spain*

In the final siege Cortés divided his forces into separate armies commanded by himself and his captains, Pedro de Alvarado, Cristóbal de Olid, and Gonzalo de Sandoval. Bernal Díaz was in Alvarado's camp, and so in this excerpt he often had to write based on what he heard rather than what he saw. Included here is his description of some of the Spanish captains followed by the operations of the forces from the viewpoint of the common soldier involved in the bitter fighting of the final stages.

. . . I wish now to record the age and appearance of Don Pedro de Alvarado, who was Commander of Santiago and Adelantado and Governor of Guatemala, Honduras, and Chiapa. He was about thirty-four years old when he came here, of good size, and well proportioned, with a very cheerful countenance and a winning smile, and because he was so handsome the Mexican Indians gave him the name of Tonatio, which means the Sun. He was very active and a good horseman, and above all was very frankhearted and a good talker, and he was very neat in his attire but with rich and costly clothes. He wore a small gold chain round his neck with a jewel, and a ring with a good diamond. As I have already stated where he died and other things about him, I will say no more here. . . .

Bernal Díaz del Castillo, *The True History of the Conquest of New Spain,* trans. Alfred P. Maudslay, 2d series (London: Printed for the Hakluyt Society, 1908), 116–18, 128–30, 148–52, 179–84, 252–55.

Captain Gonzalo de Sandoval was a very valiant Captain, and was about twenty-four years of age when he came here; he was Chief Alguacil of New Spain and for a matter of ten months was Governor of New Spain together with the Treasurer, Alonso de Estrada. He was not very tall but was very well made and robust, with a broad and deep chest, as were his shoulders. He was somewhat bowlegged, and was a very good horseman. His countenance tended towards the coarse, and his chestnut hair and beard were rather curly. His voice was not very clear, but slightly hesitating and lisping, more or less so. He was not a man of letters but of good average knowledge, nor was he covetous of anything but to be of good repute and act like a good and valiant Captain. In the wars which we waged in New Spain he always showed consideration for the soldiers who appeared to him to be behaving like men, and he protected and helped them. He was not a man to wear rich apparel but was always plainly clad. He owned the best horse, the best galloper and most easily turned to one side or the other, and they said that its like had never been seen in Castile or elsewhere. It was a chestnut with a star on its forehead and a white stocking on its near hind leg. It was named Motilla, and now when men dispute about good horses it is the custom to say in proof of excellence, "It is as good as was Motilla." I must stop talking about horses and say about this valiant Captain that he died in the town of Palos [back in Spain].

. . . As Cortés and all our captains and soldiers understood that without the launches [brigantines] we could not advance along the causeways to fight [our way] to Mexico, he sent four of them to Pedro de Alvarado,* and he left six at his own camp (which was that of Cristóbal de Olid) and he sent two launches to Gonzalo de Sandoval at the Tepeaquilla Causeway, and he ordered the smallest one not to be sent any more on the lake lest the canoes should upset it, for it was of small burden, and he ordered the people and sailors that were in it to be distributed among the other twelve, for there were already twenty men badly wounded among those who manned them.

When we saw ourselves reinforced with these launches in our camp at Tacuba Pedro de Alvarado ordered two of them to go on one side of the causeway and two on the other side, and we began to fight very successfully, for the launches vanquished the canoes which were wont to attack us from the water, and so we had an opportunity to capture several bridges and barricades, and while we were fighting, so numerous

*Cortés had broken a way through the Iztapalapa Causeway so that the ships could pass to the west side.

were the stones from the slings and the javelins and arrows that they shot at us that although all the soldiers were well protected by armor they were injured and wounded, and not until night parted us did we cease contending and fighting.

I wish to say that from time to time the Mexicans changed about and relieved their squadrons [as we could tell] by the devices and distinguishing marks on their armor. Then, as to the launches, they were checked by the darts, arrows and stones with which they were attacked from the azoteas which fell thicker than hail, and I do not know how to describe it here nor would anyone be able to understand it except those who were present, for they were more numerous than hail stones, and quickly covered the causeway. Then, whenever we left a bridge or barricade unguarded after having captured it with much labor, they would retake and deepen it that same night, and construct stronger defenses and even make hidden pits in the water, so that the next day when we were fighting, and it was time for us to retire, we should get entangled [among the defenses] and fall into the pits and they would be able to vanquish us from their canoes, for they had also got ready many canoes for the purpose, stationed in places where our launches could not see them, so that when we were in distress in the pits some [were prepared] to fall upon us by land, and others by water. To prevent the launches from coming to our assistance, they had fixed many stakes hidden in the water so that they should get impaled on them.

In this way we fought every day, I have already said before that the cavalry were of little use on the causeways for if they charged or gave chase to the squadrons that fought with us the Mexicans at once threw themselves into the water, and other squadrons were posted behind breastworks, which they had raised on the causeway, waiting [for the horsemen] with long lances or scythes made very long with the arms captured at the time of the great defeat which they inflicted on us in Mexico. With these lances and great showers of arrows and javelins shot from the lake they wounded and killed the horses before the horsemen could do damage to the enemy. In addition to this those who owned horses did not want to risk them, for at that time a horse cost eight hundred pesos and some even cost more than a thousand, and they could accomplish nothing to speak of, as they could overtake very few of the enemy on the causeway.

. . . I want to say that at this time the Mexicans were quite close to us as we kept watch, and they too had their sentinels and changed them in watches, and it was in this way; they lighted great fires that burned all night through, but those who were on guard stood away from the fires and from afar we were not able to distinguish them, and although on account of the brightness of the wood that was always burning we could not see the Indians who were watching, yet we could always tell when they were changing guard, for then they came to feed the fire. On many nights, as it rained heavily at that season it happened that their fire was put out, and they rekindled it without making any noise nor a word spoken among them, for they understood one another by means of whistles.

I wish to say that very often our musketeers and crossbowmen when we knew that they [the enemy] were going to change guard threw stones and shot arrows at a venture at groups of them, but they did them no harm, because they were in a place which even if we had wished to get at them in the night we should not have been able to reach them on account of another great and very deep opening of the canal, which they had made by hand and of the barricades and walls they had raised, and they also shot at us volleys of javelins and arrows.

Let us stop speaking about keeping watch and say how each day we advanced along the causeway fighting in the most regular order and we captured the opening, which I have spoken of, where they kept guard; but such was the multitude of the enemy who came against us every day, and the javelins, arrows and stones they shot, that they wounded us all, although we proceeded with the greatest caution and were well armored.

Then after having passed all the day fighting, when it was growing late and there was no opportunity for a further advance, only of turning back in retreat, that would be the [very] time they held many squadrons in readiness, believing that with the great energy of their attacks as we retired, they would be able to rout us, for they came on as fierce as tigers and fought us hand to hand. As soon as we found out this plan of theirs, we made the following arrangement for retreating; the first thing we did was to get our friends the Tlaxcalans off the causeway, for as they were very numerous, they longed with our support to get to blows with the Mexicans, and as the Mexicans were cunning, they wished nothing better than to see us entangled with our friends, thus they made fierce attacks on us from two or three directions, so as to enclose us in the middle and intercept some of us, and, with the many Tlaxcalans who embarrassed us, prevent us from fighting on all sides, and this was the reason that we got them [the Tlaxcalans] off the causeway to where we could place them in safety. As soon as we found ourselves no longer hampered by them, we retreated to our camp without turning our backs, but always facing the enemy, some of the crossbowmen and musketeers shooting and others loading, and with our four launches in the lake, two on each side of the causeway, protecting us against the fleets of canoes and the many stones from the azoteas and houses which were destined to be pulled down. Yet with all this caution every one of us ran great personal risk until we reached our ranchos. There we at once treated our wounds with oil and bandaged them with native cloth, and supped on the tortillas they had brought us from Tacuba, and on herbs, and such as had them, on Tunas. Then we at once mounted guard at the water-opening which I have mentioned, and the next morning we promptly returned to fight, for we could do nothing else, for however early in the morning it might be, battalions of the enemy were there ready to attack us, and they even reached our camp and shouted abuse at us, and in such manner we underwent our hardships. . . .

. . . At that time many companies of Mexicans came to the causeway and wounded the horsemen as well as all of us, and they gave Sandoval a good blow with a stone in the face. Then Pedro de Alvarado and other horsemen went to his assistance. As so many squadrons approached I and twenty other soldiers faced them, and Sandoval ordered us to retreat little by little so that they should not kill the horses, and because we did not retreat as quickly as he wished he said to us with fury "Do you wish that through your selfishness they should kill me and all these horsemen? For the love of me, dear brothers, do fall back," at that moment the enemy again wounded him and his horse. Just then we cleared our allies off the causeway, and [we retreated] little by little keeping our faces [to the enemy] and not turning our backs, as though to form a dam. Some of the crossbowmen and musketeers were shooting and others loading their guns for they did not fire them off all together, and the horsemen made charges, and Pedro Moreno Medrano, already mentioned by me, loaded and fired his cannon, yet, notwithstanding the number of Mexicans that the balls were sweeping away, we could not fend them off, on the contrary they kept on following us thinking that this very night they would carry us off to be sacrificed.

When we had retreated near to our quarters and had already crossed a great opening where there was much water, the arrows, javelins and stones could no longer reach us. Sandoval, Francisco de Lugo and Andrés de Tápia were standing with Pedro de Alvarado each one relating what had happened to him and what Cortés had ordered, when again there was sounded the dismal drum of Huichilobos and many other shells and horns and things like trumpets and the sound of them all was terrifying, and we all looked towards the lofty Cue where they were being sounded, and saw that our comrades whom they had captured when they defeated Cortés were being carried by force up the steps, and they were taking them to be sacrificed. When they got them up to a small square in [front of] the oratory, where their accursed idols are kept, we saw them place plumes on the heads of many of them and with things like fans [in their hands?] they forced them to dance before Huichilobos, and after they had danced they immediately placed them on their backs on some rather narrow stones which had been prepared as [places for] sacrifice, and with stone knives they sawed open their chests and drew out their palpitating hearts and offered them to the idols that were there, and they kicked the bodies down the steps, and Indian butchers who were waiting below cut off the arms and feet and flayed [the skin off] the faces, and prepared it afterwards like glove leather with the beards on, and kept those for the festivals when they celebrated drunken orgies, and the flesh they ate in chilmole [*chilmolli*]. In the same way they sacrificed all the others and ate the legs and arms and offered the hearts and blood to their idols, as I have said, and the bodies, that is their entrails and feet, they threw to the tigers and lions which they kept in the house of the carnivores which I have spoken about in an earlier chapter.

When we saw those cruelties all of us in our camp and Pedro de Alvarado and Gonzalo de Sandoval and all the other captains (let the interested readers who peruse this, note what ills we suffered from them [the Mexicans]) said the one to the other "thank God that they are not carrying me off to day to be sacrificed."

. . . Then, at the moment that they were making the sacrifices, great squadrons of Mexicans fell on us suddenly and gave us plenty to do on all sides and neither in one way or the other could we prevail against them.

And they cried: — "Look, that is the way in which you will all have to die, for our gods have promised it to us many times." Then the words and threats which they said to our friends the Tlaxcalans were so injurious and evil that they disheartened them, and they threw them roasted legs of Indians and the arms of our soldiers and cried to them: — "Eat of the flesh of these Teules and of your brothers for we are already glutted with it, and you can stuff yourselves with this which is over, and observe that as for the houses which you have destroyed, we shall have to bring you to rebuild them much better with white stone and well worked masonry, so go on helping the Teules, for you will see them all sacrificed."

There was another thing that Guatemoc ordered to be done when he won that victory, he sent to all the towns of our allies and friends and to their relations, the hands and feet of our soldiers and the flayed faces with the beards, and the heads of the horses that they had killed, and he sent word that more than half of us were dead and he would soon finish us off, and he told them to give up their friendship [with us] and come to Mexico and if they did not give it up promptly, he would come and destroy them, and he sent to tell them many other things to induce them to leave our camp and desert us, and then we should be killed by his hands.

As they still went on attacking us both by day and by night, all of us in our camp kept watch together, Gonzalo de Sandoval and Pedro de Alvarado and the other captains keeping us company during our watch, and although during the night great companies of warriors came [against us] we withstood them. Both by day and night half the horsemen remained in Tacuba and the other half were on the causeway.

There was another greater evil that they did us; no matter how carefully we had filled in [the water spaces] since we advanced along the causeway, they returned and opened them all and constructed barricades stronger than before. Then our friends of the cities of the lake who had again accepted our friendship and had come to aid us with their canoes believed that they "came to gather wool and went back shorn" for many of them lost their lives and many more returned wounded, and they lost more than half of the canoes they had brought with them, but, even with all this, thenceforward they did not help the Mexicans, for they were hostile to them, but they carefully watched events as they happened. . . .

As I have said Cortés not only saw that the catapult was useless but was angry with the soldier who advised him to have it made, and in consequence of Guatemoc and his Captains not wishing for peace of any sort, he ordered Gonzalo de Sandoval to invade that part of the City where Guatemoc had taken refuge with all the flower of his Captains and the most distinguished persons that were in Mexico, and he ordered him not to kill or wound any Indians unless they should attack him, and even if they did attack him, he was only to defend himself and not do them any other harm, but he should destroy their houses and the many defenses they had erected in the lake. Cortés ascended the great Cue of Tlatelolco to see how Sandoval advanced with the launches, and at that time Pedro de Alvarado, Francisco Verdugo, Luis Marin and other soldiers were there with Cortés.

Sandoval advanced with great ardor upon the place where the Houses of Guatemoc stood, and when Guatemoc saw himself surrounded, he was afraid that they would capture him or kill him, and he had got ready fifty great piraguas [canoes] with good rowers so that when he saw himself hard pressed he could save himself by going to hide in some reed beds and get from thence to land and hide himself in another town, and those were the instructions he had given his captains and the persons of most importance who were with him in that fortified part of the city, so that they should do the same.

When they saw that the launches were getting among the houses they embarked in the fifty canoes, and they had already placed [on board] the property and gold and jewels of Guatemoc and all his family and women, and he had embarked himself and shot out into the lake ahead, accompanied by many Captains. As many other canoes set out at the same time, the lake was full of them, and Sandoval quickly received the news that Guatemoc was fleeing, and ordered all the launches to stop destroying the houses and fortifications and follow the flight of the canoes, and to have a care that they kept track of where Guatemoc was going, and not to molest him or do him any injury but try to capture him without using violence.

As a certain García Holguín a friend of Sandoval, was captain of a launch which was very fast and a good sailor and was manned by good rowers Sandoval ordered him to follow in the direction in which they told him that Guatemoc was fleeing with his great piraguas, and instructed him not to do him [Guatemoc] any injury whatever beyond capturing him in case he should overtake him, and Sandoval went in another direction with other launches which kept him company. It pleased our Lord God that García Holguín should overtake the canoes and piraguas in which Guatemoc was travelling, and from the style and the awnings and the seat he was using he knew that it was Guatemoc the great Lord of Mexico, and he made signals for them to stop, but they would not stop, so he made as though he were going to discharge muskets and crossbows. When Guatemoc saw that, he was afraid and said "Do not shoot, I am the king of this City and they call me Guatemoc, and what I ask of you is not to disturb my things that I am taking with me nor my wife nor my relations, but carry me at once to Malinche." When Holguín heard him he was greatly delighted, and with much respect he embraced him and placed him in the launch, him and his wife and about thirty chieftains and seated him in the poop on some mats and cloths, and gave him to eat of the food that he had brought with him, and he touched nothing whatever in the canoes that carried his [Guatemoc's] property but brought it along with the launch.

By this time Gonzalo de Sandoval had ordered all the launches to assemble together, and he knew that Holguín had captured Guatemoc and was carrying him to Cortés, and when he heard it he told the rowers on board his launch to make all the speed possible and he overtook Holguín and claimed the prisoner, and Holguín would not give him up and said that he had captured him and not Sandoval, and Sandoval replied that that was true, but that he was the Captain General of the launches, and that García Holguín sailed under his command and banner, and it was because he was his friend and his launch the fastest that he had ordered him to follow after Guatemoc, to capture him, and that to him as his General he must give up his prisoner. Still Holguín contended that he did not wish to do so, and at that moment another launch went in great haste to Cortés (who was very close by in Tlatelolco, watching from the top of the Cue how Sandoval was advancing) to demand a reward for the good news, and they told Cortés of the dispute which Sandoval was having with Holguín over the capture of the prisoner. When Cortés knew of it he at once dispatched Captain Luis Marin and Francisco de Verdugo to summon Sandoval and Holguín to come as they were in their launches without further discussion, and to bring Guatemoc and his wife and family with all [signs of] respect, and that he would settle whose was the prisoner and to whom was due the honor of it [the capture].

While they were bringing him, Cortés ordered a guest chamber to be prepared as well as could be done at the time, with mats and cloths and seats, and a good supply of the food which Cortés had reserved for himself. Sandoval and Holguín soon arrived with Guatemoc, and the two captains between them led him up to Cortés, and when he came in front of him he paid him great respect, and Cortés embraced Guatemoc with delight, and was very affectionate to him and his captains. Then Guatemoc said to Cortés "Señor Malinche, I have surely done my duty in defense of my City, and I can do no more and I come by force and a prisoner into your presence and into your power, take that dagger that you have in your belt and kill me at once with it" and when he said this he wept tears and sobbed and other great Lords whom he had brought with him also wept. Cortés answered him through Doña Marina and Aguilar our interpreters, very affectionately, that he esteemed him all the more for having been so brave as to defend the City, and he was deserving of no blame, on the contrary [this circumstance] must be more in his favor than otherwise.

What he wished was that he [Guatemoc] had made peace of his own free will before the city had been so far destroyed, and so many of his Mexicans had died, but now, that both had happened there was no help for it and it could not be mended, let his spirit and the spirit of his Captains take rest, and he should rule in Mexico and over his provinces as he did before. Then Guatemoc and his Captains said that they accepted his favor, and Cortés asked after his wife and other great ladies, the wives of other Captains who, he had been told, had come with Guatemoc. Guatemoc himself answered and said that he had begged Gonzalo de Sandoval and Garcia Holguin that they might remain in the canoes while he came to see what orders Malinche gave them. Cortés at once sent for them and ordered them all to be given of the best that at that time there was in the camp to eat, and as it was late and was beginning to rain, Cortés arranged for them to go to Coyoacan, and took Guatemoc and all his family and household and many chieftains with him and he ordered Pedro de Alvarado, Gonzalo de Sandoval and the other captains each to go to his own quarters and camp, and we went to Tacuba, Sandoval to Tepeaquilla and Cortés to Coyoacan. Guatemoc and his captains were captured on the thirteenth day of August at the time of vespers on the day of Señor San Hipólito in the year one thousand five hundred and twenty-one, thanks to our Lord Jesus Christ and Our Lady the Virgin Santa Maria, His Blessed Mother, Amen.

It rained and thundered and lightning flashed that afternoon and up to midnight heavier rain fell than usual. After Guatemoc had been captured all the soldiers turned as deaf as if some one had stood shouting from the top of a belfry with many bells clanging and in the midst of their ringing all of a sudden they had ceased to sound. I say this purposely, for during all the ninety-three days that we were besieging this city, both by night and day, some of the Mexican Captains kept on uttering so many shouts and yells, whilst they were mustering the squadrons and warriors who were to fight on the causeway, and others were calling out to those in the canoes who were to fight with the launches, and with us on the bridges, again others to those driving in piles and opening and deepening the water openings and bridges and making breastworks, or those who were making javelins and arrows, or to the women preparing rounded stones to hurl from the slings, while from the oratories and towers of the Idols, the accursed drums, trumpets and mournful kettledrums never ceased sounding, and in this way both by night and by day, there was such a great din that we could not hear one another. On the capture of Guatemoc, the shouts and all the clamor ceased, and it is for this reason I have said that up to then we seemed to be standing in a belfry. . . .

29

Nahua Poetry

From the *Cantares Mexicanos*

This selection includes some Nahua poetry from the Cantares mexicanos, *which bemoans the loss of Tenochtitlan. These elegies serve as a fitting conclusion to the tragedy of the conquest and the loss it represented.*

THE FALL OF TENOCHTITLAN

Our cries of grief rise up
and our tears rain down,
for Tlatelolco is lost.
The Aztecs are fleeing across the lake;
They are running away like women.

How can we save our homes, my people?
The Aztecs are deserting the city:
the city is in flames, and all
is darkness and destruction.

Motelchiuhtzin the Huiznahuacatl,
Tlacotzin the Tlailotlacatl,
Oquitzin the Tlacatecuhtli
are greeted with tears.

Weep, my people:
know that with these disasters
we have lost the Mexican nation.
The water has turned bitter,
our food is bitter!
These are the acts of the Giver of Life....

The Aztecs are besieged in the city;
the Tlatelolcas are besieged in the city!
The walls are black,
the air is black with smoke,

Miguel León-Portilla, *The Broken Spears: The Aztec Account of the Conquest of Mexico*, 2nd ed. (Boston: Beacon Press, 1992), 71–78, 80–81.

the guns flash in the darkness.
They have captured Cuauhtemoc;
they have captured the princes of Mexico.

The Aztecs are besieged in the city;
the Tlatelolcas are besieged in the city!

After nine days, they were taken to Coyoacan:
Cuauhtemoc, Coanacoch, Tetlepanquetzaltzin.
The kings are prisoners now,

Tlacotzin consoled them:
"Oh my nephews, take heart!
The kings are prisoners now;
They are bound with chains."

The king Cuauhtemoc replied:
"Oh my nephew, you are a prisoner;
they, have bound you in irons,

"But who is that at the side of the Captain-General
Ah, it is Doña Isabel, my little niece!
Ah, it is true: the kings are prisoners now!

"You will be a slave and belong to another:
the collar will be fashioned in Coyoacan,
where the quetzal feathers will be woven.
Ah, it is Doña Isabel, my little niece.
Ah, it is true: the kings are prisoners now!"

FLOWERS AND SONGS OF SORROW

Nothing but flowers and songs of sorrow
are left in Mexico and Tlatelolco,
where once we saw warriors and wise men.

We know it is true
that we must perish,
for we are mortal men.
You, the Giver of Life,
You have ordained it.

We wander here and there
in our desolate poverty.

We are mortal men.
We have seen bloodshed and pain
where once we saw beauty and valor.

We are crushed to the ground;
we lie in ruins.
There is nothing but grief and suffering
in Mexico and Tlatelolco,
where once we saw beauty and valor.

Have you grown weary of your servants?
Are you angry with your servants,
O Giver of Life?

8

Aftermath: Tradition and Transformation

The military victory and defeat of the Mexica was one of a number of wars that took place in the Americas during the sixteenth century. The fall of Tenochtitlan signaled both an end and a beginning. Cortés decided to make the city, now in ruins, the capital of Spanish government. From there expeditions were sent out to pacify or take control of regions formerly under the Mexica and also beyond to other parts of present-day Mexico and Central America. Tlaxcalans, as well as troops from other city-states, were co-conquistadors in these ventures, supplying large numbers of the fighting men. The Zapotecs, the Maya, and other Indigenous societies resisted Spanish claims to sovereignty, but within a decade most of central Mexico and large parts of the rest of what the crown called New Spain were under colonial governance, though to varying degrees of bureaucratic control.

The Spaniards set about creating institutions to establish an ordered Christian society and to make the new provinces or kingdoms profitable to the Spanish king and to the victors as "colonies," although that word was never used at the time. *Encomiendas*, grants of Indigenous laborers or tribute, were awarded to many conquistadors despite some royal objections. Disputes over these grants and their effects plagued colonial society for several generations. On the religious front, the crown dispatched groups of missionaries starting in 1524; first the Franciscans and then the Dominicans and Augustinians took up the task of proselytization and conversion of the Indigenous peoples. In 1528 a bishop, Juan de Zumárraga, was appointed to organize the secular church (the "regular" or missionary orders remained separate). In terms of governance, a royal court of appeals or high court (*audiencia*) was established in 1528; royal fiscal officers set up a system of taxes and tribute; and in 1535 the first viceroy, the energetic and able Antonio de Mendoza, arrived to begin his service as the direct royal representative and chief administrator.

The main personalities of the conquest suffered various fates. Cortés executed Cuauhtémoc, the last independent Mexica leader, in 1525, accused of allegedly fomenting rebellion. Bernal Díaz ended his days in 1584 as a respected if not very wealthy resident of a town in Guatemala where he had settled. Doña Marina (Malintzin), who had borne Cortés a son, eventually married another conquistador, Juan Jaramillo, and had a number of children, including a daughter who later sued to inherit a larger part of her mother's sizeable estate. A short excerpt from this case is included in this chapter, as well as a depiction from the *Florentine Codex* of Doña Marina's work as translator and advisor.

Cortés was amply rewarded. In 1529, Emperor Charles V made him a marquis (*Marqués del Valle*) — a noble title and grant that gave him the control of extensive lands and Indigenous vassals and that also made him fabulously wealthy. His coat of arms made chilling reference to his victories: "And in the bottom right [of the shield], you may depict the city of Tenustitlan, built over water, in memory of you having subjugated the city by force of arms to our Lordship."[1] In his remaining years, Cortés was often in conflict with the king over the extent of his powers and authority in New Spain. Ruthless men of private ambition were ideal for winning wars but made kings uneasy thereafter. Cortés died near Seville in 1547. By the 1550s and 1560s, the generation of the conquest was dying off and their legacy was still in the process of definition and transformation.

Nahua society proved remarkably resilient and adaptable.[2] Indigenous communities adapted to Spanish institutions, and in some ways life continued on much as before. The Nahua *altepetl* organization and the old rank distinctions and tribute arrangements were adapted to meet Spanish bureaucratic demands, and it served colonial purposes to leave them intact.

The conversion of Indigenous peoples to Christianity justified colonialism from the very beginning. The first missionaries embarked on what they considered to be a great utopian effort. This religious zeal led to a great program of missionary activity and church construction, and also to the study of Indigenous language and culture as an adjunct to this effort. The work of Bernardino de Sahagún is an outstanding example

---

[1]A. Paz y Meliá, *Nobiliario de conquistadores de Indias* (Madrid: Impr. de M. Tello, 1892), 31–32.

[2]The most comprehensive work on the Nahua world after contact is James Lockhart, *The Nahuas after the Conquest: A Social and Cultural History of the Indians of Central Mexico, Sixteenth through Eighteenth Centuries* (Stanford University Press, 1992). Lockhart trained a whole generation of ethnohistorians who have fundamentally changed how we understand Nahua society in the post-contact period.

of the result. In time, the euphoria of the early mass conversions and the elimination of the old imperial cults and temple pyramids eventually gave way to an understanding that the victories over the minds and hearts of men and women were neither easy nor clearly defined.

Still another conquest, the biological one, accompanied and transformed these processes. The horrific impact of epidemic disease, already apparent during the final siege of Tenochtitlan, catastrophically decimated native populations, thereby upsetting existing social and political arrangements as members of the ruling dynasties perished and the number of tributaries shrank. The "great dying" in the sixteenth century, especially after the great plague of 1576–81, eventually contributed to a flagging of missionary vigor and perhaps led converts to question the new religion.

Meanwhile, as the native population contracted, the growth of Spanish industries, including sugar plantations and textile production, required an influx of labor, which colonists acquired through the Atlantic slave trade, which delivered hundreds of thousands of enslaved Africans to Mexico.[3] Other arrivals, European livestock and flora, changed diets and agricultural practices and transformed Mexico's ecosystem, at times producing negative consequences. Worse still was the devastation of silver mining, which degraded the environment with broad social impacts.[4]

Accompanying all these "conquests" was a growing social interaction between Spaniards and Indigenous peoples, more intense to be sure in the cities and large towns where Europeans concentrated, but expanding continually into many regions and social situations. Generations of children of mixed ancestry changed the face of Mexico, now complicated by people of varied origins, identities, and cultures, as well as by an ever more complicated social hierarchy. A great question that remains in Mexican history is how, at the local level, this process of social transformation was worked out as people created new identities and made new affiliations in a context of continuing traditions of ethnic, linguistic, and social practices.

The documents in this chapter reveal how contemporaries perceived the process of change and transformation. The excerpt from

[3]For this historiography, see Tatiana Seijas and Pablo Miguel Sierra Silva, "The Persistence of the Slave Market in Seventeenth-Century Central Mexico," *Slavery & Abolition: A Journal of Slave and Post-Slave Studies 37*, no. 2 (2016).

[4]Daviken Studnicki-Gizbert and David Schecter, "The Environmental Dynamics of a Colonial Fuel-Rush: Silver Mining and Deforestation in New Spain, 1522 to 1810," *Environmental History* 15, no. 1 (2010).

Bernal Díaz attempts to justify the conquest by extoling indigenous artistry and industry. The materials on Doña Marina/Malintzin reveal how a number of native people positioned themselves to benefit economically from the change in regime. As examples of the kinds of documents produced by indigenous peoples after the fall of the Mexica Empire, we include selections from the *Codex Mendoza, Relaciones geográficas*, the *Mapa Uppsala*, and the *Huejotzingo Census*. These sources illustrate how Indigenous peoples adapted new skills like the command of alphabetic writing for their own communal and personal interests, as well as to shape the memory of the events of the fall of Tenochtitlan and Spanish colonization. The chapter ends with two variant versions of the death of Cuauhtémoc, offering Nahua (from the *Codex Chimalpahin*) and Maya perspectives, which demonstrate the selective and creative nature of writing history.

30

BERNAL DÍAZ

From *The True History of the Conquest of New Spain*

While Bernal Díaz was often candid about his desire for wealth and women, he like many other conquistadors sought to justify his actions by his role in the spreading of Christianity. In this passage he reviews the impact of the conquest on everyday life and praises Indians for their acquisition of European culture. From his description, little appears of the continuation of Indigenous traditions and beliefs or the oppression of the colonial regime.

After getting rid of the idolatries and all the evil vices they practiced, it pleased our Lord god that with his holy aid and with the good fortunes and the holy Christianity of our most Christian Emperor Don Carlos . . . there were baptized, after we conquered the country, all,

Bernal Díaz del Castillo, *The True History of the Conquest of New Spain,* trans. Alfred P. Maudslay, 2d series (London: Printed for the Hakluyt Society, 1908), 265–70.

both men and women, and children who have since been born, whose souls formerly went, lost, to the Infernal regions. Now there are many and good monks of [the order of] Señor San Francisco and of Santo Domingo and of other Orders, who go among the pueblos preaching, and, when a child is of the age our holy Mother Church of Rome ordains, they baptize it.

Furthermore, through the holy sermons preached, the Holy Gospel is firmly planted in their hearts, and they go to Confession every year, and some of them, who have most knowledge of our holy faith, receive the Sacrament. In addition to this they have their Churches richly adorned with altars and all pertaining to the holy divine worship, with crosses and candlesticks and wax tapers and chalice and patens and silver plates, some large and some small, and censers all worked in silver. . . .

There is another good thing they do [namely] that both men, women and children, who are of the age to learn them, know all the holy prayers in their own languages and are obliged to know them. They have other good customs about their holy Christianity, that when they pass near a sacred altar or Cross they bow their heads with humility, bend their knees, and say the prayer "Our Father," which we Conquistadores have taught them, and they place lighted wax candles before the holy altars and crosses, for formerly they did not know how to use wax in making candles. . . .

Let us get on, and state how most of the Indian natives of these lands have successfully learned all the trades that there are among us in Castile, and have their shops of the trades, and artisans, and gain a living by it. There are gold and silver smiths, both of chased and of hollow work, and they are very excellent craftsman, also lapidaries and painters. Carvers also do most beautiful work with their delicate burins of iron, especially in carving jades, and in them depict all the phases of the holy passion of our Lord Redeemer and Savior Jesus Christ, such that, if one had not seen them, one would never believe that Indians had done. It seems in my judgment that the most renowned painter, such as was Apelles in ancient times, or in our times a certain Berruguete and Michaelangelo . . . , could not emulate with their most skilful pencils the works of art in jade, nor the reliquaries, which are executed by three Mexican Indian craftsmen of that trade, named Andrés de Aquino, Juan de la Cruz, and El Crespillo. In addition to this nearly all the sons of Chieftains are usually grammarians, and would have become expert, if the holy synod had not commanded them to abandon that which the very reverend Archbishop of Mexico had ordered to be done.

Many sons of Chieftains know how to read and write, and to compose books of plainchant, and there are craftsmen in weaving satin and taffeta and making woolen cloth. . . . They are carders, wool combers, and weavers in the same manner as there are in Segovia and in Cuenca, and others are hat makers and soap makers. There are only two crafts they have not been able to undertake, although they have tried: these are to make glass, and to become druggists, but I believe them to be so intelligent that they will acquire them very well. Some of them are surgeons and herbalists. They understand conjuring and working puppets and make very good guitars, indeed they were craftsmen by nature before we came to New Spain. Now they breed cattle of all sorts, and break in oxen, and plough the land, and sow wheat, and thresh harvest, and sell it, and make bread and biscuit, and they have planted their lands and hereditaments with all the trees and fruits which we have brought from Spain, and sell the fruit which they produce. They have planted so many trees that, because the peaches are not good for the health, and the banana plantations give them too much shade, they have cut and are cutting down many of them and putting in quinces and apples and pears, which they hold in higher esteem.

Let us go on, and I will speak of the laws which we have shown them how to guard and execute, and how every year they are to choose the Alcaldes ordinaries and Regidores, Notaries, Alguacils, Fiscals, and Mayordomos, and have their municipal houses (Cabildos) where they meet two days in the week, and they place doorkeepers in them, and give judgment and order debts to be paid which are owed by one to another. For some criminal acts they flog and chastise, and if it is for a death or something atrocious they remit it [the case] to the Governors, if there is no Royal Audiencia. According to what people, who know very well, have told me, in Tlaxcala, Texcoco, Cholula, Oaxaca and Tepeaca and in other great cities, when the Indians hold Court (Cabildo), Macebearers with gilt maces precede those who are Governors and Alcaldes (the same as the Viceroys of New Spain take with them), and justice is done with as much propriety and authority as among ourselves, and they appreciate and desire to know much of the laws of the kingdom.

In addition to this, many of the Caciques are rich, and possess horses, and bring good saddles with trappings, and ride abroad through the cities and towns and places where they are going for amusement, or of which they are natives, and bring Indians and pages to accompany them. In some pueblos, they even play at tilting with reeds and have bull fights, and they tilt at the ring, especially on Corpus Christi day or the day of San Juan or Señor Santiago . . . [M]any of them are horsemen, especially in a pueblo named Chiapa of the Indians, and, even those who are not Caciques, nearly all of them own horses, and some own herds of mares and mules, and use them to bring in firewood and maize and lime and other things of the kind which they sell in the Plazas, and many of them are carriers in the same way as we have in our Castile.

Not to waste more words, they carry on all trades very perfectly — and even know how to weave tapestry cloths.

I will stop talking further on this subject and will tell of many other grandeurs which, through us, there have been and still are in New Spain.

31

From the *Proof of the Faithful Service of Doña Marina (Malintzin) during the Conquest of New Spain*

In 1542, Doña Marina's daughter María Jaramillo and her husband Luis de Quesada initiated a judicial inquest in Mexico City regarding Malintzin's role in the fall of Tenochtitlan. This legal effort included gathering testimonies of numerous people who had known Doña Marina and witnessed her considerable political influence. The couple sought to garner validation from the crown of her social stature for their own economic ends, primarily to secure a greater share of Doña Marina's property, which included an encomienda *grant of Indian laborers and tribute from the town of Xilotepec. Doña Marina's husband (and María's father) Juan Jaramillo had disapproved of the marriage to Luis de Quesada and punished the couple by restricting their share of the estate in his will.*

Translation by T. Seijas. "Información de los méritos y servicios de doña Marina [Malintzin], india, mujer de Juan Jaramillo, que auxilió a Hernán Cortés y a su gente en la conquista de México, dándoles noticias fidedignas de lo que observaba dentro de la población, a fin de que les sirviese de gobierno." Archive of the Indies [AGI], Patronato 56 N.3 R.4 f.13, 34v.

*The excerpt below is from Marina's "Proof of Merits" (*Probanza de
meritos*) —a standardized colonial document employed by numerous participants in Spain's conquest campaigns to receive compensation for their good
service to the Spanish king. The format included a list of leading questions
for witnesses who were called upon to elaborate on the person's contributions. From the* Probanza's *questions and witnesses' answers, it is clear
that Doña Marina was widely remembered as a key player in orchestrating
the downfall of the Triple Alliance. Doña Marina and her descendants
benefited considerably from her efforts, illustrated by the fact that she rose in
social position from being an enslaved woman to a highly respected property
owner. Like Bernal Díaz's text, this kind of documentation speaks to the
importance for future generations—Spanish and Indian—of having participated in the collapse of the Mexica Empire to secure social and economic
standing in the new colonial order.*

Excerpt from *Probanza* Questionnaire

If [the witness] knows that because the said Doña Marina was a native
[*natural*] of this land at the time when the captain [Cortés] and Spaniards who accompanied him, industriously and with good judgment
towards warring Indians, who needed food with which to sustain the
army, that she was able to provide provisions, and that she did so many
times, and that Indians would give her the food and the she would bring
it back [to the camp] in order to share with everyone, and that it was
because of [her efforts] that Spaniards did not perish, and that the land
was afterwards won. . . .

Excerpt from Witness's Answers (Spanish Captain)

. . . It was almost through divine intervention that in order to conquer
New Spain everyone understood one another, which [made it possible]
to declare that God and King rule [this land]; and that the said Doña
Marina, [who was] very faithful and loyal to don Hernando Cortés and
the conquering Spaniards, had a talent for speaking with Indigenous
people and ways of making them understand that there was no way to
tame the Spaniards.

Figure 12. *Doña Marina/Malintzin as Interlocutor.*

This representation from the *Florentine Codex* portrays Doña Marina as Cortés's translator, political advisor, and cultural mediator. She stands at center, listening to Nahuatl and Spanish speakers and interpreting both languages to enable each side to understand the other. This affirmation of her importance is borne out in the testimonies of dozens of witnesses who described her efforts decades after the war.

Fray Bernardino de Sahagún, *The Florentine Codex: Historia general de las cosas de Nueva España*, Libro 12, f.47v, 1577.

32

Three Folios
From the *Codex Mendoza*

The Codex Mendoza, *commissioned by Viceroy Mendoza, was produced from 1541 to 1542 under the direction of Francisco Gualpuyogualcatl (Cuauhpoyouacatl), the head master of the painter's guild of Mexico City.*[1] *He and other Nahua scribes painted a history of the Mexica that included an explanation of their political system, social rankings, and various aspects of precontact culture, as well as a listing of tribute obligations* (Matrícula de Tributos). *The manuscript was sent to Spain but lost to French pirates. It eventually ended up in the hands of the English scholar Richard Hakluyt and is now housed at the Bodelain Library at Oxford University.*

This document, produced a generation after the fall of Tenochtitlan, displays the continuing usage of Nahua artistic conventions and the preservation of Mexica historical memory. The combination of the traditional figures with a Spanish gloss or commentary denotes the culturally mixed nature of the project. Included here are three folios. The first folio is a pictorial representation of the foundation of Tenochtitlan.[2] *The next folio is a portion of a tribute list; the glyphs for the subject towns are listed in a column along the left margin of the page, and then the tribute required of each is presented in a row across the page. The third folio records the duties of precontact priests and the rank of warriors.*

---

[1]An excellent English edition is Frances Berdan and Patricia Rieff Anawalt, eds., *The Codex Mendoza*, 4 vols. (Berkeley: University of California Press, 1992).

[2]For an art historical reading of this map, see Barbara E. Mundy, *The Death of Aztec Tenochtitlan, the Life of Mexico City* (Austin: University of Texas Press, 2015).

Codíce Mendoza, edición digital (México: INAH; Arqueología Mexicana, 2014). http://codicemendoza.inah.gob.mx/index.php?lang=english. *Codex Mendoza*, c.1541, located at the Bodleian Library, Oxford University.

The Foundation of Tenochtitlan.

At center is an eagle (associated with Huitzilopochtli) atop a prickly pear cactus, and below it is a shield and arrows that represent war. The two crossing lines representing canals separate the city into its four quarters or wards. The seated figures are the ten leaders of the original clans (*calpulli*); their leader Tenuch is the one painted black. The city is enclosed in a lake, which here is represented as a rectangular border. Below are two scenes of conquest of neighboring towns, shown by the traditional symbols of prisoners taken and temples burned. The representation of history and social organization is as important as place in this map.

Codíce Mendoza, f.2. *Codex Mendoza,* c.1541. Original at the Bodleian, Oxford University Library.

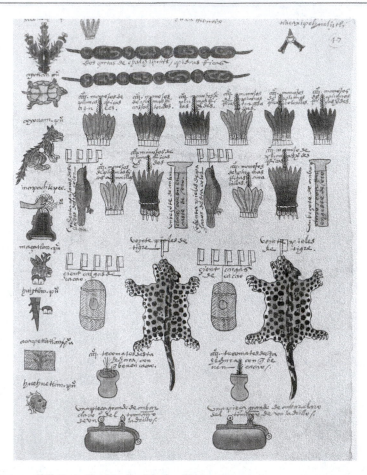

Inventory of Tribute Paid to the Mexica Emperor.

This folio enumerates the objects delivered by each tributary town, located today in southern Mexico and Guatemala.[3] From top to bottom these places are (with present-day locations): Xoconochco (Soconusco, Chiapas); Ayotlan (Ayutla, Guatemala); Coyoacan (Ayutla, Guatemala); Mapachtepec (Mapastepec, Chiapas); Maçatlan (Mazatán, Chiapas); Huiztlan (Huixtla, Chiapas); Acapetlatlan (Acapetahua, Chiapas); Huehuetlan (Huehuetán, Chiapas). *Codíce Mendoza, f.47. Codex Mendoza, c.1541.* Original at the Bodleian, Oxford University Library.

[3] For more information on these tributary cities and their identification in the Codex Mendoza, see Pedro Carrasco Pizana, *The Tenochca Empire of Ancient Mexico: The Triple Alliance of Tenochtitlan, Tetzcoco, and Tlacopan* (Norman: University of Oklahoma Press, 1999).

Caption continued to next pages

Caption continued from previous page

The combined listing of items paid in tribute every six months is as follows:
    Strings of green stones (chalchihuitl)
    Hundreds of handfuls of blue, green, red, and yellow feathers
    160 bird skins (turquoise and purple feathers)
    800 handfuls of rich quetzal feathers
    2 lip plugs of clear amber with gold settings
    200 loads of cacao beans
    40 jaguar skins
    800 gourd vessels for drinking cacao
    2 brick-sized pieces of clear amber.

The Work of Priests and the Military Ranks of Mexica Soldiers.

Caption continued to next pages

Caption continued from previous page

First row or register: The first scene depicts a soldier belonging to the two-prisoner warrior rank. The second is a soldier belonging to the three-captive warrior rank. The third is a soldier belonging to the four-captive warrior rank; he is wearing a jaguar costume befitting his military accomplishments.

Second row: The first scene is a soldier belonging to rank awarded for special bravery (rashness) in battle. The second is a soldier belonging to the Quachic warrior rank—identified by their distinct hair style (sheared head except for a lock of hair above the left ear). The final scene is a soldier belonging to the Tlacatecatl warrior rank. Men who achieved this military class were the army's commanding generals and also served as special emissaries for the emperor; they bore headbands with quetzal feathers as a sign of their high prestige.

33

The Shape of the Land

From the *Relaciónes geográficas* and the *Mapa Uppsala*

After contact, Indigenous mapmakers adapted and transformed their cartographic tradition in response to the Spanish crown's administrative needs. Some fifty years or so after the fall of Tenochtitlan, Philip II desired a better understanding of the nature and potential of his various possessions. To that end, he set up a commission that issued a series of questionnaires designed to gather information on demographics, political jurisdictions, languages spoken, physical terrain, and other topics. The responses, called the Relaciónes geográficas, *were returned from many places in the empire. In New Spain they were prepared in many communities, providing local histories, descriptions of present conditions, and a wealth of other information.*[1] *Often, accompanying maps were*

[1]For an analysis of the maps from central Mexico, see Barbara E. Mundy, *The Mapping of New Spain: Indigenous Cartography and the Maps of the Relaciones geográficas* (Chicago: University of Chicago Press, 2000). For an analysis of mapping practices and the consideration of space in the Maya region, see Amara Solari, *Maya Ideologies of the Sacred: The Transfiguration of Space in Colonial Yucatan* (Austin: University of Texas Press, 2013).

Uppsala Library: http://art.alvin-portal.org/alvin/view.jsf?file=4289. It can also be accessed at the World Digital Library: https://www.wdl.org/en/item/503/.

prepared by Indian cartographers who continued to work in traditional ways, using glyphs and symbols to indicate water, hills, buildings, and other features, and who continued to encode histories in their maps.

In Mesoamerican tradition, maps primarily recorded social, political, and historical events and realities in relationship to a particular place. As such, the maps sent to Spain were not what the crown expected and were generally considered geometrically inaccurate. These maps, however, reveal that Indigenous concepts of space and place persisted, alongside the adoption (to varying degrees) of European conventions and forms.

The Uppsala Map *(also known as the* Mapa de Santa Cruz*), from circa 1541 and housed at the Uppsala University Library in Sweden, provides another example of the adaptability of Indigenous mapmaking practices.*[2] *It depicts Mexico City's urban plan (much of which can be corroborated with the capital's historic center as it stands today) surrounded by an area of about 60 kilometers in all directions. Covering the landscape is a web-like network of the roads and river systems of Mexico's Central Valley. The representations of two hundred mostly native inhabitants engaged in various activities point to the region's economic vibrancy. Like the* Relaciónes Geográficas, *the map contains dozens of Nahua place glyphs, revealing the persistence of Indigenous political and cultural identities. Cartographic elements that both symbolized and represented the community, rather than topography, continued to be the focus of native cartography.*

---

[2]For more on the *Mapa Uppsala*, see Alonso de Santa Cruz, "*Mapa de México Tenochtitlan y sus contornos hacia 1550,*" ed. Miguel León Portilla and María del Carmen Aguilera García (México: Celanese Mexicana, S.A., 1986); Jennifer R. Saracino, "Shifting Landscape: Depictions of Environmental and Cultural Disruption in the Mapa Uppsala of Mexico-Tenochtitlan" (PhD, Tulane University, 2018).

Map of Amoltepec, Oaxaca.

This map from 1580 uses Mixtec conventions to represent space. Here the traditional symbol for a stream sets one boundary, while a semicircle of glyphs represents the names of different places that marked the limits or borders of the community. Within this circular frame the church and the palace of the ruler are represented along with glyphs for the names of places within the altepetl.

Nettie Lee Benson Latin American Collection, University of Texas Libraries, The University of Texas at Austin.

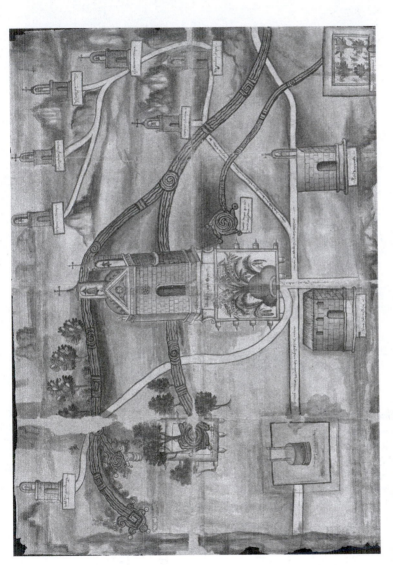

Map of Guaxtepec (Oaxtepec, Morelos).

This map, also from 1580, includes a glyph identifying the town's name (Hill of the Guaje Tree) and Nahua symbols for streams and springs. It also displays a network of roads and churches used to mark settlements; the Dominican monastery Santo Domingo de Guzmán Oaxtepec is at center. Nettie Lee Benson Latin American Collection, University of Texas Libraries, The University of Texas at Austin.

Uppsala Map.

This map of Mexico City–Tenochtitlan displays the city's urban plan and its surroundings. A cartouche in the lower right contains a dedication to Charles V. Its composition points to the need to satisfy the crown's ethnographic curiosity, while the inclusion of Nahua place glyphs reveals the persistence of Indigenous conceptions of space and place.

Map of Mexico (Uppsala Map), ca. 1540–1550.

34

TOWN COUNCIL OF HUEJOTZINGO

Letter to Philip II

Indigenous peoples continued to record things in their traditional ways, but they also wrote their own languages using the Roman alphabet. Nahuatl, Mayan, Mixtec, Purépecha, and other languages were adapted in this way. Native municipal councils often kept their town records in their own language, and thereby a tradition of alphabetic writing developed. Eventually, Indian and mixed-ancestry (mestizo) historians also recorded the histories of their local communities, often extending that story back into the ancient past, but also including a record of more recent events that reflected a broad variety of interests.

Nahuas' attachment to their altepetl *persisted. There were often good political or economic reasons to emphasize these ancient identities and traditional claims to land and water rights. In this letter of 1560, written in Nahuatl, from the town council of Huejotzingo, an* altepetl *that had allied with Cortés, the councilors emphasize their community's services and compare them favorably to those of Tlaxcala. Notice too the formulas of subservience in address now applied to Philip II of Spain rather than to a Nahua ruler. Despite the flourishes, the objective of the letter is quite practical.*

Our lord sovereign, you the king don Felipe our lord, we bow low in great reverence to your high dignity, we prostrate and humble ourselves before you, very high and feared king through omnipotent God, giver of life. We do not deserve to kiss your feet, only from afar we bow down to you, you who are most high and Christian and very pleasing to God our Lord, for you are his true representative here on earth, you who govern us and lead us in things of Christianity. All of us creatures and subjects of the life-giving God, we vassals and servants of your majesty, we people here, we who dwell here in New Spain, all together we look to you, our eyes and hearts go out toward you; we have complete

---

Arthur J. O. Anderson, Frances Berdan, and James Lockhart, eds., *Beyond the Codices: The Nahua View of Colonial Mexico* (Berkeley: University of California Press, 1976), 179–91.

confidence in you in the eyes of our Lord God, for he put us in your hands to guard us, and he assigned us to you for us to be your servants and your helpers. By our Lord God and by your very honored and very high majesty, remember us, have compassion with us, for very great is the poverty and affliction visited on us who dwell here in New Spain.

Our lord sovereign, king don Felipe our lord, with our words we appear and stand before you, we of Huejotzingo who guard for you your city—we citizens, I the governor and we the alcaldes and councilmen and we the lords and nobles, your men and your servants. Very humbly we implore you: Oh unfortunate are we, very great and heavy sadness and affliction lie upon us, nowhere do your pity and compassion extend over us and reach us, we do not deserve, we do not attain your rulership. And all the while since your subjects the Spaniards arrived among us, all the while we have been looking toward you, we have been confidently expecting that sometime your pity would reach us, as we also had confidence in and were awaiting the mercy of your very revered dear father the ruler of the world, don Carlos the late emperor. Therefore now, our lord sovereign, we bow humbly before you; may we deserve your pity, may the very greatly compassionate and merciful God enlighten you so that your pity is exercised on us, for we hear, and so it is said to us, that you are very merciful and humane towards all your vassals; and as to the time when you pity someone, when before you appears a vassal of yours in poverty, so it is said, then you have pity on him with your very revered majesty, and by the grace of omnipotent God you do it for him. May we now also deserve and attain the same, for every day such poverty and affliction reaches us and is visited on us that we weep and mourn. Oh unfortunate are we, what will happen to us, we your poor vassals of Huejotzingo, we who live in your city? If you were not so far away, many times we would appear before you. Though we greatly wish and desire to reach you and appear before you, we are unable, because we are very poor and do not have what is needed for the journey on the boat nor things to eatnor anything to pay people in order to be able to reach you. Therefore now we appear before you only in our words; we set before you our poor prayer. May you only in your very great Christianity and very revered high majesty attend well to this our prayer.

Our lord sovereign, before anyone told us of or made us acquainted with your fame and your story, most high and feared universal king who rules all, and before we were told or taught the glory and name of our Lord God, before the faith reached us, and before we were Christians, when your servants the Spaniards reached us and your captain general don Hernando Cortés arrived, although we were not yet acquainted with the omnipotent, very compassionate holy Trinity, our Lord God the ruler of heaven and possessor of earth caused us to deserve that in his mercy he enlightened us so that we took you as our king to belong to you and become your people and your subjects; not a single town surpassed us here in New Spain in that first and earliest we threw ourselves toward you, we gave ourselves to you, and furthermore no one intimidated us, no one forced us into it, but truly God caused us to deserve that voluntarily we adhered to you so that we gladly received the newly arrived Spaniards who reached us here in New Spain, for we left our homes behind to go a great distance to meet them; we went twenty leagues to greet captain general don Hernando Cortés and the others whom he led. We received them very gladly, we embraced them, we saluted them with many tears, though we were not acquainted with them, and our fathers and grandfathers also did not know them; but by the mercy of our Lord God we truly came to know them. Since they are our neighbors, therefore we loved them; nowhere did we attack them. Truly we fed them and served them; some arrived sick, so that we carried them in our arms and on our backs, and we served them in many other ways which we are not able to say here. Although the people who are called and named Tlaxcalans indeed helped, yet we strongly pressed them to give aid, and we admonished them not to make war; but though we so admonished them, they made war and fought for fifteen days. But we, when a Spaniard was afflicted, without fail at once we managed to reach him; [there was no one else]. We do not lie in this, for all the conquerors know it well, those who have died and some now living.

And when they began their conquest and war-making, then also we well prepared ourselves to aid them, for out came all of our war gear, our arms and provisions and all our equipment, and we not merely named someone, we went in person, we who rule, and we brought all our nobles and all of our vassals to aid the Spaniards. We helped not only in warfare, but also we gave them everything they needed; we fed and clothed them, and we would carry in our arms and on our backs those whom they wounded in war or who were very ill, and we did all the tasks in preparing for war. And so that they could fight the Mexica with boats, we worked hard; we gave them the wood and pitch with which the Spaniards made the boats. And when they conquered the Mexica and all belonging to them, we never abandoned them or left them behind in it. And when they went to conquer Michoacán, Jalisco, and Colhuacan, and there at Pánuco and there at Oaxaca and Tehuantepec and Guatemala, (we were) the only ones who went along while they conquered and made war here in New Spain until they finished the conquest; we never abandoned them, in no way did we prejudice their war-making, though some of us were destroyed in it [nor was there a single one of our subjects left?], for we did our duty very well. But as to those Tlaxcalans, several of their nobles were hanged for making war poorly; in many places they ran away, and often did badly in the war. In this we do not lie, for the conquerors know it well.

Our lord sovereign, we also say and declare before you that your fathers the twelve sons of St. Francis reached us, whom the very high priestly ruler the Holy Father sent and whom you sent, both taking pity on us so that they came to teach us the gospel, to teach us the holy Catholic faith and belief, to make us acquainted with the single deity God our Lord, and likewise God favored us and enlightened us, us of Huejotzingo, who dwell in your city, so that we gladly received them. When they entered the city of Huejotzingo, of our own free will we honored them and showed them esteem. When they embraced us so that we would abandon the wicked belief in many gods, we forthwith voluntarily left it; likewise they did us the good deed (of telling us) to destroy and burn the stones and wood that we worshipped as gods, and we did it; very willingly we destroyed, demolished, and burned the temples. Also when they gave us the holy gospel, the holy Catholic faith, with very good will and desire we received and grasped it; no one frightened us into it, no one forced us, but very willingly we seized it, and they gave us all the sacraments. Quietly and peacefully we arranged and ordered it among ourselves; no one, neither nobleman nor commoner, was ever tortured or burned for this, as was done on every hand here in New Spain. (The people of) many towns were forced and tortured, were hanged or burned because they did not want to leave idolatry, and unwillingly they received the gospel and faith. Especially those Tlaxcalans pushed out and rejected the fathers, and would not receive the faith, for many of the high nobles were burned, and some hanged, for combating the advocacy and service of our Lord God. But we of Huejotzingo, we your poor vassals, we never did anything in your harm, always we served you in every command you sent or what at your command we were ordered. Very quietly, peacefully we take and grasp it all, though only through the mercy of God do we do it, since it is not within our personal power. Therefore now, in and through God, may you hear these our words, all that we say and declare before you, so that you will take pity on us, so that you will exercise on us your rulership to console us and aid us in (this trouble) with which daily we weep and are sad. We are afflicted and sore pressed, and your town and city of Huejotzingo is as if it is about to disappear and be destroyed. Here is what is being done to us: now your stewards the royal officials and the prosecuting attorney Dr. Maldonado are assessing us a very great tribute to belong to you. The tribute we are to give is 14,800 pesos in money, and also all the bushels of maize.

Our lord sovereign, never has such happened to us in all the time since your servants and vassals the Spaniards came to us, for your servant don Hernando Cortés, late captain general, the Marqués del Valle, in all the time he lived here with us, always greatly cherished us and kept us happy; he never disturbed nor agitated us. Although we gave him tribute, he assigned it to us only with moderation; even though we gave him gold, it was only very little; no matter how much, no matter in what way, or if not very pure, he just received it gladly. He never reprimanded us or afflicted us, because it was evident to him and he understood well how very greatly we served and aided him. Also he told us many times that he would speak in our favor before you, that he would help us and inform you of all the ways in which we have aided and served you. And when he went before you, then you confirmed him and were merciful to him, you honored and rewarded him for the way he had served you here in New Spain. But perhaps before you he forgot us. How then shall we speak? We did not reach you, we were not given audience before you. Who then will speak for us? Unfortunate are we. Therefore now we place ourselves before you, our sovereign lord. And when you sent your representatives, the President and Bishop don Sebastián Ramírez, and the judges, Licentiate Salmerón, Licentiates Ceinos, Quiroga, and Maldonado, they well affirmed and sustained the orders you gave for us people here, us who live in New Spain. In many things they aided us and lightened the very great tribute we had, and from many things that were our tasks they always delivered us, they pardoned us all of it. And we your poor vassals, we of Huejotzingo who dwell in your city, when Licentiate Salmerón came to us and entered the city of Huejotzingo, then he saw how troubled the town was with our tribute in gold, sixty pieces that we gave each year, and that it troubled us because gold does not appear here, and is not to be found in our province, though we searched for it everywhere; then at once Licentiate Salmerón pardoned it on your behalf, so that he made a replacement and substitution of the money. He set our tribute in money at 2,050 pesos. And in all the time he thus assessed us, all the time we kept doing it, we hastened to give it to you, since we are your subjects and belong to you; we never neglected it, we never did poorly, we made it all up. But now we are taken aback and very afraid and we ask, have we done something wrong, have we somehow behaved badly and ill toward you, our lord sovereign, or have we committed some sin against almighty God? Perhaps you have heard something of our wickedness and for that reason now this very great tribute has fallen upon us, seven times exceeding all we had paid before, the 2,000 pesos. And we declare to you that it will not be long before your city of Huejotzingo completely disappears and perishes, because our fathers, grandfathers, and ancestors knew no tribute and gave tribute to no one, but were independent, and we nobles who guard your subjects are now truly very poor. Nobility is seen among us no longer; now we resemble the commoners. As they eat and dress, so do we; we have been very greatly afflicted, and our poverty has reached its culmination. Of the way in which our fathers and grandfathers and forebears were rich and honored, there is no longer the slightest trace among us.

O our lord sovereign king, we rely on you as on God the one deity who dwells in heaven, we trust in you as our father. Take pity on us, have compassion with us. May you especially remember those who live and subsist in the wilds, those who move us to tears and pity; we truly live with them in just such poverty as theirs, wherefore we speak out before you so that afterwards you will not become angry with us when your subjects have disappeared or perished. There ends this our prayer.

We cannot write here for you the very many ways in which your city of Huejotzingo is poor and stricken; we are leaving that to our dear father Fray Alonso de Buendia, son of St. Francis, if God the one deity wills that he should arrive safely before you. He will be able to tell you much more about our anguish and poverty, since he learned and saw it well while he was prior here in the city of Huejotzingo for two years. We hope that he will tell and read this to you, for we have much confidence in him and have placed ourselves completely in his hands. This is all with which we come and appear before you. This letter was done in the city of Huejotzingo on the 30th day of the month of July, in the year of the birth of our Lord Jesus Christ 1560.

Your poor vassals who bow down humbly to you from afar,

Don Leonardo Ramírez, governor. Don Mateo de la Corona, alcalde. Diego Alameda, alcalde. Don Felipe de Mendoza, alcalde. Hernando de Meneses. Miguel de Alvarado. Alonso Pimentel, Augustin Osorio. Don Francisco Vázquez. Don Diego de Chaves. Juan de Almo[. . .]. Diego de Niza. Agustín de Santo Tomás. Diego Suárez. Toribio de San [Cristó]bal Motolinia.

35

Three Folios
From the *Huejotzingo Census (Matrícula de Huexotzinco)*

This manuscript (originally consisting of more than 440 folios) from 1560 lists the towns in the province of Huejotzingo (in present-day Puebla), along with population figures and the status and occupations of residents. The audiencia *of Mexico City had this census drawn up in response to the municipal council's (*cabildo*) appeal to the Spanish colonial government to reduce their tribute obligations due to population loss and other economic factors. It should thus be read in conjunction with the previous letter as part of the same story and in order to get a sense of the voluminous documentation produced by Indians within Spanish bureaucratic structures. This record serves as testament for the legal culture that developed after the conquest, and the success of native litigants in employing colonial law to their own advantage, be it to settle land disputes among Indian communities or to receive licenses for trade, among other matters.*

This folio shows the continuity of the Nahua pictorial writing used for accounting and how it was employed alongside Nahua and Spanish written in alphabetic writing. The images also illustrate new ways of expressing local pride: Huejotzingo townsmen built one of the greatest Franciscan monasteries and temples in central Mexico, in affirmation of the new state religion, as well as to celebrate the artistry and wealth of their province.

Matrícula de Huexotzinco, f.704, 708v (Paris: Bibliothèque Nationale, 1560). http://hdl. loc.gov/loc.wdl/frpbf.15282. There is a partial copy of the census at the Huntington Library.

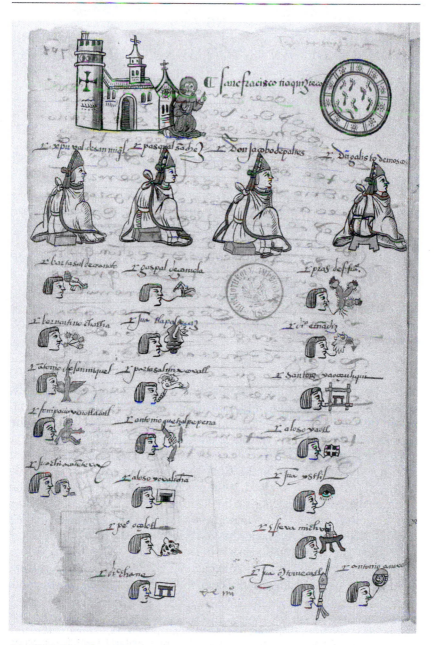

San Francisco Naquisteco.
Paris: Bibliothèque Nationale, 1560.

36

DOMINGO DE SAN ANTÓN MUÑÓN CHIMALPAHIN

The Death of Cuauhtémoc
From the *Codex Chimalpahin*

This selection presents a Nahua interpretation of the death of Cuauhtémoc, the last independent tlahtoani *of Tenochtitlan. It was written by Domingo de San Antón Muñón Chimalpahin, one of that generation of Nahua and mestizo historians who emerged in the years following the fall of Tenochtitlan. Born in 1579 to a family with perhaps distant claims to nobility in the region of Chalco to the south of Mexico–Tenochtitlan, he was sent as a youth to live in the capital, where he worked for many years as the manager of a church and dedicated himself to studying the history of the region. Chimalpahin wrote about his birthplace Chalco in the annals tradition, paying particular attention to the ties of lineage and genealogy of the Nahua elite. In this short excerpt on the death of Cuauhtémoc we see these concerns expressed in his defense of the last Mexica ruler.*

The year Three House, 1521. At this time the lord Quauhtemoctzin was installed as ruler of Tenochtitlan in Izcalli in the ancient month count, and in [the month of] February in the Christian month count, when the Spaniards still occupied Tlaxcala. He was a son of Ahuitzotzin.

And in this same said year, Three House, in Toçoztontli in the ancient month count and in April in the Christian month count, the great lords named above, sons of the lord Moteucçoma Xocoyotl, were killed. The first was named Tzihuacpopoca; the second was named Xoxopehualloc; the third was named Tzihuactzin; the fourth was named Tecuecuenotl; the fifth was named Axayaca; the sixth was named Totlehuicol. They were killed on Quauhtemoctzin's orders.

And Ahuitzol's son named Atlixcatzin Tlacateccatl begot and from him issued one son named don Diego Cahualtzin, as well as a second,

Domingo Francisco de San Antón Muñón Chimalpahin Cuauhtlehuanitzin. *Codex Chimalpahin: Society and Politics in Mexico Tenochtitlan, Tlatelolco, Texcoco, Culhuacan, and other Nahua Altepetl in Central Mexico.* Eds. and trans. Arthur J. O. Anderson, Susan Schroeder, and Wayne Ruwet. 2 vols. Vol. 1. (Norman: University of Oklahoma Press, 1997), 167-89.

named don Martín Ezmalintzin. And don Diego Cahualtzin begot two sons. The first was named don Diego Atlixcatzin; the second was named don Antonio de Mendoza Tlacacuitlahuatzin Temazcalxollotzin.

And the son of Axayacatzin, ruler of Tenochtitlan, named Teçoçomocth Aculnahuacatl, begot two sons. The first was named don Diego Huanitzin who later became ruler of Tenochtitlan. The second was named don Carlos Oquiztzin, a great lord of Tenochtitlan. However, don Diego Huanitzin had first been ruler of Ectapec at the time that the Spaniards arrived, and don Carlos Oquiztzin was ruler in Azcapotzalco Mexicapan.

The year Seven House, 1525. At this time they falsely accused the ruler Quauhtemoctzin and the other rulers. Those who made false accusations were the Tlatelolca and the Michhuaque at Huey Mollan when don Hernando Cortés, Marquis del Valle, took them there. And thus did they falsely accuse the rulers, Quauhtemoctzin, ruler of Tenochtitlan, and Tetlepanquetzatzin, ruler of Tlacopan: they falsely claimed that it was said that they would once more make war upon the Spaniards. The one who falsely accused them was a resident of Tlatelolco named Cotztemexi.

And when the Marquis heard the false statement, he at once baptized the rulers Quauhtemoctzin, Tetlepanquetzatzin, and Tlacotzin Cihuacoatl. And when they were baptized, here is what their names became: the name of the first became don Hernando Quauhtemoctzin; the name of the second became don Pedro Tetlepanquetzatzin; the name of the third became don Juan Velázquez Tlacotzin Cihuacoatl. And when they had baptized don Hernando Quauhtemoctzin and don Pedro Tetlepanquetzatzin, then in a trial the Marquis condemned both rulers. They died in Huey Mollan. They hanged them on a ceiba tree.

37

From the *Title of Acalan-Tixel*

This selection is drawn from the Chontal Maya-speaking region of Tabasco through which Cortés traveled on his way to Guatemala after the fall of Tenochtitlan. This account is really part of a título, a type of document found throughout Mesoamerica in which indigenous

Matthew Restall, *Maya Conquistador* (Boston: Beacon Press, 1988), 63–65.

*communities sought to use history and genealogy to back up their claims
to land, water, or other rights. Here, the Maya lord emphasizes his cooperation with the Spaniards as a way of claiming legitimacy for his family
and community.*

. . . Therefore the Captain said to them, "Let the ruler come, for I wish
to see him. I do not come to make war; I wish only to go and see the
whole country. I will be good to him if he receives me well." This he
said to the men who had come on behalf of their ruler, who returned
to tell their ruler Paxbolonacha, who was in the *cah* [town/commu-
nity] of Itzamkanac. All the rulers of the province's *cahob* [towns] were
thus gathered together—this was for the second time—and he said
to them, "Fine! I shall go and see and hear what he wants, the Castilian man who has come." And so the ruler Paxbolonacha went. And
the Capitán del Valle went out to meet him with many gifts—honey,
turkeys, maize, copal, and a great quantity of fruit. Then he said to Ruler
Paxbolon, "I have come here to your lands, for I am sent by the lord of
the earth [*u yum cab*], the emperor [*enperador*] seated on his throne
in Castile; he sends me to see the land and those who live in it, not for
the purpose of wars. I wish only to ask for the way to Ulua, to the land
where gold and plumage and cacao come from, as I have heard." Then
he [Paxbolonacha] replied that it would be good if he left, but that he
should come first to his land, to his home, to his *cah*, where they would
discuss what would be best. "Let us rest first," the Capitán del Valle
then told him; therefore they rested for twenty days. The ruler [*ahau*]
Cuauhtemoc was there, having come with him [Cortés] from Mexico.
And it happened that he said to the aforementioned ruler Paxbolonacha, "My lord ruler, these Castilian [TAT:72v] men will one day give you
much misery and kill your people. In my opinion we should kill them,
for I bring many officers and you also are many." This is what Cuauhtemoc said to Paxbolonacha, ruler of the people of Tamactun, who, upon
hearing this speech of Cuauhtemoc's, replied that he would first think
about what he wished to do about his speech. And, in considering his
speech fully, he observed that the Castilian men behaved well, that
they neither killed a single man nor beat a single man, and that they
wished only to be given honey, turkey hens, maize, and various fruits,
day after day. Thus he concluded, "I cannot therefore display two faces,
two hearts, to the Castilian men." But Cuauhtemoc, the aforementioned
ruler from Mexico, continued to press him about it, for he wished to
kill the Castilian men. Because of this, the ruler Paxbolonacha told the

Capitán del Valle, "My lord Capitán del Valle, this ruler Cuauhtemoc who is with you, observe him so that he does not revolt and betray you, for three or four times he talked to me about killing you." Upon hearing these words the Capitán del Valle seized him [Cuauhtemoc] and had him bound in chains. He was in chains for three days. Then they baptized him. It is not known what his baptismal name was; some say he was named don Juan and some say he was named don Hernando. After he was named, his head was cut off, and it was impaled on a ceiba tree in front of the pagan temple [*otot ciçin*, devil's home] at Yaxdzan. . . .

Chronology of the Conquest of Tenochtitlan (1485–1568)

1485	Birth of Hernando (Hernán) Cortés
1496	Birth of Bernal Díaz del Castillo
1502	Moctezuma II, called the Younger (*Xocoyotl*), becomes *tlahtoani* or ruler of Tenochtitlan
1511– 1514	Colonization of Cuba
1517	*February to April* Hernández de Córdoba sails from Cuba to Yucatan and encounters the Maya peoples
1518	*May to November* Governor of Cuba, Diego Velázquez, sends second expedition to Yucatan under Juan de Grijalva
1519	Velázquez sends new expedition under Hernando Cortés
	February Founding of Vera Cruz
	February 10 Cortés sails for Yucatan
	June 3 Spaniards reach Cempoala
	September 2–20 Spaniards battle and then ally with Tlaxcalans
	October 15 (?) Massacre at Cholula
	November 8 Spaniards and Tlaxcalans enter Tenochtitlan
	November 14 Spaniards seize Moctezuma
1520	*early May* Cortés marches against Pánfilo de Narváez
	May 16 (?) Toxcatl festival; Pedro de Alvarado massacres celebrants
	June Cuitlahuac is chosen *tlahtoani*
	June 24 Cortés reenters Tenochtitlan
	June 29 Moctezuma is killed
	June 30–July 31 *Noche triste*: Spaniards and allies escape Tenochtitlan with great losses

231

July 12   Fleeing Spaniards reach Tlaxcala

July–December   Recovery of Spanish forces; isolation of Tenochtitlan; Spanish expeditions to win allies and supporters

October   Plague devastates Tenochtitlan

December 4   Cuitlahuac dies from smallpox

1521   *February*   Cuauhtémoc becomes *tlahtoani*

February–April   Cortés campaigns around the lake and garners additional city-states as allies

May 10–13   Siege of Tenochtitlan begins

May 26   Fresh water to the city is cut off

May 31   Fight for Iztapalapa

June 1   Spaniards begin to enter Tenochtitlan

June 16   Palaces of Moctezuma burned

June 30   Spaniards set back between Tenochtitlan and Tlatelolco

July 18   Mexica propose peace if Spaniards leave

July 20–25   Main plaza of Tenochtitlan cleared of Mexica resistance

August 7   Ongoing fighting in Tlatelolco

August 13   Starving defenders trapped; capture of Cuahtémoc and surrender of the city

1522–1523   Cortés's first three letters published in Seville

1525   Cuahtémoc executed by Cortés

1535   First Viceroy of Mexica arrives; Cortés's power is weakened.

1540–1541   *Relación de Michoacán* is completed

1547   Cortés dies in Spain

1560   *Matrícula de Huexotzinco* is completed

1568   Bernal Diaz completes first draft of *Historia verdadera de la conquista de la Nueva España*

Questions for Consideration

1. Is history always written by the winners? If so, how do we recapture the "other side" in the past?
2. What is a "true" history?

1. Omens

1. Why did Indigenous people associate the Spanish arrival with omens? And why did Europeans similarly look for natural and supernatural signs of great events?
2. Might these documents be better placed in the last section, "Aftermath"?

2. Preparations

1. In what ways were the early Spanish expeditions business ventures rather than "explorations" or "conquests"?
2. What were the economic and political motivations that drove Spaniards to venture to the mainland from Cuba?

3. Encounters

1. How did Cortés evaluate the land and the peoples he encountered in Mexico? And what was his agenda in describing this territory to the Spanish crown?
2. How do the Spanish and Nahua descriptions and understandings of the first meetings differ? What aspects of behavior most preoccupy the Spaniards? The Nahuas?
3. How might Indigenous women's views of Spaniards have differed from those of men given their status and economic roles in native societies?

4. The March Inland: Tlaxcala and Cholula

1. How do the Tlaxcalans come across in the Mexica account?
2. What are the advantages of employing pictorial elements and nonalphabetic writing systems to convey information?

5. Tenochtitlan

1. From the perspective of Tenochtitlan's residents, what were the most memorable aspects of the Spanish-Tlaxcalan entourage upon arrival?
2. In what ways did European preconceptions and beliefs influence Díaz's description of Mexica culture?
3. Apart from translation, in what ways might Doña Marina (Malintzin) have influenced the interactions between Cortés and Moctezuma?

6. Things Fall Apart: Toxcatl and The *Noche triste*

1. What actions did the Mexica emphasize in their memory of the Toxcatl massacre? The Spaniards?
2. How can the two distinct versions of the death of Moctezuma be explained?

7. The Siege and Fall of Tenochtitlan

1. What was the role of Cortés's native allies in bringing about the fall of the Triple Alliance?
2. What do the decisions and choices of Nahua elites from city-states like Texcoco tell us about the nature of Mexica power?
3. In what ways did disease contribute to the Mexica defeat?
4. From the *Florentine Codex*, what does the meeting between Nahua lords and the mention of tribute tell us about the way the Mexica conceived of their surrender?

8. Aftermath: Tradition and Transformation

1. In what ways did Spaniards rely on pre-existing power structures to establish bureaucratic government in Tenochtitlan-Mexico City?
2. What aspects of the *Relaciones Geográficas* and the *Uppsala Map* reflect attributes of the Indigenous mapmaking tradition? What about the influence of European cartography?
3. Identify the occupations noted in the Huejotzingo Census. What do these activities tell us about the perseverance of precontact industries? What evidence is there for new economic activities?
4. Did the fall of the Mexica Empire represent a radical change in central Mexican history? Or were Spaniards incorporated into Nahua society as other conquerors (including the Mexica) had been before?

Biographical Notes

Aguilar, Gerónimo de (1489–1531)   A Spaniard thought lost in a shipwreck in 1511, he was washed ashore in Yucatan, where Maya leaders held him captive until the arrival of Cortés in 1519. During these years he learned the Yucatec Mayan language, and he later served as a translator for the Spanish.

Alva Ixtlilxochitl, Fernando de (1578?–1650)   Descendant of Texcoco royalty, including Nezahualcoyotl, Nezahualpilli, and the conquest-era leader Fernando Cortés Ixtlilxochitl. He served in a number of high positions in colonial government and was a prolific writer of Nahua history.

Alvarado, Pedro de (1485–1541)   A member of both Grijalva's (1518) and Cortés's (1519) expeditions to Mexico from Cuba, he served as a commander in one of Cortés's three armies during the conquest. He was responsible for the Toxcatl massacre in Tenochtitlan.

Cacamatzin (Cacama)   Ruler of Texcoco at the time of Spanish arrival in Tenochtitlan. His passing prompted a dynastic crisis that resulted in Fernando Cortés Ixtlilxochitl becoming the new *tlahtoani* of Texcoco. The latter's alliance with Cortés proved crucial for the subsequent attack on Tenochtitlan.

Carlos V (Charles V) (1500–1558)   Holy Roman Emperor from 1519–56 and the king of Spain as Charles I from 1516–56.

Chimalpahin Cuauhtlehuanitzin, Domingo Francisco de San Antón Muñón (1579–1660?)   A Nahua intellectual and prolific writer from Chalco. He wrote an extensive history of his region in the late sixteenth century, today known as the *Codex Chimalpahin.*

Cortés, Hernando (Hernán) (1485?–1547)   Born in Medellin, Spain, he arrived in Hispaniola in 1504. He led the third expedition to Mexico in 1519 and, with the fall of Tenochtitlan two years later, became one of the wealthiest men in the Spanish Empire and an inspiration to subsequent conquistadors.

Cortés, Martín (1523?–1595?)   Son of Hernando Cortés and Doña Marina (Malintzin); he was raised in Spain, where he suffered from court conspiracies against his family. His half-brother of the same name inherited their father's title Marquis of the Valley of Oaxaca.

Cuauhtémoc *(Guatemoc–Díaz del Castillo; Quauhtemoctzin–Lockhart)* **(1497?–1525)**   The eleventh and last *tlahtoani* of Tenochtitlan (r. 1520–21). Known as "Descending Eagle," the son of Ahuitzol (eighth Mexica ruler) and grandson of Moctezuma I (fifth Mexica ruler) ruled from December 1520 until the fall of Tenochtitlan in August 1521. Spaniards murdered him to strengthen their own political standing.

Cuitlahuac (1476?–1520)   The tenth *tlahtoani* of Tenochtitlan (r. September 16, 1520–December 4, 1520). The son of Axayacatl (sixth Mexica ruler, 1468–81), Cuitlahuac was the ruler of Ixtapalapa before succeeding his brother, Moctezuma II, in 1520. After ruling for only eighty days, he died of smallpox.

Díaz del Castillo, Bernal (1495?–1584?)   He arrived in the Caribbean in 1514 and was a member of all three expeditions from Cuba to Mexico (Córdoba 1517, Grijalva 1518, Cortés 1519). A foot soldier in Cortés's army, he eventually wrote a history of the fall of Tenochtitlan in response to another book (by López de Gómara) on the war that he considered incorrect.

Durán, Diego (1537?–1588)   Born in Seville, he arrived in Mexico in 1542, entered the Dominican Order in 1556, and thereafter chronicled Nahua religion and history in some of the most revealing and detailed books written during this period.

Guerrero, Gonzalo   Presumed lost in a shipwreck with Gerónimo de Aguilar in 1511, he washed ashore in Yucatan and was captured by the Mayas. After marrying a local woman, he achieved high status in Maya society and refused to join Cortés after he landed in Yucatan in 1519. He allegedly died fighting alongside Maya soldiers in a battle against Spanish forces.

Itzcoatl (?–1440)   The fourth *tlahtoani* of Tenochtitlan (r. 1426–1440). He was one of three nobles responsible for the founding of the Triple Alliance in 1428, with the Mexica of Tenochtitlan leading; he was instrumental in expanding the geographic reach of the Mexica Empire.

Las Casas, Bartolomé de (1484–1576)   Born in Seville, he arrived in Hispaniola in 1502 and participated in the colonization of the island. After witnessing the massacre and enslavement of the Indigenous population, he entered the Dominican Order, after which he devoted his life to the protection and defense of native peoples. He published several books denouncing Spanish colonial claims over the New World, including *Short Account of the Destruction of the Indies (1542)*.

López de Gómara, Francisco (1511–1566)   Using his patron Cortés's written documents and memoirs, he wrote a history of the conquest of the Mexica Empire, even though he never set foot in the Americas. Heralding Cortés as a hero, this is the book that inspired Díaz del Castillo to tell his own "true" version of the events.

**Malintzin (Doña Marina, baptized as Marina; Malinche)
(1500?–1529?)** Nahua woman who was held as a slave by a Maya leader, who then gifted her to Cortés after the battle of Potonchan. Speaking both Nahuatl and Yucatec Mayan, she became a crucial interpreter for Cortés as he entered the world of the Mexica. She was also the mother of Cortés's son, Martín, and later married Juan Jaramillo, with whom she had several more children. Her sizeable estate became a source of conflict among her heirs.

Mendoza, Antonio de (1494–1552) Of elite Spanish nobility and a diplomat in the Spanish court, he was personally selected by King Charles I in 1535 to serve as the first viceroy of New Spain and as president of the *audiencia* (high court) of Mexico City. He arrived in Mexico later that year and remained as viceroy until 1551.

Moctezuma Ilhuicamina (I) *(Moteczoma–Durán; Motecçoma–Lockhart; Montezuma–Díaz del Castillo; Motecuhzoma–León Portilla)* (?–1469) The fifth *tlahtoani* of Tenochtitlan (r. 1440–68). He was the son of the second Mexica emperor, Huitzilhuitl (?–1417), and the grandfather of Moctezuma II.

Moctezuma Xocoyotl (II) *(Moteczoma–Durán; Motecçoma–Lockhart; Montezuma–Dian del Castillo; Motecuhzoma–León Portilla)* (1466?–1520) "He Scowls Like a Lord." The ninth *tlahtoani* of Tenochtitlan (r. 1502–20) and Mexica emperor when Cortés arrived in Mexico. The son of Axayacatl (sixth *tlahtoani* of Tenochtitlan) and the grandson of Moctezuma I; he died on June 29, 1520, while being held hostage by the Spanish in his own palace.

Narváez, Pánfilo de (1480?–1528?) Governor Diego Velázquez placed him in command of a large fleet and ordered him to sail from Hispaniola to Mexico to capture and return Cortés. After landing on the coast, Cortés defeated Narváez's forces in May 1520 and employed the captured men and supplies to reinforce his own armies by taking them back to Tenochtitlan.

Olid, Cristóbal de (1488?–1524) Along with Alvarado and Sandoval, a commander of one of Cortés's three armies during the siege of Tenochtitlan. He later rebelled against Cortés after staking a claim to territory in Honduras, much as Cortés had previously done to Diego Velázquez.

Olmedo, Bartolomé de (1484?–1524) A Mercedarian friar who sailed to Mexico from Cuba with Cortés and accompanied him to Tenochtitlan, he performed some of the first baptisms of Nahua nobility in Mexico.

Sahagún, Bernardino de (1499?–1590) A Franciscan friar who arrived in New Spain in 1529, he spent the rest of his life studying, documenting, and chronicling Nahua culture, history, and religion. He used interviews with Nahua elders in central Mexico to collect his information. His lifelong work, known as the *Florentine Codex,* is the most detailed and thorough work on Nahua life and culture that exists today.

Sandoval, Gonzalo de (1497?–1529?)   Along with Olid and Alvarado, a commander of one of Cortés's three armies during the siege of Tenochtitlan. Loyal to Cortés until his death, he served as co-governor of New Spain for a short period.

Tlacaelel (?–1487?)   Nephew of Emperor Itzcoatl, he served as commanding general of the Triple Alliance after 1428 and held the advisory position of *cihuacoatl*—a sort of prime minister—to a number of Mexica rulers. Although the reach of his power has been disputed, it is certain that he was a central figure in the political and military expansion of the Mexica Empire throughout the fifteenth century.

Tzintzicha Tangaxoan (?–1530)   Ruler *(cazonci)* of the Purépecha Empire in present day Michoacán during the siege of Tenochtitlan. He was the son of the previous Purépecha ruler, Zuangua (?–1520).

Velázquez, Diego de (1465–1524)   Accompanied Columbus on his second voyage to the New World in 1493 and later colonized Cuba in 1511–14, becoming its first governor. He ordered the first exploratory expeditions to Mexico.

Xicotencatl I (the Elder) *(Xicotenga–Díaz del Castillo)* (?–1522)   *Tlahtoani* of Tizatlan and father of the Tlaxcalan general Xicotencatl the Younger. Having lived through the increasing economic and political demands of the surrounding Mexica Empire, he saw the Spanish as potential partners for the Tlaxcalans to overthrow the Mexica and free themselves from the pressures of that dominating empire. He successfully lobbied for an alliance between the Spanish and Tlaxcalans.

Xicotencatl II (the Younger) *(Xicotenga–Díaz del Castillo)* (?–1521)   Son of Xicotencatl the Elder, he was a Tlaxcalan general who resisted Cortés's arrival in Tlaxcala. Vehemently opposed to the Spanish invasion, he remained so even after the alliance was formed with them, and was eventually hanged in Texcoco by Cortés for allegedly planning a revolt with the Mexica against the Spanish.

Zorita, Alonso de (1511?–1585?)   Arriving in New Spain in 1548, he became a royal judge of the *audiencia* in Mexico City. Twenty years later, he returned to Spain in 1568. Sympathetic to the plight of Indigenous peoples, he wrote a *Brief and Summary Relation of the Lords of New Spain*.

Glossary of Terms in Nahuatl and Other Indigenous Languages

A NOTE ON PRONUNCIATION

Nahuatl, the language of the Mexica, Tlaxcalans, and other Nahua peoples, is a living language still spoken in Mexico. Languages change over time, and Nahuatl is no different, but its basic structure and pronunciation remain similar to its form in the sixteenth century. Spaniards who first tried to write down what they heard in Nahuatl often only approximated the sounds and sometimes found the Spanish alphabet inadequate to the task. Pronunciation will be made easier for modern readers if it is remembered that:

x is pronounced as sh   (Mexica = Meshica)
tl is pronounced like English "atlas"   (Tlaxcala, Tlaloc)

altepetl   city or city-state; sovereign political unit

atlatl   spear thrower; instrument used to fire projectiles with long shafts and sharp obsidian tips

Aztlán   legendary name of the mythical home of the Mexica people

cacique/cacica   a Taino word meaning ruler; employed by Spanish colonists to refer to Indigenous rulers in Mexico and Latin America in general

calmecac   Mexica school for the children of nobles and elites; served as a theological college for priests, and a military academy for Mexica leaders

calpulli   "big house"; referred to core territorial unit of Nahua social organization, usually related to a neighborhood or barrio-like section of the town or city; often likened to a clan

Camaxtli   god of the hunt and war; patron deity of Tlaxcala and Huejotzingo; related to Xipe Totec and Mixcoatl; often depicted wearing a flayed skin

cazonci   Purépecha word for ruler

chinampas   rectangular plots of silt constructed in a lake by building dirt-filled enclosures, on which multiple harvests could be made in a single year; similar to hydroponic agriculture; also called "floating gardens"

Cihuacoatl   "woman-snake"; earth deity; related to Quilaztli as creation goddess; also the title of the Mexica ruler's main advisor

Huitzilopochtli   "hummingbird of the south"; god of war and associated with the sun; patron deity of the Mexica; said to have led the Mexica from Aztlán to the Central Valley of Mexico; deity shared the largest temple (*Templo Mayor*) in Tenochtitlan's ceremonial precinct with Tlaloc, god of rain

izahuatl   also *zauatl*; smallpox, rash

Iztaccíhuatl   "white woman"; one of two volcanic mountains to the east of Tenochtitlan-Mexico City through which Cortés and his army passed en route to the Mexica capital

macehualtin   the people, commoners; social class of majority in Nahua society

pipiltin   nobility; elite social class in Nahua society

pochteca/pochtecah (pl.)   long-distance merchants; wielded great economic control from their base in Tlatelolco, home of the largest market in Mesoamerica

Popocatepetl   "smoking mountain"; one of two volcanic mountains to the east of Tenochtitlan-Mexico City through which Cortés and his army passed en route to the Mexica capital; highest peak in Mexico, exceeding 17,000 feet above sea level

Quetzalcoatl   "plumed or feathered serpent"; ancient Mesoamerican deity; god of light and knowledge; associated with Ce Acatl Topiltzin Quetzalcoatl, historical ruler of Tula

telpochcalli   Mexica school for the children of commoners; served as a civics school and military academy, training included accompanying active soldiers on campaigns

Tenochtitlan   Mexica capital; founded on an island in Lake Texcoco around 1325 after the Mexica were pushed out by enemy city-states; the Mexica defeated rivals on the lakeshore by 1428, and over the next decades became the most powerful city-state in central Mexico

tepoztli   "copper"; became word for iron and other metals; employed in descriptions of cannonballs

Tezcatlipoca (Tezcatepuca-Díaz del Castillo)   "smoking black mirror"; ancient Mesoamerican deity; god of war, the night sky, and divination; celebrated at Toxcatl festival (event where Spanish massacred Mexica participants in 1520)

tlacateuctli   Nahua sovereign ruler, similar to *tlahtoani*

tlahcuiloh Nahua artist-scribe, known as "master of the red and black ink"; produced books, codices, and lienzos for use by the priesthood, rulers, and nobility

Tlaloc ancient Mesoamerica deity; for the Mexica, god of rain, lightning, and earthquakes; deity shared the largest temple (*Templo Mayor*) in Tenochtitlan's ceremonial precinct with Huitzilopochtli

Tlamamah/tlamemeh (pl.) also *tameme;* a human carrier or porter

tlahtoani "orator"; dynastic ruler of a Nahua *altepetl*

Xiuhtecuhtli "lord of the grass"; god of fire and heat; associated with youthful rulers and military men

Xochipilli "prince of flowers"; god of love, beauty, and sport; associated with festivity and harvest

Xochiquetzal "flower quetzal"; goddess of love, beauty and art; associated with harvest and childbirth

xochiyaoyotl "flower war"; ritual combat between two Mesoamerican polities aimed at demonstrating military prowess, included the acquisition of captives for ritual killings

Selected Bibliography

The following items provide an introduction to the rapidly growing literature in this field.

PRIMARY SOURCES

Acuña, René, ed. *Relaciones geográficas del siglo XVI.* 10 vols. México: UNAM, 1981–88.

Alva Ixtlilxochitl, Fernando de. *Obras históricas.* México: Secretaría de Fomento, 1891. https://archive.org/details/obrashistricasd00chavgoog.

———. *The Native Conquistador: Alva Ixtlilxochitl's Account of the Conquest of New Spain.* Eds. and trans. Amber Brian, Bradley Benton, and Pablo García Loaeza. State College: Penn State University Press, 2015.

Anderson, Arthur J. O., Frances Berdan, and James Lockhart, eds. and trans. *Beyond the Codices: The Nahua View of Colonial Mexico.* Berkeley: University of California Press, 1976.

Bakewell, Liza, and Byron E. Hamann. *Mesolore: Exploring Mesoamerican Culture.* Prolarti Enterprise, LLC and Brown University. http://mesolore.org.

Bierhorst, John, ed. and trans. *Cantares mexicanos: Songs of the Aztecs.* Stanford: Stanford University Press, 1985.

———. *History and Mythology of the Aztecs: The Codex Chimalpopoca.* Tucson: University of Arizona Press, 1992.

Burkhart, Louise M., Stafford Poole, Barry D. Sell, Gregory Spira, and Elizabeth R. Wright, eds. and trans. *Nahuatl Theater.* 4 vols. Norman: University of Oklahoma Press, 2004–09.

Chimalpahin Cuauhtlehuanitzin, Domingo Francisco de San Antón Muñón. *Codex Chimalpahin: Society and Politics in Mexico Tenochtitlan, Tlatelolco, Texcoco, Culhuacan, and other Nahua Altepetl in Central Mexico.* Eds. and trans. Arthur J. O. Anderson, Susan Schroeder, and Wayne Ruwet. 2 vols. Norman: University of Oklahoma Press, 1997.

———. *Annals of His Time: Don Domingo de San Antón Muñón Chimalpahin Quauhtlehuanitzin.* Eds. and trans. James Lockhart, Susan Schroeder, and Doris Namala. Stanford: Stanford University Press, 2006.

———. *Chimalpahin's Conquest: A Nahua Historian's Rewriting of Francisco López de Gómara's* La conquista de México. Eds. and trans. Susan

Schroeder, Anne J. Cruz, Cristián Roa-de-la-Carrera, and David E. Tavárez. Stanford: Stanford University Press, 2010.

The Chronicles of Michoacán. Eds. and trans. Eugene R. Craine and Reginald C. Reindorp. Norman: University of Oklahoma Press, 1970.

Codex Aubin [copy]. Princeton University, c.1775–1825. http://arks. princeton.edu/ark:/88435/mg74qn39s.

———. *Histoire de la nation mexicaine depuis le départ d'Aztlan jusqu'a l'arrivée des conquérants espagnols (et au dela 1607).* Paris: E. Leroux, 1893. https://archive.org/details/histoiredelanati00aubi.

———. *Historia de la nación mexicana; reproducción a todo color del Códice de 1576 (Códice Aubin).* Ed. Charles E. Dibble. Madrid: J. Porrúa Turanzas, 1963.

The Codex Mendoza. Ed. and trans. Frances F. Berdan and Patricia Rieff Anawalt. 4 vols. Berkeley: University of California Press, 1992.

———. *The Essential Codex Mendoza.* Ed. and trans. Frances F. Berdan and Patricia Rieff Anawalt. Berkeley: University of California Press, 1997. https://archive.org/details/bub_gb_JQeAQZHev0IC.

———. *Codíce Mendoza,* edición digital. México: INAH; Arqueología Mexicana, 2014. http://codicemendoza.inah.gob.mx/index. php?lang=english.

Cortés, Hernando. "Cartas de Relación." *In Historiadores primitivos de Indias.* Ed. Enrique de Vedia. Madrid: Impr. de M. Rivadeneyra, 1852. https://archive.org/details/historiadorespr00unkngoog.

———. *Letters from Mexico.* Eds. and trans. Anthony Pagden. New Haven: Yale University Press, 1986.

Díaz del Castillo, Bernal. *The True History of the Conquest of New Spain.* Trans. Alfred P. Maudslay. 2d series. London: Printed for the Hakluyt Society, 1908.

———. *The History of the Conquest of New Spain.* Ed. and trans. Davíd Carrasco. Albuquerque: University of New Mexico Press, 2008.

Durán, Diego. *Historia de las Indias de Nueva España e islas de Tierra Firme.* 2 vols. México: Imprenta de Ignacio Escalante, 1880.

———. *The Aztecs: The History of the Indies of New Spain.* Eds. and trans. Doris Heyden and Fernando Horcasitas. New York: Orion Press, 1964.

Fuentes, Patricia de, ed. and trans. *The Conquistadors: First-Person Accounts of the Conquest of Mexico.* Norman: University of Oklahoma Press, 1993.

Lienzo of Tlaxcala [copy]. Tulane University. https://digitallibrary.tulane. edu/islandora/object/tulane%3A19311

López de Gómara, Francisco. *The pleasant historie of the conquest of the West India, now called New Spaine, atchieued by the most woorthie prince Hernando Cortes.* London: Thomas Creede, 1596. http://www.openlibrary. org/books/OL25126448M.

———. *Cortés: The Life of the Conqueror.* Ed. and trans. Lesley B. Simpson. Berkeley: University of California Press, 1966.

Muñoz Camargo, Diego. *Historia de Tlaxcala*. México: Oficina tip. de la Secretaría de Fomento, 1892. http://archive.org/details/historiadetlaxca00muno.

Restall, Matthew, and Florine G. L. Asselbergs, eds. and trans. *Invading Guatemala: Spanish, Nahua, and Maya Accounts of the Conquest Wars*. University Park: Pennsylvania State University Press, 2007.

Sahagún, Fray Bernardino de. *Historia general de las cosas de Nueva España*. 1577. https://www.wdl.org/en/item/10096/.

———. *Florentine Codex: General History of the Things of New Spain*. Eds. and trans. Arthur J. O. Anderson and Charles E. Dibble. 12 vols. Salt Lake City: University of Utah Press, 1982.

———. *We People Here: Nahuatl Accounts of the Conquest of Mexico*. Ed. and trans James Lockhart. Los Angeles: University of California Press, 1993.

Tapia, Andrés de. "Relación." In *Colección de documentos para la historia de México* (versión actualizada). Ed. Joaquín García Icazbalceta. México: J.M. Andrade, 1858. http://www.cervantesvirtual.com/obra-visor/coleccion-de-documentos-para-la-historia-de-mexico-version-actualizada--0/html/21bcd5af-6c6c-4b27-a9a5-5edf8315e835_49.htm#121.

Townsend, Camila, ed. *Here in This Year: Seventeenth-Century Nahuatl Annals of the Tlaxcala-Puebla Valley*. Stanford: Stanford University Press, 2010.

Zorita, Alonso de. *Life and Labor in Ancient Mexico: The Brief and Summary Relation of the Lords of New Spain*. Ed. and trans. Benjamin Keen. Norman: University of Oklahoma Press, 1994.

SECONDARY SOURCES

Adorno, Rolena. *The Polemics of Possession in Spanish American Narrative*. New Haven: Yale University Press, 2007.

Aguilar-Moreno, Manuel. *Handbook to Life in the Aztec World*. New York: Oxford University Press, 2007.

Aguilera, Carmen. "The Matrícula de Huexotzinco: A Pictorial Census from New Spain." *Huntington Library Quarterly* 59, no. 4 (1996): 529–41.

Alchon, Suzanne A. *A Pest in the Land: New World Epidemics in a Global Perspective*. Albuquerque: University of New Mexico Press, 2003.

Altman, Ida. *The War for Mexico's West: Indians and Spaniards in New Galicia, 1524–1550*. Albuquerque: University of New Mexico Press, 2010.

Asselbergs, Florine G. L. *Conquered Conquistadors: The Lienzo de Quauhquechollan, A Nahua Vision of the Conquest of Guatemala*. Boulder: University Press of Colorado, 2008.

Baudot, Georges. *Utopia and History in Mexico: The First Chroniclers of Mexican Civilization*. Niwot, CO: University Press of Colorado, 1995.

Benton, Bradley. *The Lords of Tetzcoco: The Transformation of Indigenous Rule in Postconquest Central Mexico*. New York: Cambridge University Press, 2017.

Boone, Elizabeth H. *Stories in Red and Black: Pictorial Histories of the Aztecs and Mixtecs*. Austin: University of Texas Press, 2000.

Brian, Amber. *Alva Ixtlilxochitl's Native Archive and the Circulation of Knowledge in Colonial Mexico*. Nashville: Vanderbilt University Press, 2016.

Brienen, Rebecca P., and Margaret A. Jackson, eds. *Invasion and Transformation: Interdisciplinary Perspectives on the Conquest of Mexico*. Boulder: University Press of Colorado, 2008.

Carrasco, David. *The Aztecs: A Very Short Introduction*. Oxford: Oxford University Press, 2012.

Carrasco Pizana, Pedro. *The Tenochca Empire of Ancient Mexico: The Triple Alliance of Tenochtitlan, Tetzcoco, and Tlacopan*. Norman: University of Oklahoma Press, 1999.

Cerwin, Herbert. *Bernal Díaz: Historian of the Conquest*. Norman: University of Oklahoma Press, 1963.

Chipman, Donald E. *Moctezuma's Children: Aztec Royalty under Spanish Rule, 1520–1700*. Austin: University of Texas Press, 2005.

Christensen, Mark Z. *Nahua and Maya Catholicisms: Texts and Religion in Colonial Central Mexico and Yucatan*. Stanford: Stanford University Press, 2013.

Clendennen, Inga. *The Aztecs*. Cambridge: Cambridge University Press, 1991.

———. *The Cost of Courage in Aztec Society: Essays on Mesoamerican Society and Culture*. New York: Cambridge University Press, 2010.

Connell, William F. *After Moctezuma: Indigenous Politics and Self-Government in Mexico City, 1524–1730*. Norman: University of Oklahoma Press, 2011.

Conway, Richard. "Lakes, Canoes, and the Aquatic Communities of Xochimilco and Chalco, New Spain." *Ethnohistory* 59, no. 3 (2012): 541–68.

Davies, Nigel. *The Aztec Empire: The Toltec Resurgence*. Norman: University of Oklahoma Press, 1987.

Florescano, Enrique. *Los orígenes del poder en Mesoamérica*. México: Fondo de Cultura Económica, 2009.

Gardiner, C. Harvey. *Naval Power in the Conquest of Mexico*. Austin: University of Texas Press, 1956.

Gibson, Charles. *The Aztecs under Spanish Rule: A History of the Indians of the Valley of Mexico, 1519–1810*. Stanford: Stanford University Press, 1964.

———. *Tlaxcala in the Sixteenth Century*. Stanford: Stanford University Press, 1967.

Gillespie, Susan D. *The Aztec Kings: The Construction of Rulership in Mexica History*. Tucson: University of Arizona Press, 1989.

Gruzinski, Serge. *Painting the Conquest: The Mexican Indians and the European Renaissance.* Paris: Flammarion-UNESCO, 1992.

Hajovsky, Patrick T. *On the Lips of Others: Moteuczoma's Fame in Aztec Monuments and Rituals.* Austin: University of Texas Press, 2015.

Hamann, Byron E. "Object, Image, Cleverness: The Lienzo de Tlaxcala." *Art History* 36, no. 3 (2013): 518–45.

Haskett, Robert. *Indigenous Rulers: An Ethnohistory of Town Government in Colonial Cuernavaca.* Albuquerque: University of New Mexico Press, 1991.

———. *Visions of Paradise: Primordial Titles and Mesoamerican History in Cuernavaca.* Norman: University of Oklahoma Press, 2005.

Hassig, Ross. *Aztec Warfare: Imperial Expansion and Political Control.* Norman: University of Oklahoma Press, 1988.

———. *Mexico and the Spanish Conquest.* 2 ed. Norman: University of Oklahoma Press, 2006.

Henige, David P. *Numbers from Nowhere: The American Indian Contact Population Debate.* Norman: University of Oklahoma Press, 1998.

Hirth, Kenneth G., ed. *Housework: Craft Production and Domestic Economy in Ancient Mesoamerica.* Hoboken, NJ: Wiley, 2009.

Horn, Rebecca. *Postconquest Coyoacan: Nahua-Spanish Relations in Central Mexico, 1519–1650.* Stanford: Stanford University Press, 1997.

Joyce, Rosemary A. *Gender and Power in Prehispanic Mesoamerica.* Austin: University of Texas Press, 2000.

Kellogg, Susan. *Law and the Transformation of Aztec Culture, 1500–1700.* Norman: University of Oklahoma Press, 1995.

Krippner-Martínez, James. *Rereading the Conquest: Power, Politics, and the History of Early Colonial Michoacán, Mexico, 1521–1565.* University Park: Pennsylvania State University Press, 2001.

Leibsohn, Dana. *Script and Glyph: Pre-Hispanic History, Colonial Bookmaking, and the* Historia Tolteca-Chichimeca. Washington, DC: Dumbarton Oaks Research Library and Collection, 2009.

León Portilla, Miguel. *Pre-Columbian Literatures of Mexico.* Trans. Grace Lobanov. Norman: University of Oklahoma Press, 1986.

———. *Aztec Thought and Culture.* Trans. Jack Emory Davis. 2 ed. Norman: University of Oklahoma Press, 1990.

———. *The Broken Spears: The Aztec Account of the Conquest of Mexico.* Trans. Lysander Kemp. Expanded ed. Boston: Beacon Press, 1992.

Lockhart, James. *The Nahuas after the Conquest: A Social and Cultural History of the Indians of Central Mexico, Sixteenth through Eighteenth Centuries.* Stanford: Stanford University Press, 1992.

López Austin, Alfredo. *The Myth of Quetzalcoatl: Politics, Religion, and History in the Nahua World.* Trans. Russ Davidson and Guilhem Olivier. Boulder: University Press of Colorado, 2015.

Magaloni Kerpel, Diana, and Cuauhtémoc Medina. *The Colors of the New World: Artists, Materials, and the Creation of the Florentine Codex.* Los Angeles: Getty Publications, 2014.

Martínez Baracs, Rodrigo. *Convivencia y utopía: El gobierno indio y español de la "ciudad Mechuacan" 1521–1580.* México: INAH, 2005.

Marcus, Joyce. *Mesoamerican Writing Systems: Propaganda, Myth, and History in Four Ancient Civilizations.* Princeton: Princeton University Press, 1992.

Matthew, Laura E., and Michel R. Oudijk, eds. *Indian Conquistadors: Indigenous Allies in the Conquest of Mesoamerica.* Norman: University of Oklahoma Press, 2007.

McDonough, Kelly S. *The Learned Ones: Nahua Intellectuals in Postconquest Mexico.* Tucson: University of Arizona Press, 2014.

McEnroe, Sean F. *From Colony to Nationhood in Mexico: Laying the Foundations, 1560–1840.* New York: Cambridge University Press, 2012.

Mundy, Barbara E. *The Mapping of New Spain: Indigenous Cartography and the Maps of the* Relaciones geográficas. Chicago: University of Chicago Press, 2000.

———. *The Death of Aztec Tenochtitlan, the Life of Mexico City.* Austin: University of Texas Press, 2015.

Nichols, Deborah L., and Enrique Rodríguez-Alegría, eds. *The Oxford Handbook of the Aztecs.* New York: Oxford University Press, 2016.

Pastor Bodmer, Beatriz. *The Armature of Conquest: Spanish Accounts of the Discovery of America, 1492–1589.* Stanford: Stanford University Press, 1992.

Pollard, Helen Perlstein. *Taríacuri's Legacy: The Prehispanic Tarascan State.* Norman: University of Oklahoma Press, 1993.

Rabasa, José. *Tell Me the Story of How I Conquered You: Elsewheres and Ethnosuicide in the Colonial Mesoamerican World.* Austin: University of Texas Press, 2011.

Ramos, Gabriela, and Yanna Yannakakis, eds. *Indigenous Intellectuals: Knowledge, Power, and Colonial Culture in Mexico and the Andes.* Durham: Duke University Press, 2014.

Restall, Matthew. *Maya Conquistador.* Boston: Beacon Press, 1998.

———. *Seven Myths of the Spanish Conquest.* New York: Oxford University Press, 2003.

———. "The New Conquest History." *History Compass* 10, no. 2 (2012): 151–66.

———. *When Montezuma Met Cortés: The True Story of the Meeting that Changed History.* New York: Ecco/HarperCollins, 2018.

Restall, Matthew, and Felipe Fernández-Armesto. *The Conquistadors: A Very Short Introduction.* Oxford: Oxford University Press, 2012.

Roa-de-la-Carrera, Cristián A. *Histories of Infamy: Francisco López de Gómara and the Ethics of Spanish Imperialism.* Boulder: University Press of Colorado, 2005.

Robertson, Donald. *Mexican Manuscript Painting of the Early Colonial Period: The Metropolitan Schools.* Norman: University of Oklahoma Press, 1994.

Rojas Rabiela, Teresa. *La agricultura chinampera: compilación histórica.* 2 ed. Chapingo: Universidad Autónoma de Chapingo, 1993.

Rosado, Juan José Batalla. "The Scribes Who Painted the *Matrícula De Tributos* and the *Codex Mendoza.*" *Ancient Mesoamerica* 18, no. 1 (Apr 2007): 31–51.

Ruiz Medrano, Ethelia, and Susan Kellogg, eds. *Negotiation within Domination: New Spain's Indian Pueblos Confront the Spanish State.* Boulder: University Press of Colorado, 2010.

Sáenz de Santa María, Carmelo. *Historia de una historia: La crónica de Bernal Díaz del Castillo.* Madrid: CSIC, 1984.

Saracino, Jennifer R. "Shifting Landscape: Depictions of Environmental and Cultural Disruption in the Mapa Uppsala of Mexico-Tenochitlan." PhD, Tulane University, 2018.

Schroeder, Susan. *Chimalpahin and the Kingdoms of Chalco.* Tucson: University of Arizona Press, 1991.

———, ed. *The Conquest All Over Again: Nahuas and Zapotecs Thinking, Writing, and Painting Spanish Colonialism.* Eastbourne: Sussex Academic Press, 2010.

Schroeder, Susan, Stephanie G. Wood, and Robert Haskett, eds. *Indian Women of Early Mexico.* Norman: University of Oklahoma Press, 1997.

Schwaller, John F., "The Expansion of Nahuatl as a Lingua Franca among Priests in Sixteenth-Century Mexico," *Ethnohistory* 59, no. 4 (2012): 675–690.

Schwaller, John F., and Miguel Leon-Pórtilla. "Broken Spears or Broken Bones: Evolution of the Most Famous Line in Nahuatl." *The Americas* 66, no. 2 (2009): 241–54.

Schwaller, John F., and Helen Nader. *The First Letter from New Spain: The Lost Petition of Cortés and His Company, June 20, 1519.* Austin: University of Texas Press, 2014.

Seijas, Tatiana, and Pablo Miguel Sierra Silva. "The Persistence of the Slave Market in Seventeenth-Century Central Mexico." *Slavery & Abolition: A Journal of Slave and Post-Slave Studies* 37, no. 2 (2016): 307–33.

Smith, Michael E. *The Aztecs.* 3 ed. Malden, MA: Wiley-Blackwell, 2012.

———. *At Home with the Aztecs: An Archaeologist Uncovers their Daily Life.* London: Routledge, Taylor & Francis Group, 2016.

Solari, Amara. *Maya Ideologies of the Sacred: The Transfiguration of Space in Colonial Yucatan.* Austin: University of Texas Press, 2013.

Sousa, Lisa. *The Woman Who Turned Into a Jaguar, and Other Narratives of Native Women in Archives of Colonial Mexico.* Stanford: Stanford University Press, 2017.

Sousa, Lisa, and Kevin Terraciano. "The 'Original Conquest' of Oaxaca: Spanish and Mixtec Accounts of the Spanish Conquest." *Ethnohistory* 50, no. 2 (2003): 349–400.

Studnicki-Gizbert, Daviken, and David Schecter. "The Environmental Dynamics of a Colonial Fuel-Rush: Silver Mining and Deforestation in New Spain, 1522 to 1810." *Environmental History* 15, no. 1 (2010): 94–119.

Terraciano, Kevin. *The Mixtecs of Colonial Oaxaca: Ñudzahui History, Sixteenth through Eighteenth Centuries*. Stanford: Stanford University Press, 2001.

Thomas, Hugh. *Conquest: Montezuma, Cortés, and the Fall of Old Mexico*. New York: Simon & Schuster, 1993.

Townsend, Camilla. "Burying the White Gods: New Perspectives on the Conquest of Mexico." *American Historical Review* 108, no. 3 (2003): 658–87.

———. *Malintzin's Choices: An Indian Woman in the Conquest of Mexico*. Albuquerque: University of New Mexico Press, 2006.

———. "Glimpsing Native American Historiography: The Cellular Principle in Sixteenth-Century Nahuatl Annals." *Ethnohistory* 56, no. 4 (2009): 625–50.

———. *Annals of Native America: How the Nahuas of Colonial Mexico Kept Their History Alive*. New York: Oxford University Press, 2016.

Villella, Peter B. *Indigenous Elites and Creole Identity in Colonial Mexico, 1500–1800*. New York: Cambridge University Press, 2016.

Wauchope, Robert, ed. *Handbook of Middle American Indians*. 16 vols. Austin: University of Texas Press, 1964-76.

Wood, Stephanie G. *Transcending Conquest: Nahua Views of Spanish Colonial Mexico*. Norman: University of Oklahoma Press, 2003.

Acknowledgments (*continued from p. ii*)

Documents 2, 10, 13, 15, 23, 27: Excerpts from *We People Here: Nahuatl Accounts of the Conquest of Mexico, Repertorium Columbianum*, UCLA Center for Medieval and Renaissance Studies, Volume 1, by James Lockhart. Copyright 1993 by The Regents of the University of California. Used with permission of the University of California, Center for Medieval and Renaissance Studies.

Documents 3 and 26: Excerpts from *The Chronicles of Michoacan*, translated and edited by Eugene R. Crane and Reginald C. Reindorp. Copyright 1970, University of Oklahoma Press. Reprinted by permission of University of Oklahoma Press, Norman.

Document 7: From *The First Letter from New Spain: The Lost Petitition of Cortes and His Company*, June 20, 1519 by John F. Schwaller with Helen Nader. Copyright (c) 2014. By permission of the University of Texas Press.

Document 20: Excerpts from *Broken Spears*, by Miguel Leon-Portilla. Copyright 1962, 1990 by Miguel Leon-Portilla. Expanded and Updated Copyright 1992 by Miguel Leon-Portilla. Reprinted by permission of Beacon Press, Boston.

Document 25: Excerpts from *The Native Conquistador: Alva Ixtlilxochitl's Account of the Conquest of New Spain*, eds. and trans. Amber Brian, Bradley Benton, et al. Copyright 2015. Used with permission of the Penn State University Press.

Document 29: Excerpts from *Broken Spears*, by Miguel Leon-Portilla. Copyright 1962, 1990 by Miguel Leon-Portilla. Expanded and Updated Copyright 1992 by Miguel Leon-Portilla. Reprinted by permission of Beacon Press, Boston.

Document 34: Excerpts from *Beyond the Codice: The Nahua View of Colonial Mexico*, edited by Arthur J. O. Anderson, Frances Berdan, and James Lockhart. Copyright 1976 by The Regents of the University of California. Reprinted by permission of University of California Press, Berkeley.

Document 36: Excerpt from *Codex Chimalpahin: Society and Politics in Mexico Tenochtitlan, Tlateloco, Culhuacan, and Other Nahua Altepetl in Central Mexico*, edited and translated by Arthur J. O. Anderson and Susan Schroeder. Copyright 1997, University of Oklahoma Press. Reprinted by permission of University of Oklahoma Press, Norman.

Document 37: Excerpt from *Maya Conquistador* by Matthew Restall. Copyright 1988. Reprinted with permission from Beacon Press, Boston.

Index